States and Markets

Political economy is the study of decentralized and centralized mechanisms for allocating resources and distributing incomes: markets and states. Both markets and states can be organized and combined in a variety of ways and they jointly determine what the economy produces as well as who gets what.

The purpose of this book is to introduce the reader to the concepts and tools for studying relations between states and markets. The focus is methodological. Both the economy and the state are analyzed as networks of relations between principals and agents, occupying particular places in the institutional structure.

Having introduced the principal-agent framework, the book analyzes systematically the effect of the organization of the state on the functioning of the economy. The central question is under what conditions governments will do what they should be doing and not do what they should not.

Adam Przeworski is the Caroll and Milton Petrie Professor of Politics at New York University. His previous books include *Democracy and the Rule of Law*, coedited with José María Maravall (Cambridge, 2002); *Democracy and Development*, cowritten with Michael Alvarez, Jose Antonio Cheibub, and Fernando Limongi (Cambridge, 2000); and *Democracy, Accountability, and Representation*, coedited with Susan C. Strokes and Bernard Manin (Cambridge, 1999).

States and Markets

A Primer in Political Economy

Adam Przeworski
New York University

 CAMBRIDGE
UNIVERSITY PRESS

PUBLISHED BY THE PRESS SYNDICATE OF THE UNIVERSITY OF CAMBRIDGE
The Pitt Building, Trumpington Street, Cambridge, United Kingdom

CAMBRIDGE UNIVERSITY PRESS
The Edinburgh Building, Cambridge CB2 2RU, UK
40 West 20th Street, New York, NY 10011-4211, USA
477 Williamstown Road, Port Melbourne, VIC 3207, Australia
Ruiz de Alarcón 13, 28014 Madrid, Spain
Dock House, The Waterfront, Cape Town 8001, South Africa

http://www.cambridge.org

First published 2003

Printed in the United States of America

Typeface Times 10/13pt.   *System* LATEX 2_ε * [TB]

A catalog record for this book is available from the British Library.

Library of Congress Cataloging in Publication Data
Przeworski, Adam.
    States and markets : a primer in political economy / Adam Przeworski.
        p.   cm.
    Includes bibliographical references.
    ISBN 0-521-82804-X – ISBN 0-521-53524-7 (pb.)
    1. Economic policy.   2. Capitalism.   3. Decision making.
    4. Economics.   I. Title.
    HD87.P79   2003
    330.12 – dc21   2003043587

ISBN 0 521 82804 X hardback
ISBN 0 521 53524 7 paperback

Contents

Preface

"I would like to study, among all the moderate governments we know, what is the distribution of the three powers, and to calculate in this way the degrees of liberty which each of them can enjoy. But one should not always exhaust a subject to such an extent that nothing is left for the reader to do. The point is not to make read but make think."

(Montesquieu, *De l'Esprit des Lois*, Livre XI)

These are, only slightly polished, notes for lectures I used to give at the University of Chicago and now offer at New York University. They are based on the belief that political scientists cannot study political economy without knowing some economics. This was certainly my problem. Many years ago, I taught a course on the Marxist Theory of the State, only to conclude that neither the writers we studied nor I knew enough economics to make sense of the role of the state in a market economy. Hence, I decided to bite the bullet and, with the guidance of a graduate student at the time, Michael Wallerstein, I plunged. One unexpected consequence was that "Marxist" was dropped from the course title: I discovered that there are other sensible theories of the state. But, as I continued to learn economics, by that time by reading Joseph E. Stiglitz, I also discovered that there are many theories of markets. Thus I came to the conclusion that both "the state" and "the market" must be deconstructed. This conclusion provides the motivation for the course as it now stands.

I give this course to graduate students who have taken a basic course in microeconomics, with calculus. A former student in this course, James Vreeland, offers it to upper-level undergraduates at Yale. My motivation in making these notes public, however, is mainly to make the material accessible to colleagues. I know that there are many political scientists who were not taught this kind of material in graduate school, who run in the publishing race, but in the back of their minds always plan that one day they will "retool." Having gone through a retooling process more than once – indeed, having spent most of my life retooling – I know this is not an easy feat. But it can be done, and these notes are intended to help.

The emphasis of the course is on concepts and tools. Its purpose is to teach the reader how to analyze markets and states and how to evaluate their functioning. The course prepares you to read the substantive literature but it does not review it systematically. If you want to continue, the best places are the textbook by Jean-Jaques Laffonte and Jean Tirole that, in spite of its foreboding title, *Theory of Incentives in Procurement and Regulation*, is in fact an excellent introduction to political economy, and Allan Drazen's magisterial review of the literature in *Political Economy for Macroeconomics*. Avinash Dixit's *The Making of Economic Policy* will then put everything in perspective before you start reading frontier research.

Some of the chapters offer general introductions to particular concepts or techniques, but some are no more than explanations of representative articles or book chapters. I engage in mathematics only to illustrate general techniques needed to understand the substantive findings. However, some chapters do nothing more than fill gaps in mathematical derivations that were skipped by authors writing to an economic audience.

Each of the chapters is preceded by a list of readings. You should at least skim the items indicated as "Read" before studying each chapter and you should reread them afterward.

A note about the necessary mathematical background: You will need elementary calculus and a lot of courage. I found that students who cheat, entering the class without any knowledge of calculus, make it successfully through. They do work harder, often consulting some calculus textbook. But there is a lot of repetition in the course, and in the end they learn by having done it over and over. Hence, even if at the beginning your understanding is only fuzzy, by the end you should find it easier than it seemed.

States and Markets

CHAPTER 1

Introduction

1.1 Decentralized allocation mechanisms

Suppose each of you in the class has an *endowment* of some apples and some pears. Some of you like apples more than pears; some like pears more than apples. Each of you can rank all baskets of apples and pears by a *preference relation* such that for all baskets you can tell whether you prefer a particular basket to another or you are *indifferent* between them. For example, you may prefer to have 7 apples and 6 pears to having 6 apples and 7 pears, so that $\{7a, 6p\} \succ \{6a, 7p\}$, where $\succ$ stands for "prefers." In turn, you may be indifferent between having a basket of 7 apples and 6 pears and a basket of 4 apples and 11 pears, so that $\{7a, 6p\} \sim \{4a, 11p\}$. Your preferences can be also represented by a *utility function* $U_i(a, p)$, increasing in both arguments. If $\{7a, 6p\} \succ \{6a, 7p\}$, then $U(7a, 6p) > U(6a, 7p)$. If $\{7a, 6p\} \sim \{4a, 11p\}$, then $U(7a, 6p) = U(4a, 11p)$. Utility is just some number **you**, i, attach to the value of a particular basket.

Suppose now that each of you wants to *maximize* the utility you derive from consuming apples and pears by exchanging them with others. Once the exchange is completed, but not before, you eat the apples and the pears you have.

How can this exchange process be organized? Suppose we do it like this:

(1) Each of you puts your apples and your pears on the table. When this is done, a bell rings and each of you takes all the apples and pears you want and leaves the room with them.

What will happen? Obviously, a fight. What will be the final *allocation*? Bullies will take more and some black-and-blue marks will be inflicted.

Is this *allocation mechanism* a "market"? It does not quite look like one, since people grab, using force, rather than exchange voluntarily. There is nothing to safeguard your endowments and nothing to protect your allocation: only your big muscles and swift feet. But notice that this is a *decentralized mechanism*: Everyone acts independently. Moreover, the allocation process is completely free: You do what you want.

The outcome is bad. Some people will get injured. If it is possible to generate the same allocation of apples and pears without fighting, some people would be better off (without bruises) without anyone being worse off. Hence, if people care about bruises, this outcome is *inefficient*: Someone can be better off without anyone being worse off. Moreover, strong people may get a lot; weak people nothing, which somehow does not seem right. Even our most vague moral intuitions tell us that the allocation should be related to something like *effort* or *need*, not just the good *luck* of being physically strong. It should be *equitable*. Hence, this is not a good way to allocate.

(2) Suppose then we do it in a different way. All the apple owners can exchange their apples for pieces of paper on which pear owners write the number of pears they will give in return for each apple tomorrow. Hence, *i* gives *j* an apple and *j* gives *i* a piece of paper that says "*p*": the pear *price* *j* is willing to pay tomorrow.

Let us ask again what will happen. What will be the final allocation? The obvious answer is that nothing will be exchanged. The final allocation will be the same as the original endowments. The reason is that if the exchange were to occur, it would not be in the interest of *j* tomorrow to fulfill her promise. Hence, the promise is not *credible*: *j* may well write some number "*p*" on a piece of paper, but she will not deliver on her promise. In turn, if *i* knows that *j* will not fulfill her promise, *i* will not alienate his apples.

Note that this mechanism looks more like a market. An exchange could now occur. But something is missing, namely, *enforcement institutions*. The fact that the promises concern tomorrow does not matter. Suppose that they were for one hour from now, one minute from now, or even one second from now. In the end, the exchange of apples for pears may be almost simultaneous: The question still remains who will lift his hand off the apples and pears first.

Is the final allocation a good one? Let us stipulate that *i* has $\{3a, 2p\}$ but would like more $\{1a, 3p\}$ while *j* has $\{1a, 2p\}$ but prefers $\{3a, 1p\}$. Hence, if *i* could give *j* 2*a* in exchange for 1*p*, they would both be happier. Because the initial endowments can be improved on and because no exchange occurs under this allocation mechanism, the final allocation is inefficient. Hence, the mechanism "exchange apples for promises of pears" is free and decentralized but it is bad in the sense of leading to an inefficient allocation.

(3) Yet another way. Suppose that there is someone who can and will, can **and** will, force the owners of pears to deliver them to the sellers of apples in quantities written on the pieces of paper, so that the pieces of paper are as good as real pears. Moreover, to make exchanges easier, one can also write pieces of papers promising apples in exchange for pears.

What will the outcome be? First, we need to answer the following question: Will the exchange process ever stop? There are many students in this class, each with some initial endowment. Now i sells $2a$ to j for $1p$. But k comes along and offers to buy each of i's pears for a price of $3a$. Suppose that, given the number of apples i has, he is willing to give up a pear for 3 apples. Then i will sell her pears to k. But, and so on. As you see, the stopping question is not a trivial one. But you know from your microeconomics course – and we will cover this material remedially in the next chapter – that this exchange will come to a stop. It will reach some allocation such that no one will want to trade anymore, an *equilibrium*.

What will be true of this equilibrium? First, all the potential gains from trade will be exhausted: No one will be able to benefit from continuing the exchange. Second, no one can be better off without someone else being worse off: The only way i could increase her utility is by someone else losing his. Finally, if we were to take a vote whether to alter the equilibrium allocation, then at least one person would vote against changing it: This allocation would not be defeated under unanimity rule. *These three conditions are equivalent, and they fully describe efficiency in the sense of Pareto or Pareto optimality.*

Note that we have smuggled in a number of assumptions. One is that no one eats during the exchange process. If you were to consume before the equilibrium allocation is reached, *out of equilibrium*, then some of you would be consuming apples or pears for which you would have paid too little or too much. You may have consumed an apple for which you paid $2p$ while there may have been someone who would have sold you an apple for $1p$, so that you could have consumed more apples and pears. We assumed that trading is costless, that is, that it has no *transaction costs*.

Second, we assumed that everyone knows everything and everyone knows the same. Suppose that the pears are not all the same – some are rotten – and that only the sellers know their quality. Then you may suspect that if someone is willing to sell you a pear for a low apple price, this may be because she knows that the pear is of poor quality. You may be unwilling to buy pears at all, so that there may be no market for pears (Ackerlof 1970).

Suppose for the moment that these assumptions hold. We know that the equilibrium allocation will be Pareto efficient. Does it mean that this mechanism that generated this allocation is a good one? In the example we discussed thus far the initial endowments and the equilibrium allocation were

$$i : 3a, 2p \Rightarrow 1a, 3p$$
$$j : 1a, 2p \Rightarrow 3a, 1p$$

But suppose that the initial endowments were different and the exchange led to a different allocation:

$$i : 2a, 2p \Rightarrow 0a, 3p$$
$$j : 2a, 2p \Rightarrow 4a, 1p$$

Can these equilibrium allocations be compared by the Pareto criterion? Because the utility functions increase in both arguments, i is better off in the original than in the modified world: She has the same number of pears but one apple more. But j is better off in the new world: He has the same number of pears as in the original one but one more apple. Hence, j is better off but i is worse off. The Pareto criterion cannot be used to compare these two allocations: We cannot judge which is more efficient by this criterion. Each equilibrium allocation is *Pareto superior* to the corresponding endowment allocation: Otherwise there would have been no exchange. But each initial endowment leads to a different equilibrium allocation, and neither of them is Pareto superior to the other.

Hence, if we want to evaluate these states of the world, we need some other criteria. We could, for example, ask which of these worlds is better in terms of total societal consumption or total utility. In the first case, we would use as the criterion a function $W(C_i, C_j)$, where C stands for consumption, such that

$$W(C_i, C_j) = C_i + C_j.$$

According to this criterion, an allocation that makes this sum larger is better than one that makes it smaller. Because we are not producing anything and because nothing is lost in exchange, total consumption is the same in the two worlds, so this criterion does not work. But even if total consumption associated with different allocations was different, this criterion would be vulnerable to the criticism that the value of consumption to different individuals may be different.

So we are left with total utility, the classical utilitarian way to think of *social welfare*. This criterion is a function $W(U_i, U_j)$ such that

$$W(U_i, U_j) = U_i(C_i) + U_j(C_j).$$

In terms of our example, the original world is better than the modified one if

$$U_i(1a, 3p) + U_j(3a, 1p) > U_i(0a, 3p) + U_j(4a, 1p),$$

or

$$U_i(1a, 3p) - U_i(0a, 3p) > U_j(4a, 1p) - U_j(3a, 1p).$$

As you see, to make this evaluation, we have to compare the utilities of i and j, which is hard, if not impossible, to do. The Us are numbers individuals attach and i may attach 3 to his difference but may as well attach 102, so how are we to tell if i's difference is greater than j's? Moreover, because i prefers $\{1a, 3p\}$ to $\{0a, 3p\}$, if we asked i what her value of the difference is, she would say "1000": She would reveal her preferences strategically. Hence, this is not a promising route either.

How about comparing these allocations by the criterion of *equality*? Is this a good criterion? Note that in our example the world in which the equilibrium allocation would be perfectly equal would not be a good world: We already know that people would want to trade away from equal endowments. *Outcome-egalitarianism* does have its supporters. But even if we are egalitarians, we must ask: Equality of what? (Sen 1992).

"Utility" is an appealing answer: People should be able to be equally happy with their consumption baskets. If they do not envy other people's allocations, that is, if given their utility functions both i and j prefer their own allocation to the allocation of the other person, then these allocations are at least *fair*. But we have seen that as an operational criterion utility is hard to implement.

Perhaps what we should equalize is *opportunity*. Suppose now that what you consume is produced. Specifically, the output (you can think of it as total value of apples and pears measured in equilibrium prices) is produced by two factors of production: luck (L) and effort (E). We can write the production function generally as

$$Y = F(L, E)$$

increasing in both arguments. Suppose that the specific production function is simply

$$Y = L + E$$

Now, say that i has 8 lucks and exerts 2 efforts, while j exerts the same amount of effort but has no luck. Their output will be:

$$i : 8 + 2 = 10$$
$$j : 0 + 2 = 2$$

Note that their opportunities are very different: i can get 8 units of consumption doing nothing, while j must rely completely on her effort. We could equalize the opportunity for consumption by taking 4 lucks away from i and giving them to j. They will both have an opportunity of 4. Obviously, they may exert different amounts of effort and end up with different consumption. But their rewards will be, in Dworkin's (1981a and b) language, "ambition-" rather than "endowment-" sensitive.

But what is "luck" and what is "effort"? If I watch TV the whole day rather than work, is it because I am lazy or because I have a deficiency of laboramine in my brain? And how do luck and effort combine in production? Suppose that you observe Y but not L and E separately. How to equalize opportunity now? (The problem is not hopeless, see Roemer 1996.)

Is opportunity a good *equalisandum*? Suppose we equalized opportunity, so that everyone has 4 lucks and i turns out to be a bum, exerting no effort, and starves having only 4 to consume. Should we accept this allocation or should we ensure that everyone has some basic consumption basket? You may say with Giddens (1998), "no rights without responsibilities": i had the same chance to produce the basic basket as everyone else and if she decided to squander her opportunities it is just tough. But suppose that the reason she did not exert any effort was that she fell ill. Again, you may say that she should have insured herself against this possibility; to anticipate what follows, you may even say that she should have been *forced* to insure herself. But suppose she was not forced and did not buy insurance: A hiker climbs a mountain, breaks a leg, and is lying on a ledge, dying from the cold. A helicopter televises his agony. He could have bought rescue insurance but he did not. Should he be allowed to just die or should he be saved?

Finally, you may want to evaluate allocations by a *maximin* criterion (Rawls 1971). Suppose that we rank all the baskets of some basic goods from the largest to the smallest. Then an allocation is better if it makes larger the smallest basket.

1.2 Centralized allocation mechanisms

There are obviously other ways we can allocate and other ways we can evaluate the allocations and the mechanisms that generate them. Let us consider a few more.

(4) Here is the most obvious: i is a *dictator* and she decides who gets what for everyone. What individuals get does not depend on their actions, just on the decision of the dictator, who can enforce it using physical coercion if need be. Will the resulting allocation be a good one? Is this a good allocation mechanism? Do not jump to conclusions. Whatever the dictator decides, the allocation will be Pareto efficient: Any other allocation would make someone worse off, namely, the dictator. But this may just show that the Pareto criterion is too weak. More interestingly, the dictator may be benevolent: She may just want to implement one of the criteria we discussed above.

One question arises immediately: Will a decentralized mechanism generate the same allocation as a benevolent and omniscient dictator? This question is often posed by economists as a **counterfactual** method to evaluate allocations: It makes sense to think that an allocation chosen by a benevolent, omniscient dictator is the best possible, so that any mechanism that deviates from the *command optimum* must be in some way deficient. This is, however, an excessively demanding standard: How would the dictator know everything? We can weaken it by assuming that the dictator knows no more and not less than individuals and ask about the *constrained command optimum*. For example, we can ask whether the allocation that results from the last decentralized mechanism we considered is *constrained Pareto efficient*, that is, whether this allocation could be Pareto improved on by a benevolent dictator who knows only what the trading individuals know.

Yet even this weaker criterion is still counterfactual. Individuals know things the dictator does not know: Most obviously what makes them happy but perhaps also how much they need to survive or how much luck they enjoy and how much effort they exert. If a benevolent dictator is to act in their interest, he must somehow elicit this information. But individuals will *reveal* their private information only if they have *incentives* to do so. This may mean that even constrained Pareto efficiency may be unattainable to the dictator.

Note that what is at stake in these distinctions is what we can realistically expect as the best possible. Many debates about the virtues and vices of different allocation mechanisms hinge on this question. We will return to such issues several times.

(5) Let us consider another centralized mechanism. Say the Central Authority confiscates the initial endowments of apples and pears, puts them in baskets as before, and runs a lottery to determine who gets which basket. Once the results of the lottery are known, the Central Authority distributes to individuals the baskets they won.

Before we consider how to evaluate this mechanism, let us pause on the notion of a *centralized mechanism*. In what sense is this mechanism centralized? Is it because we have a Central Authority? But in the example of decentralized exchange of commodities for commodities through pieces of paper, that we also had some kind of an authority that used or threatened coercion if people did not deliver on their pieces of paper. We have already seen that there can be no exchange, at least no generalized anonymous exchange, without some kind of an enforcement mechanism.

It is useful to ask first why we did not pose this question with regard to the dictator. The answer is that in the case of the dictator, it is obvious that one decision generates the entire allocation to all the individuals. The dictator decides how much to give to each. But so does the lottery. Lots are thrown into an urn, a handsome television actor, smiling broadly, reaches into the urn to allocate consumption baskets to everyone. Contrast this with exchange, where i decides whether to sell to j but their exchange does not affect the allocation to k. Exchange is a decentralized mechanism because the final allocation results from independent decisions of each agent; dictatorship and lottery are centralized mechanisms because one decision allocates to everyone.

Is lottery a good mechanism? It does have its virtues. One would want to say intuitively that it is fair, but we have seen that economists reserved this term for an allocation that does not produce envy, and lottery certainly does. It equalizes chances, but they are not quite the opportunities we discussed above, because all you can do with your basket is to consume it. It is obviously inefficient and outcome-inegalitarian. We tend to employ lotteries, I suspect, when we think that exchange is not an ethically defensible mechanism and have no obvious criteria by which to allocate (on these issues, see Elster 1992). For example, some countries use lotteries to allocate scarce medical resources, including body parts. We do not think they should be exchangeable for money and we cannot see other clear criteria. Hence, we leave things to luck.

(6) One more, I promise the last, allocation mechanism. Suppose we use majority vote. Say there are three individuals so that we can easily use the

Table 1.1

	Apples	Pears
i	1	3
j	3	1
k	2	2
Total	6	6

majority criterion. The mechanism works as follows. Any individual can propose any allocation $\{\mathbf{a}, \mathbf{p}\}$ where, note, the members of this allocation are column vectors of size 3, because there are three individuals. The only condition we will impose is that of a *balanced budget*, so that the sums allocated must equal the total endowments available. For example, say that individual i proposes the following allocation to all three.

The proposal of i is then paired against the status quo (say the initial endowments of each individual) and people cast their votes either for the status quo or for i's proposal. Whichever of the two alternatives wins is the new status quo and everyone, i included, can propose a different allocation, which will be paired against the status quo, and so on. Note that this mechanism is a centralized one: Everyone together decides how to allocate to each.

The first thing we need to do is to return to the stopping problem. Will this process ever end? Or will it continue ad infinitum? Because this is an issue shrouded in confusion, let us be careful about the question we are asking. We are not asking how much time it will take to reach the final decision about allocation. This was not the question about exchange either: We asked in fact whether there exists some allocation such that, **whenever** it is reached, exchange will stop. So let us ask the same question now: Is there some allocation such that, whenever it is reached, voting will stop? Suppose that there is some allocation that beats every other possible allocation by majority vote. Say the proposal of i, which we will call X, does it. If j proposes some other allocation, say Y, $X \succ_M Y$ (read $\succ_M$ as "beats by" or "is preferred to" under majority rule). If k proposes Z, $X \succ_M Z$, and the same is true for every other proposal. Then X is the *majority (or Condorcet) winner*. And if X is the majority winner, then the voting process will "stop" at X: Nothing will defeat it. The electorate will have chosen to allocate consumption according to X, given in the Table 1.1.

Before we raise a problem, let us consider the qualities of this allocation. Is it efficient? This is the same as to ask whether individuals would want to trade their allocations after the voting process had stopped. You will see that i's proposal gives i and j the same they were being allocated in our example of free exchange. Hence, if this were the allocation, trading would stop (assuming that k does not want to trade). Moreover, someone would vote against any other allocation. So it is efficient.

The problem is that voting would not stop at X. Even worse, there is no proposal that beats every other alternative by a simple majority rule. Just think: Say that in response to X, j proposes an allocation Y that gives less to i and more to j and k. Then the latter two will vote for Y over X, so that $Y \succ_M X$. But then k will propose an allocation Z that gives more to k and i than Y, so that these two will not vote for it and $Z \succ_M Y$. But i can offer her initial proposal again. This proposal will give i and j more than Z, $X \succ_M Z$. Hence, we have $X \succ_M Z \succ_M Y \succ_M X$. There is no proposal that beats every other proposal under pairwise majority rule. Majority winner does not exist, which means that this mechanism is not *decisive*: It fails to pick one from among all alternatives.[1]

As you see, this is a different kind of a deficiency than those we discussed above. The problem here is not that the equilibrium allocation is somehow undesirable but that there is no allocation that constitutes an equilibrium. We just do not know what to expect in this situation. Perhaps this only means that we did not describe the voting mechanism adequately, but this is for later.

1.3   Political-economic equilibria

Let us first summarize what we have done thus far. We discussed three decentralized mechanisms of allocation: "grab all you can," "exchange commodities for pieces of paper," and "exchange commodities for commodities via pieces of paper." Then we discussed three centralized mechanisms: dictatorship, lottery, and majority rule. With regard to each of them, we asked first which allocation they will generate. We discovered that in some cases this question has a relatively easy answer but in one case the answer may be

---

[1] The word "cycling" is banned from this book. Nothing "cycles" here. This paragraph does not describe how proposals will be made but only a property of the function that transforms individual preferences into a collective one. All that we have learned is that this function fails to pick a unique allocation.

impossible. Then, with regard to each allocation, we asked how to evaluate it. We found that there is a number of possible criteria and that each of them is in some way problematic. Efficiency in the sense of Pareto is an appealing criterion because any allocation that is inefficient is obviously undesirable. But, first, it is a weak criterion: There are normally lots of efficient allocations and this criterion does not distinguish them any further. Second, we have to ask ourselves what is the best possible world: The fact that an allocation is not as good as it would have been under unrealistic conditions is just not very enlightening. We also considered other criteria, particularly different versions of equality, and discovered that while each has normative appeal, it is not obvious to pick one among the competing citeria.

Why did we go through this discussion using silly examples, rather than begin with big guns: "the market" and "the state"? This is what we have been discussing all along, so why use the subterfuge?

The first point I wanted to make is that there is no such thing as "the" market and "the" state. Grabbing is different from exchanging for a piece of paper, which is different from exchanging commodities via pieces of paper, and all three are different from other examples one could cook up. Dictatorship is different from lotteries, which are different from majority voting, and again they are all different from other centralized mechanisms. There are different ways of organizing production and exchange and different ways of organizing political institutions. Markets and states are always organized in some particular ways, and how they are organized matters. Hence, it is more useful to inquire about the properties of the particular decentralized and centralized mechanisms. This is what, in my view, political economy is all about.

The second conclusion is that no general anonymous exchange is possible without some centralized enforcement mechanism lurking in the background. The state is everywhere. This is a long story, which goes back to Marx before Polanyi. Capitalism is a system in which most productive resources are owned privately. Yet under capitalism property is institutionally distinct from political authority: This separation is necessary for markets to exist. The slaveowner or a feudal lord was at the same time the owner of the instruments of production and the political sovereign. The capitalist employer has no authority over the worker outside the labor contract. As Marx put it, "the mediaeval proverb *nulle terrae sans seignor* was replaced by that other proverb: *l'argent n'a pas de maitre.*" As a result, there are two mechanisms by which resources can be allocated to uses and distributed among households: markets and the state. Individuals are simultaneously market agents and political actors.

Markets are decentralized mechanisms: Households and firms decide how to allocate the resources they own. Depending on market structure, their decisions may or may not be independent, but they affect each other only via the consequences of actions of one agent for the welfare of another. The state is a centralized mechanism: It coerces economic agents to do what they would have not done voluntarily. Depending on the political structure, the decisions of the state can be made by one individual, the "dictator," or can result from a process involving all citizens. Yet, however they are reached, once reached state policies are binding.

Given the coexistence of these two mechanisms, one concept of *political-economic equilibrium* is the following. Consider the following game. First, political actors reveal their preferences for policies by a variety of mechanisms ranging from voting to bribes to rioting. Second, the state maximizes its objectives by adopting a policy such as the tax rate. Finally, economic agents choose their actions to maximize their utility, subject to the constraint of the policy. The equilibrium of this game is a policy of the state and a set of actions by individuals *qua* political actors and *qua* economic agents, such that no one would want to act differently given their beliefs and given the actions of others. Associated with this equilibrium is an allocation of resources to uses and a distribution of incomes.

One example that will be studied in the course is the following. Suppose all individuals seek to maximize their consumption, which is given by

$$c_i = (1 - \tau)w_i L_i + \tau \overline{w_i L_i}$$

where τ is the tax rate, w_i is the individual-specific hourly wage rate, L_i are labor services measured in hours, and the bar stands for "average." Individuals first vote on the tax rate and in this case the majority voting procedure considered above does yield a Condorcet winner, τ^*. Given this tax rate, each individual decides independently how much labor services to sell and the outcome is $\mathbf{L}^*(\tau^*)$. Finally, associated with $\{\tau^*, \mathbf{L}^*(\tau^*)\}$ is the allocation of consumption $\mathbf{c}[\tau^*, \mathbf{L}^*(\tau^*)]$. The equilibrium of this situation has two components: $\{\tau^*, \mathbf{L}^*\}$, where $\mathbf{L}$ is an N-vector of the amounts of labor supplied by the $i = 1, \ldots, N$ individuals. Associated with this equilibrium is a vector $\mathbf{c}^*$ of consumptions of all the N individuals. This is a political-economic equilibrium.

Exchange and production cannot occur without the presence of some centralized mechanism. To make this point clear, let us go back to the exchange of commodities example. We have seen that trades will occur only if there is some mechanism to assure the agents that promises will be fulfilled. But we did not consider what this mechanism might be; we did not even note that it must cost something. Remember that the initial endowments were traded according to

$$i : 3a, 2p \Rightarrow 1a, 3p$$
$$j : 1a, 2p \Rightarrow 3a, 1p.$$

But if the trades can occur only if there is a policeman to enforce the promises, then the policeman must earn an income. Suppose the policeman, s, who has no initial endowment, must get

$$s : 0a, 0p \Rightarrow 1a, 1p$$

to want to work as a policeman. Now the society has to decide whether it wants to bear this cost and be able to trade or to remain with the initial endowments. Suppose it decides to hire the policeman. But how is the tax decided on? Whatever is the mechanism that allocates taxes, it must be a centralized one. (Voluntary contributions will generally not work: We will discuss why in the next chapter.) Either someone is a dictator or a lottery is used or the decision is reached by voting. But some joint decision has to be made: Joint, because taxes are allocated to everyone. Hence, the only way to describe the exchange situation is in two steps: (1) A centralized decision is reached whether to employ a policeman and how to tax. (2) Given the presence of the policeman and the taxes, decentralized exchange occurs. The final allocation results from a combination of a centralized and a decentralized mechanism: It is a property of a *political-economic equilibrium*. One way, therefore, to represent the insight of Polanyi is to say that all equilibria of production and exchange situations are political-economic equilibria: They always combine a centralized with a decentralized mechanism.

Consider a slightly different example, due to Stiglitz (1994). Suppose you drive your car to some meeting place. You can park your car just in front of this place and avoid walking, but the probability that your car will be stolen in this place is not insignificant. Alternatively, you can park the car three blocks away, in a place that is safer, and walk. Suppose your car is insured and it is raining. You park in front. The situation is as follows: You paid a as your insurance premium, you will get b if your car is stolen, and the probability of this event is $\overline{p}$ in the dangerous place and $\underline{p}$ in the safe place. The amount a you pay as premium takes into account the fact that if you are insured, you will park in a dangerous place: *moral hazard*. The insurance industry is competitive, so that $a = \overline{p}b$. Suppose now that the insurance company (or you; it does not matter in this case) is taxed some amount τ and the tax revenue is spent to put a policeman in the dangerous place, which now becomes safe. Your premium is now such that $a - \tau = \underline{p}b$ or $a = \underline{p}b + \tau$. The insurance company is indifferent between the two arrangements and if $\tau < b(\overline{p} - \underline{p})$, then you are better off. The terms of a purely private exchange between you and your insurance company, which are $\{a, b\}$, depend on the number of policemen who patrol the streets, so they are in fact $\{a(\tau), b(\tau), \tau\}$. For every number of policemen, the terms of private exchange are different. The state is present in every private transaction.

But the story does not end here. Now that we have a policeman, what is to guarantee that the policeman will in fact guard the car? Even worse, who is to prevent the policeman from stealing the car himself? This is an ancient question, but it becomes particularly poignant as posed by Stigler (1975): We study economic agents as individuals who rationally pursue their interests. If these individuals were angels, then, as Madison said, no government would be necessary. But if economic agents are no angels, then why would we think that the same people are angels when they become public officials? We could optimistically believe that only those people who are motivated by public spirit enter the public realm. But we often suspect, and are faced with abundant evidence, that at least some people in the public office pursue their own interests, or the interests of their cronies, or pursue some special interests to which they are indebted. Indeed, in some countries the only way to become a public official is to indebt yourself to special interests. We have to distrust the motivations of public officials: The idea that democracy is stronger when people trust the government is a piece of wishful nonsense. True, when democracy is strong, people trust the government. But democracy is strong when public officials have incentives – when they are appropriately punished and rewarded – to act in the best interest of the public. Hence, we have to ask how the state is organized: What is its institutional structure?

What public officials do depends on their motivations and on the structure of incentives they face. This structure of incentives, in turn, is constituted by the institutional framework within which they operate. Suppose that if a car is stolen, everyone votes not to have policemen anymore and that the people who are policemen have no alternative sources of income. Then they will guard cars. The equilibrium in which people pay the tax, insurance premiums are low, and cars are not stolen is supported by the threat that people would not pay the tax if a car were to be stolen.

Consider a simple case of economic regulation, to be studied in detail later. A particular bureaucracy, referred to now as "the regulator," must decide whether to subsidize investment by a private firm. This firm either has an antiquated technology, in which case the investment is socially beneficial, or a state-of-the-art technology, in which case investment cannot improve its productivity. The regulator knows which technology the firm has but the public does not. Now, a good state intervention in the economy, to use the traditional language, would be for the regulator to subsidize investment if the firm has an old technology and not to subsidize if it has new one. Bad intervention would be not to subsidize a firm that has an old technology or to subsidize one that cannot increase productivity anyway. What will the regulator do? Well, perhaps it will act properly, that is, subsidize the firm only if it has an antiquated technology. But perhaps, the regulator will be "captured": It will subsidize a firm with the new technology, share the rents with the firm, and hide from the public the fact that the subsidy was not necessary. Obviously, the honesty of the regulator matters: If he cannot be swayed by the prospect of becoming the senior vice president of the firm and becoming rich on leaving the public office, he will act in the public interest. But perhaps it also matters whether there is another public office that monitors his actions. Perhaps it matters whether citizens can and will vote out of office the government that tolerates corruption or colludes with special interests. The point is that what the regulator will do may depend on the structure of incentives it confronts. In this sense, *regulation is endogenous*: What it will be depends on the consequences for the regulator of the alternative courses of action he can choose.

These were only examples and we could go on. Indeed, we will go on.

1.4   Plan of the book

In the old days, we would say that the purpose of the book is to study the relations between states and markets. But we already know better: Our goal is to investigate the positive and normative properties of different political-economic equilibria.

We open with a more serious examination of markets. Even though you are expected to have followed a basic course in microeconomics, we begin with a remedial chapter on the miracles and the failures of markets. This chapter is followed by a discussion of markets that are incomplete and in which information is imperfect. Our conclusion is that instead of thinking that there is some ideal market that sometimes fails, it is better to begin with markets as they always are, incomplete and not fully informative. We also discover that instead of thinking of identical market individuals, it is useful to think of the economy as a network of relations between different classes of *principals and agents*. Hence, we need to learn how to analyze relations between principals and agents.

We then apply the principal-agent framework to study the structure of the state. First, we consider the relation between governments and private economic agents. Having analyzed the logic of regulation, we study what happens when regulation is endogenous, that is, when it results from a political process. Second, we study the relation between elected politicians and appointed bureaucrats. Finally, we delve into the relation between voters and elected politicians.

All throughout these discussions we ask positive questions: Will there be an equilibrium? Will it be unique? How much will people produce and consume in equilibrium? How much will they pay in taxes? What will be the distribution of income? We also pose normative questions: Will the equilibrium allocation be efficient? Will it be egalitarian? Will it be just?

Having learned concepts and techniques of analysis, we focus on the role of the state in a market economy. We ask what the state should do to promote economic development, to redistribute, and to ensure against bad luck. But we also keep asking whether there are reasons to expect that governments will do what they should and not do what they should not. In particular, we repeatedly ask whether the allocations generated by government actions are efficient from the economic point of view. But even when we discover that they are not, we ask whether more efficient, Pareto-superior, allocations are feasible.

A brief overview closes the book.

Decentralized mechanisms

CHAPTER 2

Market miracles and market failures

2.1　Readings

Read the most difficult you can from the following. The readings are listed from the easiest to the most difficult:

Johansson, Per-Olov. 1991. Appendix, Chapters 2 and 5 (in this order) of *An Introduction to Modern Welfare Economics*. Cambridge: Cambridge University Press.

Silberberg, Eugene. 1978. Chapter 15 of *The Structure of Economics*. New York: McGraw-Hill.

Varian, Hal R. 1984. Chapters 5, 6, and 7 of *Microeconomic Analysis*. New York: Norton.

Campbell, Donald E. 1987. Chapters 3 and 7 and Appendix 2 of *Resource Allocation Mechanisms*. Cambridge: Cambridge University Press.
Background: (These are classical articles on market failures.)

Bator, Francis M. 1958. "The Anatomy of Market Failure." *Quarterly Journal of Economics 72*: 351–379.

Musgrave, Richard A. 1971. "Provision for Social Goods in the Market System." *Public Finance 26*: 304–320.

Coase, R. H. 1960. "The Problem of Social Cost." *The Journal of Law and Economics 3*: 1–44.

2.2　Introduction

This chapter is largely remedial: just to remind you what you should have learned in your microeconomics course and to establish a benchmark of what everyone should know. It is not a substitute for a rigorous microcourse.

I skirt over some technical issues and compromise on rigor to convey the central intuitions. We begin by discussing the Walrasian, "perfect," market and continue to consider some, "traditional," market failures.

2.3   Walrasian market

Suppose there are $i = 1, \ldots, N$ individuals,[1] where N is a large number. They are households in a pure exchange economy or households and firms in an economy with production. There is some vector, $\mathbf{x} = \{x_1, \ldots, x_k\}$, of *commodities*. These commodities may include a blue button-down shirt, a four-wheel drive station wagon, a seventeen-inch television set four years from now, Internet services, car insurance, and an umbrella if it rains. For simplicity, whenever no generality is lost, we think in terms of a two-commodity world.

Individuals derive *utility* from consuming commodities and from leisure. In general, $U_i(\mathbf{x})$ is the utility derived by the $i-th$ individual from consuming a basket $\mathbf{x}$. Utilities need not be the same for all the individuals: This is why they are indexed by i. Given the utility function of an individual, we can represent it by an *indifference map*. A particular indifference (or isoutility) curve represents all combinations of commodities that give an individual the same utility, $U(\mathbf{x}) = \overline{U}$. (I will drop the index i.) Two such indifference curves for individual i are presented in Figure 2.1.

You are indifferent between any combination of x_l and x_k along the same curve. You prefer to be at any point in the North-East direction (such geographical references are customarily used), so that you prefer to be at any point of U' rather than U''. Note that the indifference curves are convex to the origin (the intuitive way to think about convexity is that all tangents are below the line). This assumption is synonymous with the assumption that marginal rates of substitution between commodities are diminishing, where the *marginal rate of substitution* between l and k is the number of units of commodity x_l an individual is willing to give in exchange for a little more of x_k for utility to remain the same. If you have a few units of x_k, you will be willing to give up many x_l to get a little more x_k (point A); if you have many units of x_k, you will be willing to give up few x_l to get a little more x_k

---

[1] Strangely enough when economists speak of decision-making units operating in the market they call them "agents," while sociologists call them "actors." I decided to speak whenever possible of "individuals," whether these are physical individuals, households, or firms, and to reserve the term "agents" for the principal-agent framework.

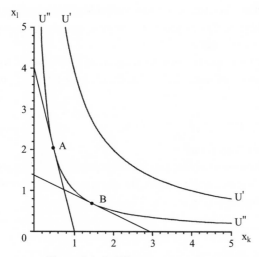

Figure 2.1. Indifference curves for individual i.

(point B). Let

$$U(x_k, x_l) = \overline{U}.$$

Differentiating with regard to x_k and setting the derivative to zero (to maintain U constant) yields

$$\frac{d\overline{U}}{dx_k} = \frac{\partial U}{\partial x_k} + \frac{\partial U}{\partial x_l}\frac{dx_l}{dx_k} = 0,$$

which implies that

$$\frac{\partial U/\partial x_k}{\partial U/\partial x_l} = -\frac{dx_l}{dx_k} = MRS_{lk}$$

The marginal rate of substitution (MRS) is thus the slope of the indifference curve, represented by the straight lines tangent to the indifference curves.

Households face a *budget constraint.* They have income (or endowment) y. (In problems including production, it is also customary to assume that individuals have a unit of time, which they can divide between labor and leisure.) Let the price of x_k be p_k and let the price of x_l be p_l. A household can purchase at most

$$y = p_k x_k + p_l x_l.$$

We assume that the actions of a single individual do not affect prices, so that each individual is a *price taker. A competitive market is a market in which everyone is a price taker.*

Each household seeks to *maximize $U(x_k, x_l)$* under the budget constraint. Hence, the problem of the household is to decide how much x_k and x_l to purchase so as to

$$\max_{x_l, x_k} U(x_k, x_l) \; s.t. \; y = p_k x_k + p_l x_l,$$

where *s.t.* stands for *"subject to."*

Given that we have only two commodities and that y, p_k, and p_l are fixed, one can use the budget constraint to write the quantity of x_l that a household can purchase as a function of x_k:

$$x_l = \frac{y}{p_l} - \frac{p_k}{p_l} x_k$$

and reduce the problem to a simple maximization in one variable[2]

$$\max_{x_k} U\left(x_k, \frac{y}{p_l} - \frac{p_k}{p_l} x_k\right).$$

The first-order condition for this problem is

$$\frac{dU}{dx_k} = U_k + U_l \left[\frac{d}{dx_k}\left(\frac{y}{p_l} - \frac{p_k}{p_l} x_k\right)\right] = 0,$$

where, **note**, we have written partial derivatives using subscripts, so that $\frac{\partial U}{\partial x_k} \equiv U_k$ and $\frac{\partial U}{\partial x_l} \equiv U_l$. Taking the derivative in the square bracket yields

$$U_k - U_l \frac{p_k}{p_l} = 0,$$

or

$$\frac{U_k}{U_l} = \frac{p_k}{p_l}.$$

But what is $\frac{U_k}{U_l}$? It is the marginal rate of substitution. Hence, the maximum is reached when

$$\frac{\partial U/\partial x_k}{\partial U/\partial x_l} = -\frac{dx_l}{dx_k} = MRS_{lk} = \frac{p_k}{p_l}.$$

This is a result of profound significance, so let us understand what happened here. Take two price ratios $\frac{p_k}{p_l}$, differing only in p_k: p_l is the *numeraire.*

---

[2] There is also a more general, but slightly more difficult, way to handle this problem.

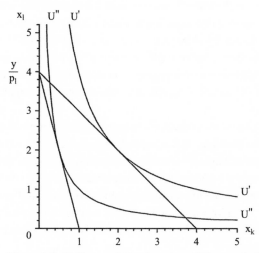

Figure 2.2. Utility maximization given different relative prices.

We can draw the functions $x_l = \frac{y}{p_l} - \frac{p_k}{p_l} x_k$ for each price ratio. Their intercept is in both cases $\frac{y}{p_l}$, so that they differ only in slopes, given by $\frac{p_k}{p_l}$. (See Figure 2.2.)

Each household is trying to reach the highest indifference curve compatible with its budget constraint: This is what maximization means. The highest one possible is the one tangent to the budget constraint line. If the price of x_k is low relative to the price of x_l, so that $\frac{p_k}{p_l}$ is low, they can reach U'. When $\frac{p_k}{p_l}$ is high, they can reach only U''. Moreover, note that the mix of x_k, x_l will be different. Given the relative prices, households adjust their consumption so that their marginal rate of substitution, the ratio of their marginal utilities, equals the ratio of prices. At their optimal solution, what they are willing to give up in x_k to get a units of x_l depends on their relative prices.

Note that this will be true for all households. Their utility functions need not be the same. But each household will adjust its consumption basket in such a way that for each household its marginal rate of substitution will equal the price ratio. And if the marginal rate of substitution of all households equals the ratio of the prices, then the marginal rates of substitution must be equal for all households.

Why is it so? Prices have a fundamental role in this story. They fully inform each individual what opportunities she gives up by consuming (or using in production) a unit of each commodity. This is the miracle of the market. By looking at the price, you know how many pears you will not be able to eat every time you devour an apple. I know it seems obvious, but just imagine that you do not know what the pear price of apples is. How could you now decide whether to eat an apple? Perhaps when you ate an apple you would be giving only one pear, but perhaps you would be giving up ten! And although one pear for an apple may be just fine if you prefer apples, what about ten pears?

Note that if you knew everyone's tastes and everyone's endowments you could still solve the problem: These endowments and the individual utility functions uniquely determine the (equilibrium) prices, so you could calculate the equilibrium directly, without a recourse to prices. But even if you knew all this, each time an idea of eating an apple would cross your mind you would need a computer. Yet if you just know this one number – the pear price of apples – you can decide immediately. It is easy to be a utility maximizer in a competitive market.

But this story is not about apples and pears, so the time has come to drop silly examples. Prices inform not just about the pear price of apples but about everything price of apples, about all the possible bundles of consumption, now and forever, of every commodity. They tell you that if you consume a unit of x_k you will be giving up going to a movie, or taking a day of unpaid leave next year, or being able to buy $(1 + r)^{10}$ units of x_k ten years from now, or being able to buy an umbrella if it rains. They represent the *opportunity cost* of every *dated commodity* in every *contingent state of nature*.

Because this is the greatest virtue of the market, let us go over some examples. When you know the price of the blue shirt you find attractive and the price of movie tickets, you know how many movies you would have to give up if you buy this shirt. This much is trivial. But prices tell you not just about going to the movie tonight; they also inform you how many movies you will have to give up one year from now, ten years from now, and one hundred years from now. This is what is meant by dated commodities. Moreover, it may be that if there is no earthquake in Hollywood, prices of movies will be low but if an earthquake does strike, they will be high. Hence, prices tell you how many movies you will be giving up for your shirt if there is an earthquake and if there is none: in every contingent state of nature. If you are to make decisions rationally, you need to know all this, and prices allow you to make rational decisions.

Consider two special examples. Suppose you are asking yourself whether buying this blue shirt is worth working an hour more. You are solving a problem of maximizing the utility derived from consumption (of blue shirts) and leisure, so that your problem is

$$\max_l U(c, l) \ s.t. \ l = 1 - L,$$

where $c = wL$ stands for consumption, l stands for leisure, and $L = 1 - l$ stands for labor. The first-order condition for this problem is

$$U_c \frac{dc}{dl} + U_l = 0,$$

which yields

$$\frac{U_l}{U_c} = -\frac{dc}{dl} = w.$$

The wage rate, the price of your labor services in consumption units, tells you how much you can buy if you give up a fraction of your leisure, or work a fraction of your time more. Hence, this price enables you to decide whether it is worth it for you to work more and buy the shirt.

You may also want to know what is the price of your current consumption in terms of your future consumption: If you buy this shirt now (N), how many shirts will you be unable to buy in the future (F)? Your problem now is to maximize your utility from consumption now and in the future, subject to the budget constraint:

$$\max_{c^N} U(c^N, c^F) \ s.t. \ c^F = (1 + r)(y^N - c^N),$$

with first-order condition

$$U_N + U_F \frac{dc^F}{dc^N} = 0,$$

so that

$$\frac{U_N}{U_F} = -\frac{dc^F}{dc^N} = 1 + r,$$

where r is the interest rate. Given that you know the price of consuming now in terms of consuming in the future, all you need to ask yourself is whether you prefer to consume now or to wait.

Enough examples. Let me now just state, informally and without proofs, two central theorems of welfare economics. The first one asserts that *if the price vector p and allocation x constitute a competitive equilibrium, then this allocation is Pareto efficient*. In a competitive equilibrium, no single individual can affect the prices facing other individuals and markets must be

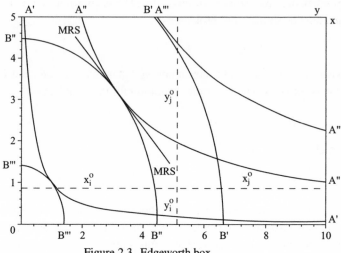

Figure 2.3. Edgeworth box.

"complete," which means that there is a market for every commodity. This is intuitively clear: If there is no market for car insurance, how could you compare the value of a shirt with the expected cost of car theft?

The intuition behind this theorem, "the first theorem of welfare economics," is best explained using a heuristic device developed more than one hundred years ago, popularly called the "Edgeworth box" (see Figure 2.3). The story goes as follows: There are two individuals, i and j, and two commodities, x and y. The two individuals have convex utility functions $U(x, y)$ and initial endowments $\{x, y\}$. Now we enter into a pure exchange economy (nothing is produced). Any allocation must satisfy the constraints

$$x_i + x_j = x$$
$$y_i + y_j = y$$

Because both individuals want to consume as much as possible, they want to reach an indifference curve as far as possible from their origin. Let the origin be at the point $\{0, 0\}$ for individual i and at the point $\{x, y\}$ for individual j. Then individual i prefers any point on the indifference curve A''' to any point at A'' to any point at A'. In turn, j prefers any point at B''' to any point at B'' to any point at B'. Now, suppose that the initial endowments are $\{x_i^o, y_i^o; x_j^o, y_j^o\}$ such that the point determined by them lies in the open cone above B'' and below A''. Now draw the indifference curves that pass through this point; call them A^o, B^o. Can both i and j be better off if they exchange? Consider the allocation defined by the point of tangency of A'' and B'', $\{x_i'', y_i''; x_j'', y_j''\}$. Since i prefers any point at A'' to any point at A^o and j prefers any point at B'' to any point at B^o, both are better off. Hence, the exchange that led from $\{x_i^o, y_i^o; x_j^o, y_j^o\}$ to $\{x_i'', y_i''; x_j'', y_j''\}$ generated gains for both. The question remains, however, whether either of them can be still better off without the other one being worse off. Will they want to exchange further? Any deviation from $\{x_i'', y_i''; x_j'', y_j''\}$ makes someone worse off. If they were to move closer to the $\{0, 0\}$ point, i would suffer; if they were to move closer to the $\{x, y\}$ point, j would; if they were to move to some point above B'' and below A'', both would. Hence, the point $\{x_i'', y_i''; x_j'', y_j''\}$ is an equilibrium: an allocation from which no one would want to deviate.

Now note that at this point the marginal rate of substitution is tangent to the indifference curves of both individuals. Hence, it must be the same, and we already know that it must equal the ratio of prices. Hence, in equilibrium the marginal rates of substitution are the same for all households and they equal the ratios of prices.

At the risk of boring you, note again that at the equilibrium all gains from trade are exhausted, no one can be better off without someone else being worse off, and someone would vote against changing it. Hence, the allocation associated with the equilibrium is efficient. A "Walrasian economy," one in which there are markets for everything, everyone is a price taker, and some other conditions hold, generates, therefore, an efficient allocation of resources. Note that we considered only a pure exchange economy but you can consult any microeconomics textbook to see that the same is true of an economy with production.

Now the second theorem. It asserts, again very roughly, that *if the economy is Walrasian and if redistribution of initial endowments is costless, then any efficient allocation can be reached by a suitable redistribution of initial endowments followed by decentralized exchange.*

To see the intuition, let us go back to the Edgeworth box. We already know that from the initial endowment $\{x_i^o, y_i^o; x_j^o, y_j^o\}$, the individuals will trade to $\{x_i'', y_i''; x_j'', y_j''\}$. But from a different initial endowment they will trade to a different equilibrium. Indeed, the set of all equilibria – called the *contract curve* – is a line that connects all the points of tangency of the indifference curves. Hence, the equilibrium allocation depends on the initial endowments. In our initial illustration, individual i had a lot of x but little y, while j had a lot of y but little x. Suppose that j is just poor in initial endowments, so that she has little x and little y. Then the equilibrium will be at the point of tangency of A''', B' and j will still be poor, after all the gains from trade have been exhausted. What the second theorem of welfare economics asserts is that if it is possible to costlessly reallocate the initial endowments, then any point on the contract curve can be reached. All that is needed to generate the relatively outcome-egalitarian equilibrium given by the tangency of A'', B'' is to reallocate endowments to $\{x_i^o, y_i^o; x_j^o, y_j^o\}$.

This, then, is the miracle of the market. Households or firms do not need to know anything about other households or firms: All the information they need to act rationally is summarized by the prices. The allocation they generate by production and exchange is efficient. If a society deems a particular allocation undesirable, all it needs to do is to reallocate endowments. Markets enable individual rationality and generate collective rationality.

2.4   Market failures

This is a miracle, not the real world, not a description of any real economy (although some people who believe in miracles take it for such) but only a statement of the exacting conditions that are necessary for such a miracle to occur.

We now go over some conditions under which this miracle breaks down. The conditions we consider are often referred to as "market failures." But we see in the next chapter that this is not a good language, because it presupposes that the miracle is a natural state of the world that breaks only in some special cases. Such conditions are ubiquitous, so there is no sense to confuse models and realities.

Three "traditional" market failures are typically distinguished, although the distinctions are not always sharp. They are due to increasing returns to scale, nonrivalries in consumption, and externalities.

2.4.1   Increasing returns

As you know, *increasing returns to scale* are a characteristic of production: Returns are increasing if multiplying all the inputs by a factor of n leads to an increase of output by more than n. Otherwise returns are constant or decreasing. Increasing returns imply that the average costs of the firm declines as the scale of production increases. Consider an electric company. A company that has a large network faces low costs of connecting an additional consumer, while a company that has a small network must build a lot to hook up the next consumer. Hence, if the firm is large, its average cost of production is lower than when it is small.

Increasing returns to scale imply that an already large company has a competitive advantage over small companies. Because it faces lower average costs, it can drive other firms out of business and it can deter entry. Hence, increasing returns lead to "natural" monopolies. Not all monopolies result from increasing returns: Often they are a result of collusion. But increasing returns lead to monopolies without any collusion.

Increasing returns cause market failure because monopolies set prices above the competitive level, so that the society cannot consume all it would want to at competitive prices. Moreover, the gain to the monopolies is smaller than the loss to consumers and the net difference constitutes a loss to the society, *deadweight loss*.

One way to think about this situation is as follows. There is only one firm producing a particular commodity. The firm maximizes profits, which are the difference between revenues and costs. Suppose that the firm decides how much to produce, q. It faces a downward-sloping demand curve: The higher the price, the less of this commodity the consumers buy. Note that as the monopolist increases the volume of production, it must charge a lower (uniform) price on all the units it sells. The monopolist's problem is

$$\max_{q \geq 0} p(q)q - c(q),$$

where p stands for price and c for cost. The solution, q^M, must satisfy the first-order condition

$$p'(q^M)q^M + p(q^M) = c'(q^M), q^M > 0.$$

The left-hand side of this equation represents marginal revenue; the right-hand side marginal cost. Because $p'(q) < 0$, it must be true that the price exceeds marginal cost. Hence, the monopolist's output must be lower than the socially optimal (competitive) output level, call it q^S.

To see the social cost entailed, consider Figure 2.4. The output level chosen by the monopolist is $q^M < q^S$ and the price charged by the monopolist, p^M, is higher than the competitive price. The shaded area represents the deadweight loss of monopoly – the welfare loss to the society resulting from the fact that consumers would be willing to purchase more of this commodity, up to q^S, were the price competitive.

One caveat is necessary. The analysis we presented is *static*, as is the Walrasian model. If you start thinking in dynamic terms, it will become

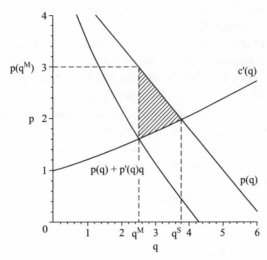

Figure 2.4. Deadweight loss of monopoly.

clear that some firms may enjoy a monopolistic position because they are the only ones who have introduced something new that consumers want. Clearly, once an innovation had been made, the society would want it to be competitively priced. But if innovations are costly to make, they would not be made unless they generate excess profits, or *entrepreneurial rents*. And the society may be better off with innovation being financed by monopoly rents than without it. Moreover, as other firms learn that these commodities generate excess profits, they will move to produce them and the rents will be dissipated. A growing economy is not efficient in the static sense: This was the great intuition of Schumpeter (1946). We touch on the topic of economic growth later on, but for the time being let us continue with a static analysis.

The society is not helpless against monopolies. It can act legally against monopolies that result simply from collusion. And even in the case of natural monopolies, it can regulate them so as to ensure that consumers face competitive prices, either by subsidizing the natural monopolies to produce more or by subsidizing prices to consumers so that they would buy more. We study the regulation of monopolies later.

2.4.2   Public goods

Public goods are commodities that are nonrival in consumption. Note that all the commodities used as examples to study the Walrasian economy were rival in consumption. If I eat the apple, you cannot eat it. If you are wearing this blue shirt, I am not. In the Walrasian model, all the commodities have this characteristic: If they are consumed by one individual, they cannot be consumed by another. But think now of clean air. The fact that I breathe it does not preclude you from breathing it as well. Or think of a lighthouse: If one ship sees it, no other ship is precluded from seeing it. Such goods are ubiquitous, and some examples are surprising. The stock of basic knowledge, national defense, and global warming are all examples of public goods. Note that public goods can be bad: "Goods" stands for commodities, not for things that are good, even if sometimes you will encounter the expression "public bads."

Pace Varian (1984, p. 253), public goods need not be jointly consumed. Indeed, no one has to consume them. Defense is a public good that is jointly consumed: If the armed forces defend one citizen, they defend all. But lighthouses are not: One ship may look for it, while another will not. What matters is only that if the first ship were to look for the light, the second one would not be impeded from looking. Nonrivalry is an attribute of goods, not of social organization of consumption. Clean air is a public good even where no one breathes.

Goods are public if they are nonrival in consumption, not when they are produced by the public sector. National defense is a public good because if the armed forces defend one citizen, no other citizen is less defended. Health services offered by the public sector are rival goods: If a doctor is seeing me, she cannot be attending you. So are obviously cars produced by a public automobile factory.

Many public goods are *subject to congestion*. A park or a highway are public goods because my lying in the grass or driving does not prevent others from doing so. But only up to a point, because parks or highways can become so full that no one else can use them.

Public goods may or may not be *excludable*. We can put a fence around a park and charge admission. We can, and do, create tollways. We may reserve beaches to residents of a particular community. You may encounter definitions that restrict the class of public goods to those that are nonexcludable. As we will see, this is wrong: What matters about goods is the nonrivalry, not excludability.

Note that by cross-classifying rivalry with excludability, we get an interesting classification of goods (see Table 2.1).

This terminology is not standard: People invent all kinds of names. But the intuition is shared. Goods that are rival and excludable are private: These

Table 2.1

	Excludable	Nonexcludable
Rival	Private	Common pool
Nonrival	Club, toll	Pure public

are the only commodities that exist in a Walrasian economy. *Common pool resources* (CPRs) are goods that are jointly exploited by several independent individuals. "The commons" in the literal sense are the communal pasture lands and this term is often used as a metaphor for all such goods. The fish pool in a lake is such a good. "Club" goods are some (not all) nonrival goods from which people can be excluded: A beach can be reserved to residents, but it would stretch the notion of "club" to say that people who pay tolls constitute one. Finally, "pure" public goods are those that are nonrival and nonexcludable.

The most obvious problem with public goods is this. Assume that the public good G is non-negatively valued by all individuals. Once the good is produced, the marginal cost of consuming it, that is, the cost of it being consumed by an additional person, is 0. Hence, the price of this good should be 0. But if the good is costly to produce, no firm will produce it if it can charge only this price. Hence, the market will undersupply nonexcludable private goods. One way to see it is to portray the situation as game, making B the benefit an individual derives from consuming G and letting $2C$ be the total cost of supplying it (see Table 2.2).

Assume that $2C > B > C > 0$ for both individuals. This means that if both were to contribute (equally) to the provision of the good, each would be better off, $B - C > 0$. Hence, it is *individually rational* for them to contribute. But if $B - 2C < 0$, then neither of them cares about this good so much as to finance it by herself. If i were to pay, j would be better off not contributing; and vice versa. Hence, this is a prisoners' dilemma, with the equilibrium $\{not\ pay,\ not\ pay\}$ and the associated payoff of $\{0, 0\}$ Pareto inferior to the allocation associated with $\{pay,\ pay\}$, which has a positive value for each individual. Thus provision of public goods entails *free riding*.

To see the same point in the Walrasian framework, let us compare the provision of public goods by the market with the command equilibrium, that is a collectively optimal decision. Suppose first that each individual contributes g_i to finance the quantity G of a public good, so that $\sum_{i \in N} g_i =$

Table 2.2

		individual i	
		pay	not pay
individual j	pay	$B_j - C, B_i - C$	$B_j - 2C, B_i$
	not pay	$B_j, B_i - 2C$	$0, 0$

G. Each individual has a utility function $U_i(x_i, G)$, where x is a private good. The budget constraint is $p_x x_i + p_G g_i = y_i$. Maximization with regard to g_i yields[3]

$$\frac{U_G}{U_x} = \frac{p_G}{p_x},$$

as if G were a private good. But in fact, each individual consumes G, not g_i: All of it. Hence, we can suspect that G will be undersupplied.

To see what would be socially optimal, in the first step let the social planner choose G to maximize a welfare function

$$\max_G W = \sum_{i \in N} \gamma_i U_i \ s.t. \ \sum_{i \in N} y_i - \left[p_x \sum_{i \in N} x_i + p_G G \right] = 0.$$

where γ_i is the weight the planner attaches to the welfare of individual i.

Comment. This is a constrained maximization problem. For most such problems,

$$\max \ maximand \ s.t. \ constraint$$

---

[3] The steps are:

$$x_i = \frac{y_i}{p_x} - \frac{p_G}{p_x} g_i,$$

$$\max_{g_i} U^i \left(\frac{y_i}{p_x} - \frac{p_G}{p_x} g_i, G \right),$$

$$U_x^i \frac{dx_i}{dg_i} + U_G^i \frac{dG}{dg_i} = 0,$$

because $\frac{dG}{dg_i} = 1$,

$$-U^i \frac{p_G}{p_x} + U_G^i = 0.$$

we first write a "Lagrangean," £, as

$$\text{£} = U + \lambda[\textit{constraint}],$$

and then we apply the first-order conditions (and check for second-order conditions). (**End of comment**)

Writing the Lagrangean, we have

$$\max_{G} \text{£} = \sum_{i \in N} \gamma_i U_i + \lambda \left[\sum_{i \in N} y_i - p_x \sum_{i \in N} x_i - p_G G \right].$$

First-order conditions imply

$$\sum_{i \in Ni} \gamma_i U_G = \lambda p_G.$$

In the second step, the planner chooses x_i to maximize $U_i(x_i, G)$ s.t. the individual's budget constraint (alternatively, each individual solves her problem and the planner attaches weights γ_i to each when aggregating) and given the decision about G, so that the problem is

$$\max_{x} \text{£} = \gamma_i U_i(x, G) + \lambda[y_i - p_x x_i - p_G G],$$

with the solution

$$\gamma_i U_x = \lambda p_x,$$

or

$$\gamma_i = \frac{\lambda p_x}{U_x}.$$

Substituting for γ above and eliminating λ yields

$$\sum_{i \in N} \frac{U_G}{U_x} = \frac{p_G}{p_x}.$$

This is Samuelson's (1954) condition for Pareto-optimality in the presence of public goods.

To see what this means, rewrite

$$\frac{U_G^i}{U_x^i} = \frac{p_G}{p_x} - \sum_{i \neq j} \frac{U_G^j}{U_x^j}.$$

If x and G are normal goods ($U_x > 0, U_G > 0$), then the last sum is positive, so that the marginal rate of substitution for the society will be

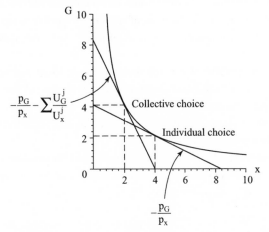

Figure 2.5. Society wants to consume more G and less x than each individual.

lower than the one associated with market equilibrium. In other words, the society wants to consume more G and less x than each individual. (See Figure 2.5.)

The slope is steeper for the society, so that it will choose less x and more G than each individual.

Suppose this good is nonrival but excludable. For example, a firm charges a $1 toll to enter the highway. But this means that all the consumers for whom the value of using the road is more than 0 but less than $1 will not use it. And because the cost of using it is 0, this is waste from a social point of view, a loss of consumer surplus.

Hence, the existence of goods that are nonrival in consumption causes inefficiency, whether or not they are excludable. If they are nonexcludable, they will be undersupplied by the market; if they are excludable, they will be underutilized.

2.4.3 Externalities

An externality is an effect of actions of an individual that affects the welfare (utility) of others. Say a factory generates smoke that dirties houses in the neighborhood. An externality is an effect of actions – production of smoke – on welfare – dirty houses. The factory produces smoke and pays for its production. Yet the smoke also inflicts a cost on home owners. In this chapter, we consider only technological externalities, in which the action of one individual directly affects the utility or profit of another. Pecuniary externalities, in which the effect is trasmitted only through prices, are discussed in the next chapter.

Externalities are *positive* if the action of one individual increases the welfare of other individuals. For example, by developing a subway line in London, the government created a positive externality for people living close to the new line. Externalities are *negative* when the effects reduce the welfare of others. We already have an example.

Consider a classical story. There are two neighbors. One produces apples; the other one produces honey. The production function of the apples is

$$A = A(T, B)$$

and of honey it is

$$H = H(B).$$

Apples are produced by trees, T, but they are pollinated by bees. Honey is produced by beehives, B. Both production functions are concave, so that for any input x, $F_x > 0$, $F_{xx} < 0$. Let the price of a beehive, $p_B = 1$, be the *numeraire*, that is, let us measure the values of everything in the price of beehives. The profit functions are then

$$\pi_A = p_A A(T, B) - p_T T,$$

and

$$\pi_H = p_H H(B) - B.$$

Each producer maximizes profits. The apple grower chooses the number of trees to plant; the honey producer chooses the number of beehives. The apple grower will thus choose the number of trees such that (subscripts on commodities denote derivatives)

$$A_T = p_T/p_A,$$

and the honey producer will choose the number of beehives such that

$$H_B = 1/p_H.$$

The number of beehives chosen by the honey producer will thus be B^M, portrayed in Figure 2.6.

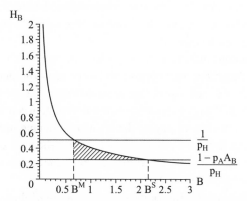

Figure 2.6. An example of a negative externality.

Now consider what would happen if the decisions to invest were made by the society, that is, in a centralized way. The profit to the society is

$$\pi_S = p_A A(T, B) + p_H H(B) - p_T T - B,$$

with first-order conditions (derived by taking partial derivatives with regard to both inputs) given by

$$A_T = p_T / p_A,$$

and

$$H_B = \frac{1 - p_A A_B}{p_H}.$$

Note that the first-order condition with regard to apples is the same as in the market decision. But the society will consider the marginal impact of beehives on the output of apples, A_B. Hence, the value of the derivative H_B chosen by the society will be lower, implying that the society will choose a higher number of beehives, B^S.

What happens here is this. The honey producer derives profits from the investment in beehives. But his beehives increase the rate of return to apple trees and the honey producer does not capture these profits, because the apples belong to someone else. Hence, the honey producer does not consider the effect on apples when he decides how many beehives to install. As a result, the private, market, rate of return is lower than the social rate of return. The market allocates resources inefficiently: The area shaded in Figure 2.6

measures the loss of consumer surplus. If the apple and the honey producers would make their decisions jointly, at least one of them would be better off without the other one being worse off.

There are two solutions that make the allocation efficient. One is to subsidize the honey producer. For each beehive, the value of the production of apples increases by $p_A A_B$. Suppose the apple producer is taxed the amount $p_A A_B (B^S - B^M)$. Then the apple producer is indifferent between not paying the tax and producing less or paying the tax and producing more. The honey producer, in turn, will have an incentive to invest at the level B^S. This is a *Pigovian subsidy*, named after Albert Pigou, a British economist. (This solution is not without problems of its own.)

The second solution is to centralize the decisions: to make them jointly. The two firms can merge; one of the firms can buy the other one; or the state can order investment. In any case, the investment in beehives will be B^S, at the efficient level.

2.4.4   Are transaction costs a source of market failure?

This is a muddled topic. Trading is always costly: It always entails some "transaction costs." Even if completing a trade takes just a phone call, the call is costly. This ubiquity of transaction costs leads some authors to see them everywhere. But if they are everywhere, they are not very illuminating for the understanding of the way markets work. Only if they can be distinguished do they offer a tool for the analysis.

Consider some definitions. North (1990, p. 27) sees transaction costs as "the costs of measuring the valuable attributes of what is being exchanged and the costs of protecting rights and policing and enforcing agreements." Williamson (1989, p. 142) defines them as "comparative costs of planning, adapting, and monitoring task completion under alternative governance structures." These definitions imply that there is no market – indeed, no situation – in which such costs are absent. Williamson's emphasis on "comparative costs ... under alternative governance structures" does point to the way in which this concept can be used as an analytical tool, but we do not yet know what these costs are.

Let us, therefore, start differently. In a Walrasian model, there are no transaction costs. But suppose that any transaction would have a fixed, exogenous cost T. What would happen? Some transactions would not occur:

Even if I could exchange from my initial endowment to an allocation I prefer, I would not do it if the costs of this exchange were so high that I would end up worse off. Suppose I sell my apples for pears, but the pears have to come from overseas and they rot in the process. Or suppose that the pears are produced locally but an expert must be flown from overseas to determine if they are rotten. Then I may not give up my apples for pears. I do not find it enlightening to say that the resulting allocation is inefficient: Pears are produced only overseas and they rot in transport. This is just a constraint on exchange and nothing can be done about it. Hence, such transaction costs are not a source of "market failure." The market allocates resources as efficiently as it is possible given exogenous constraints.

Suppose now that what we are trading are not commodities but property rights. The honey producer would be better off if she could capture the externality of bees on apples and she wants to buy the apple firm. The apple producer would be better off if he could determine the number of beehives, so he wants to buy the honey firm. Suppose that the transaction is costless. Then one of them will buy the other (or they will merge) and an efficient allocation will be reached. It makes no difference who owned what originally and who bought whom. Hence, in the absence of transaction costs, the original assignment of property rights does not matter for efficiency: The market, which now includes property rights as a tradeable commodity, will reach an efficient allocation. This is the *Coase theorem*.

What may impede this transaction? Consider a situation in which the honey producer cannot determine the value of the apple firm without hiring a well-paid accountant. The transaction does not occur because it is costly. But we are back to where we were: If accountants make good money, this is again just a constraint on the property rights market. There is no market in property rights because property transactions are inherently costly. The market allocation of property rights is not Pareto efficient, but global Pareto efficiency is not an enlightening way to evaluate this allocation.

The concept of transaction costs becomes useful only when we stop thinking of "the market" that may or may not fail, but admit that all markets are organized in some particular ways, including the ways in which they are regulated. Only then Williamson's comparative emphasis makes sense: If property rights transactions can be differently structured, then it makes sense to ask whether one way of organizing them makes them less costly than other ways. But this puts us ahead of what we know thus far.

2.5   Conclusion

Note how we have proceeded. We said first "there is a market" with some specific properties. Indeed, we said "Assume there is a complete set of competitive markets which, in addition, satisfies some properties." We discovered that this market will allocate resources efficiently and that any socially desired allocation can be reached by this market by reallocating initial endowments. Then we delved into some of the previously not specified conditions, some "absences." We observed that the market will allocate efficiently if there are no increasing returns to scale, if there are no nonrivalries in consumption, and if there are no externalities. Whenever one of these absences becomes filled, the market "fails." Hence, there is a perfect market that fails under specific circumstances.

One way of thinking, not without technical difficulties, that the market fails is that the private rate of return diverges from the social rate of return. The difficulties are because the latter is not always easy to determine. We used "command optimum" as the tool to determine the allocation by society and this tool is subject to caveats that were discussed in the first chapter. Yet if we were to apply this tool to the Walrasian economy, we would have discovered that the choice by the society is the same as the market allocation. Hence, this is a useful tool. And the intuition is clear. The private rate of return to the investment by a monopoly is higher than the social rate; the private rate of return to the investment in public goods is zero, while the social rate is positive; the private rate of return to investment producing a positive (negative) externality is lower (higher) than the social rate. If the role of the state is to maximize the social rate of return (or some equivalent criterion), then governments should undertake actions that equalize these rates.

The discovery of market failures in the early 1950s led indeed to a view of governments that could be termed "the market-failure theory of the state." This theory was best captured by the 1959 program of the German Social Democratic Party: "markets whenever possible, the state whenever necessary." The idea was that markets "should be left to themselves" to do things they do well but governments should step in to correct their functioning when they fail. Hence, the proper role of the state was to regulate monopolies, provide public goods, and correct for externalities.

This theory raised a question that is obvious, even though it was publicly formulated only in the 1970s, namely "What guarantees that when markets fail, the state will not fail as well?" This is one of central topics of this book. But this entire way of thinking is more profoundly misleading. The question is not about what the state should and will do when the market fails but "Is there anything out there to fail?" Is there something that could be termed "the market," something that "can be left to itself"?

This is the topic for the next chapter.

CHAPTER 3

Incomplete markets, imperfect information

3.1 Readings

Read:

Newbery, David M. 1990. "Missing Markets: Consequences and Remedies." In Frank Hahn (ed.), *The Economics of Missing Markets, Information,
and Games*, 211–242. Oxford: Clarendon Press.

Stiglitz, Joseph E. 1994. Chapters 3 and 4 of *Whither Socialism?*
Cambridge, MA: MIT Press.

Recommended:

Greenwald, Bruce C. and Joseph E. Stiglitz. 1986. "Externalities in
Economies with Imperfect Information and Incomplete Markets." *Quarterly
Journal of Economics 101*: 229–264.

3.2 Introduction

As Stiglitz (1994) observes, when markets are incomplete, as they must be,
and when information is not perfect, there is not even a presumption that
markets are efficient. The intuition that markets are incomplete is immediate. If there were a complete set of markets for all the present and future
dates, then we could finalize all the terms of trade once and for all and just
execute exchanges as time goes on. Yet we all think that we will trade in
the future. The prima facie evidence that information is imperfect (and often
asymmetric) is that we often think that prices inform about quality: "What
must he know to be selling this beautiful red car for such a low price?"

If some markets are always missing and if information is often imperfect,
perhaps it is better to start with markets as they are. Instead of conjuring

perfect markets and studying why they fail, we will thus start studying markets from the beginning. We will first ask why markets are always incomplete and then examine the consequences of incomplete markets for efficiency and for information. To study these consequences, we have to figure out how to think of efficiency when some markets are missing. Then we focus on imperfect information. Finally, we learn to think of an economy in a different way, as a network of relations between principals and agents.

3.3   Causes of market incompleteness

Why **must** markets be incomplete? There are several reasons.

3.3.1   Futures markets

Suppose that all the assumptions of the Walrasian model are fulfilled. For the first theorem to apply, goods must be distinguished by their physical characteristics, by their place and date of delivery, as well as by the state of the world. Newbery's (1990, p. 213) example is perfect: "Thus, a taxi to meet the 18:46 train in Cambridge on June 1, 2010 [I changed the date], if raining, is distinguished from the same taxi if sunny (and is presumably more valuable)." This assumption is often hard, and sometimes impossible, to meet.

(1) It is easy to consider the "impossible" part. The commodities for which futures markets must exist include those that have not yet been invented. Say you are in 1980 and you are considering whether to buy the blue shirt we discussed earlier. The shirt costs $29.95 in 2000 prices. Now, to make a rational decision you must know how many months of subscription to AOL you will give up in 2000 if you buy this shirt in 1980. But no one has yet thought of the Web. In 1980, there was no futures market for the Web because there was no Web.

(2) Now there is no futures market for Web services either. Indeed, the number of commodities for which futures markets do exist is very small, around thirty. There is a futures market for corn but not for e-mail and not for automobiles. The reason here is that corn of a particular variety is homogeneous: Its qualities are quite uniform. But cars vary greatly from one another. Hence, future cars or future Fords or even future Ford

station wagons may be better or worse. Cars are not something you want to buy sight unseen.

But, you may say, how about a futures market for metallic blue station wagons that have four-wheel drive, accelerate in 9.8 seconds from 0 to 50, consume 24.7 gallons in urban traffic, and have fewer than three defects? The problem here is different. As we specify the qualities of a commodity, the market for it becomes thinner and thinner: There will be fewer and fewer buyers and sellers. As Stiglitz (1994, p. 42) observes, in the end the market for labor is the market for Joe Stiglitz's labor, something with unique qualities. And if it is, then Joe Stiglitz is a monopolist, the only seller of this commodity. Hence, Stiglitz argues, markets that would distinguish all the physical characteristics, by their place and date of delivery, as well as by the states of the world, would be noncompetitive. Completeness and competition vary in inverse proportions.

3.3.2   Risk markets

Why couldn't we just insure ourselves against the variations of possible outcomes? Say we agree to buy a Ford station wagon ten years from now for some price knowing that we can sue Ford if the car is not what it is contracted to be. If Ford cannot completely predict the quality of its station wagons, because it depends on future events beyond its control, then Ford could buy an insurance against such suits. But the problem is that if Ford buys the insurance, it will have less of an incentive to control the quality (it will have nothing to lose and it will save the costs of quality control), which means that the insurance company will expect to lose money, which means in turn that it will not sell this insurance. Hence, the market for this insurance will be missing. Some risks are uninsurable because they entail too much *moral hazard.* For example, there is no (private) insurance for profit and there is none because the management would lose incentives to maximize it if the firm were insured. There is no (private) insurance against unemployment because some people would deliberately quit jobs, draw their unemployment insurance, and look for new jobs only to qualify for insurance again. The parenthetical "private" matters. There is public unemployment insurance because the state can intrusively monitor the reasons for losing jobs, whether an individual is searching actively, whether he or she is engaged in other gainful activities, and so on. These are obviously extreme cases, but for many items the transaction costs of insuring and monitoring are a very high proportion of the price.

Other risks may be uninsurable because people who face high risk, for example, knowing that they are likely to fall ill, want to buy insurance at terms under which the insurance firm is profitable only if people who face low risk also purchase the insurance at the same price. If the insurance firm does not know who faces high and low risks, there will be no private insurance market. We study *adverse selection* in detail when we discuss the welfare state.

3.3.3 Public goods and externality markets

Suppose that there are H households, N private goods, and one pure public good. Newbery's example of the public good is a television signal. Because each household may value the television signal differently (has a different MRS between the private and the public good), this economy has in fact $N + H$ goods, where each of the H goods is "TV signal for household h." Complete market would mean here that there is a market for each of the H goods, and we know from Chapter 1 that such a market would be efficient if it satisfied Samuelson's (1954) condition. Yet note that a complete market would not be competitive, because there is only one potential buyer in each market.

An important complication we encounter later is that incomplete markets can of themselves generate externalities. That is, not only externalities may lead to incomplete markets but markets incomplete for other reasons generate externalities.

3.3.4 Markets for future labor

Hahn (1990) points out that we generically do not have markets for future labor. With minor restrictions, employees are not bound by the duration of their contracts. True, I am expected to finish the academic year or perhaps someone else has to give a three-week notice. But I cannot be forced to work for my current employer two years from now even if I have a three-year contract binding on the employer. And I would not be bound by a promise to work for Boston Analytics ten years from now at $100,000 per year. The reason, Hahn says, is that our legal principles bar involuntary labor. I am not sure how far these principles extend: I am bound by a contract to deliver a 400-page book five years from now. But some trades entailing labor services are certainly nonenforceable. Hence, markets for some kinds of future labor are missing.

3.4   Consequences of missing markets

The consequences of market incompleteness are profound. The entire Walrasian conception breaks down.

(1) Note first the postmodernist tinge of the new image of markets. Instead of one market, one order, there are now lots of fragmented markets, in plural. We can now ask: "Is there a market for A, B, or C?" The modern revolution of Mandeville and Smith was to explain how a social order can emerge spontaneously out of decentralized actions, without anyone directing them, without any central authority. I remember from my introductory sociology class that Durkheim was obsessed by the fact that every morning he could open the back door of his apartment and find a bottle of milk, and he did not even know the milkman. The image of incomplete markets is much more fragmented, chaotic (we will see that there are multiple equilibria), and uncertain.

Indeed, instead of "the market," we now have to think of particular *sets of markets*. In one, there may be markets for A, B, and C, but not for D; in another, there may be markets for B, C, and D, but not A, and so on. Each of these sets of markets will generate a different equilibrium (or equilibria in plural).

(2) There is longer a presumption that markets are efficient. We cannot show that markets are always inefficient but generically, **almost always**, they are. We must investigate each set of markets separately to find out what the equilibrium or equilibria in plural will be and whether they will be efficient.

But what does efficiency mean in the context of incomplete markets? One way to think about it is that an allocation is constrained Pareto efficient if, *given the constraints*, there is no allocation that would leave household utilities unchanged while increasing government revenue.

Comment. Because we will use this concept frequently, it is useful to follow Greenwald and Stiglitz (1986) to see it in more detail. Assume that the economy is in some way imperfect, not necessarily because of missing markets, but also for reasons discussed in Chapter 1. In such an economy, the utility of a household will be $u(x, z)$, where x is the consumption vector of the household and z is the vector of other variables that affect utility, say pollution or the average quality of a good consumed. A necessary, although not sufficient (because there are other instruments that do the same) condition for a constrained Pareto optimality, where the constraint originates from the presence of z in the household utility function and perhaps in the firms' production function, is that there are taxes, subsidies, or lump sum transfers that would make households as well off while increasing government revenue. This condition is equivalent to saying that there is no wedge between consumer and producer prices. Greenwald and Stiglitz (1986) show that an allocation is constrained Pareto optimal only if there are no z's that change with taxes and affect either profits or household utilities.

When an allocation is not constrained optimal, it can be improved by income transfers. An optimal tax is then one that equates the marginal deadweight loss due to the distortion in consumption to the reduction of externalities. (**End of comment**)

Note that now we have two ways of thinking about efficiency. One is whether an allocation reached by the set of existing markets would improve (or deteriorate) if more markets were opened. Go back to apples and pears of the opening chapter, when we stipulated that, given that only these two markets existed, no one would want to trade away from the allocation $\{i : 1$ *apple*, 3 *pears*; j : 3 *apples*, 1 *pear*\}. Suppose we now open a market for plums: both individuals had plums before but there was no market for them. We discover that the individuals now trade to $\{i$: 0 *apples*, 4 *pears*, 2 *plums*; j : 4 *apples*, 0 *pears*, 1 *plum*\}. What this must mean is that allocation generated by the set of markets that included only apples and pears is inefficient. It did not exhaust the gains from trade. Somehow the traders could not each have an efficient allocation of apples and pears in the absence of a market for plums. Say that the relative prices of apples and pears depend on the weather, so that i is holding onto one apple just in case the weather is bad for apples and their price is very high. But now i buys insurance, to be paid in plums, in case the weather is bad for apples. He is now willing to trade away all his apples for the expected two plums.

The allocation produced by the apple-pear market is inefficient. But we already know that this allocation is efficient in the existing set of markets. It might have not been, for some other reasons, but within the apple-pear set of markers this allocation exhausts the gains from trade. Exchange in the existing set of markets is constrained by the absence of some other markets.

But under this constraint, it is efficient. Without opening a new market, no other allocation Pareto dominates the equilibrium allocation.

We also have a new conceptual tool: *(de)centralization.* We can ask whether an allocation would be Pareto superior if markets were to open or close. Note that opening markets may actually decrease efficiency: Study Newbery's (1990) island example.

Hence, one way to pose the relation between markets and states is to ask about decentralizability (a horrible word): Can a market be opened (or closed)? Will its opening increase or decrease efficiency? Is allocating airport slots by an auction (a market) more efficient than allocating it by command or by a lottery?

It is easy to intuit that incomplete sets of markets are often not globally Pareto efficient, that is, that opening (or closing) new markets would generate a different allocation in the previously existing set of markets. *But, the conclusion is that incomplete markets are generically, almost always, also constrained-inefficient.* That is, there exist allocations that are Pareto-superior to those generated by incomplete markets even without opening (or closing) markets. This is not a general theorem, in the vein of the theorems of welfare economics. There are no general theorems to be established because different situations are different. We must study them one by one. But it turns out that incomplete markets are generically not constrained-Pareto efficient. The most general reason for this inefficiency is that when some, mainly risk, markets are missing, no one can be certain what everyone else will be doing. But the actions of some have consequences for the utility levels reached by others. Hence, these actions create a negative externality of increased risk and in the presence of externalities the equilibrium allocation is not efficient.

Consider Stiglitz's (1994) example of market for labor (see Figure 3.1). There is one market, in which demand for labor, L^D, is a function of average quality, $\overline{q}$.

Now suppose that an unskilled worker enters the labor pool. His entrance will lower the average quality from $\overline{q}_o$ to $\overline{q}_s$, and demand will fall from $L(\overline{q}_o)$ to $L(\overline{q}_s)$. This means that a worker with quality q_o will have a lower chance of getting a job. Hence, the entrance of the less skilled worker imposes an externality on the more skilled one. Note that if the hiring firm could distinguish the quality of each worker, that is, if there was a separate market for labor of each quality, then more people would be employed and firms would be getting higher profit. Hence, the allocation is Pareto-inefficient. But it is also constrained inefficient: even if no private insurance against getting bad quality workers were available, the allocation {*profits, jobs*}

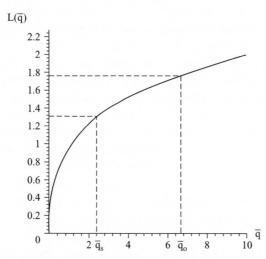

Figure 3.1. The market for labor in the presence of uncertainty.

could be improved by some set of subsidies and taxes. (Say workers pay an employment tax that is distributed to firms that happen to get workers of poor quality.)

(3) Prices no longer constitute sufficient statistics: They no longer inform uniquely about all the forsaken opportunities. If there is no future market for my labor, I do not know what I gain or lose if I continue my education instead of working. If there is no future market for station wagons, I do not know what I lose when I buy one now instead of waiting. If I cannot insure myself against having to hire a taxi when it rains, I do not know whether or not I will have to walk in the rain if I buy a beer on the train.

If markets are missing, individuals must make guesses about opportunity costs. Say there are several employers and a pool of workers. Employers must guess the quality of this labor pool, $\overline{q}$. Note that each worker knows the quality of his or her labor, q_i. But the firms do not. Hence, information is *imperfect and asymmetric:* In this case, firms do not know exactly the state of nature they are in and different firms know different things.

This fact has several consequences, but before getting to them, we need to clarify one aspect. Suppose that firms correctly guess the average quality: $E(q) = \overline{q}$, where $E(.)$ stands for *"expected value."* Do rational expectations remove the inefficiency? Is imperfect information the only channel through which incomplete markets cause inefficiency? The answer is that if firms are risk neutral, it is. But if employers are risk averse, that is, if they fear getting bad workers more than they benefit from good workers, then the rational expectations equilibrium in incomplete markets is Pareto-constrained inefficient (see Newbery 1990). If employers fear that making a mistake may cause the firm to go under, they will hire fewer workers even if they guess right the average quality of the labor pool, just because they fear that they get a particularly bad sample of this pool. Hence, imperfect information is not the only channel of inefficiency: If the profit insurance market is missing, and if individuals are risk averse, then even the rational expectations do not remove inefficiency. The effect of externalities persists even if individuals correctly guess the probability distribution of uncertain events.

But imperfect, asymmetric information does cause inefficiency of itself. We have already seen this in the example of the labor pool. What can employers do in this situation? They may be able to offer contracts in such a way that workers will sort themselves out. Let x_i stand for the output of a worker with quality q_i, and let $w(x_i)$ stand for wages. Then a *contract* is menu of pairs $\{x_i, w(x_i)\}$. Employers can design contracts such that good workers and bad workers would accept different offers. Bad workers would accept a contract $\{\underline{x}, \underline{w}\}$, while good workers would opt for $\{\overline{x}, \overline{w}\}$. But it turns out that employers will have to pay good workers for revealing their quality, so that $d\overline{x}/dL < \overline{w}$: Good workers will be paid more than their marginal product. This, in turn, implies that there will be unemployment. There is no way around it: We study such situations in the next chapter.

(4) Because the demand for labor depends on the guesses about labor quality that employers make, there is a different level of employment for each of the guesses. We know that the labor-market equilibria will lie on the demand for labor curve, but we do not know where. We no longer know what allocation the market will generate: high employment or low employment.

Because each firm knows that the other firm may know something it does not know, firms may ask "Why is the other firm (not) hiring?" "Maybe I should (not) be hiring as well?" Prices will be no longer exogenous. Individuals will treat them as conveying private information, so that someone's willingness to sell at a given price may affect my willingness to buy at this price. You can easily see that such situations may lead to "beauty contests," "bubbles," or "sunspots," as such equilibria are called.[1] If I believe that some other firm knows that the labor pool is good, I will hire. If I see that someone

---

[1] A small trader on the gold exchange tells me that it makes no sense for him to invest in information. Instead, he just needs to stand next to a large trader, who does invest, and imitate what he does.

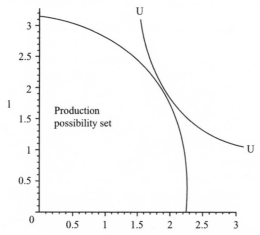

Figure 3.2. Convex production possibility set.

is selling his Brazilian currency, I will sell as well. When individuals learn from each other's actions, a multiplicity of equilibria emerges.

As we see, when markets are incomplete and information is imperfect, the concept of equilibrium loses much of its analytical and predictive power. Instead of there being a unique vector of prices, there are now many possible equilibrium prices. The theory still asserts that there are equilibria, but we no longer know which equilibrium will ensue.

Comment. If you are not an economist, you may wonder why Stiglitz is so concerned with nonconvexivities. With apologies to the mathematically trained, here is the reason. (Noneconomists should study Varian 1984, pp. 8–15). A *production possibility set* is the set of all technologically feasible combinations of outputs and inputs. It consists of points such as {2 *tons of steel*, 10 *machines*, 57 *labor hours*}. It may also include a combination of the same output, with 10 machines, but 60 labor hours, but presumably firms would not want to use more labor than they need. Now, this set is convex if and only if the *production possibility frontier* – its upper contour – is quasiconcave. What this means is the production possibility frontier looks like this (see Figure 3.2).

Now, you already know that utility indifference curves are convex to the origin. And you can easily see that if the production possibility frontier is concave and the indifference curves are convex, then there is only one straight line (hyperplane in more dimensions) that separates them. In other

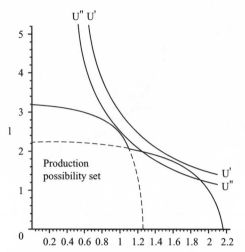

Figure 3.3. Production possibility set with several equilibria.

terms, they can touch only in one place, which is then the unique solution to the problem of maximizing utility under the constraint of the technology.

Imagine now that the production possibility set is not globally convex, so that its frontier goes in and out (see Figure 3.3).

Then there will be an equilibrium at each point of tangency of the production set and the indifference curves, and there will be more than one such point. Hence, there will be several equilibria.

(5) The second theorem of welfare economists asserts that any equilibrium allocation can be reached by a suitable redistribution of initial endowments and decentralized exchange. Hence, questions of efficiency can be separated from those of distribution. But this theorem assumes that the redistribution of endowments is costless. It is achieved by a *lump-sum tax*: a tax that does not depend on anything an individual does and therefore does not alter the incentives. A head tax is a lump sum tax: You pay it regardless of what you do, unless you were to cut off your head. Income tax, however, changes the rate of return to savings and to labor and may make individuals save or work less.

If the government does not know the utility functions of all individuals, then it does not know how to redistribute the initial endowments so as to reach a socially desired distribution. The only way it can redistribute is by taxing observables, such as income or wealth. But these observables constitute consequences of actions and taxing them will alter these actions. Hence, governments can alter the distribution only via *distortionary* taxes. Distribution and efficiency cannot be separated.

Hence, equality and efficiency are related. But it is not always obvious how: Do not take the "big trade-off" (Okun 1971) between equality and efficiency for granted. There are situations in which reducing inequality causes inefficiency but there are also situations in which it increases social welfare. We discuss this issue throughout the course, but an example may be helpful. If the poor cannot borrow to educate their talented children – and the credit market is missing because there is too much moral hazard (parents could use the money to eat, rather than to educate children) – then a redistribution of wealth would increase the supply of educated talent to the society.

When there are nonconvexivities – hence, multiple equilibria – reaching a desired distribution can be complicated. Just taxing some at a linear rate and distributing to others will not generate the desired result. Incentives have to be designed in such a way that each individual will want to behave in ways that generate a particular equilibrium. And, as we see in the next chapter, these incentives will be inevitably costly in terms of efficiency. Hence, again generically, decentralization will not work. Markets will not be constrained-efficient, so that the first-best allocations will not be reachable.

3.5 Conclusion and some implications

Some markets are always missing: These may be futures markets, risk markets, or markets for externalities. If markets are missing, prices no longer inform about all the opportunity costs. Moreover, different people may know different things and they may learn from the behavior of others. Because each set of markets is different, it is not possible to develop general theorems that would cover all the possible situations. But some generic consequences can be established. The positive consequence of missing markets is that there may be a multiplicity of equilibria. The normative consequence is that allocations by incomplete sets of markets are often inefficient, both in the sense that if a market were to be opened or closed, the equilibrium allocation would be different and in the sense that there exist allocations that would make someone better off without anyone else being worse off even without opening or closing markets.

The consequences of imperfect, and often asymmetric, information are also profound. Instead of thinking of individuals operating in the markets as anonymous, homogeneous "individuals," we now have to ask what each of them knows. My exchange with a doctor is not a trade between "individuals." The doctor knows all kinds of things I do not know: Indeed, I hire a doctor to act in my interest because I know that she knows things I do not know. A used car salesman knows more about the red Mercedes than I do, and I am suspicious if he offers to sell it at a low price. A worker knows more about his quality than the employer; an entrepreneur knows more about the risks entailed in a project than the investor; a manager knows more than the owner. In all these relations someone wants someone else to act in his or her interest but the information is imperfect and asymmetric. And because information matters, to analyze any market situation we have to take it into account.

In each of these situations one of the parties (sometimes many) is the "principal"; the other (sometimes many) is the "agent." It is not always easy to determine who is who: We will worry about it below. But think generically of classes of individuals: Investors loan money to entrepreneurs to undertake risky projects, entrepreneurs hire managers to run the project, managers hire employees to perform the tasks entailed. And there is no reason to stop here: Governments regulate incentives for market agents, politicians delegate some of the task of governing to bureaucrats, citizens elect politicians to represent them. In all these situations, someone, "the principal," hires someone else, "the agent," to act in his or her interest. In all these situations, the agents know all kinds of things the principal does not know. In all these situations, the principals are trying to set the incentives for the agents so that the agents would do most for the principals. This is what "an economy" is: a network of principal-agent relations.

CHAPTER 4

Principal-agent framework

4.1 Readings

Macho-Stadler, Inés, and David Pérez-Castrillo. 1997. Chapters 1, 2, 3, and 4 of *An Introduction to the Economics of Information*. Oxford: Oxford University Press.

Kreps, David M. 1990. Chapters 16 and 17 of *Microeconomics*. Princeton: Princeton University Press.

Note: Kreps has some nice examples, so you may want to start with him. But his mathematical presentation is more demanding, so you may wish to follow with Macho-Stadler and Pérez-Castrillo.

4.2 Introduction

The topic of this chapter is a framework for analyzing relations between principals and agents. The chapter provides some technical background and explanations necessary to understand Macho-Stadler and Pérez-Castrillo but otherwise stays close to their text. Hence, if you can follow their textbook, you can just skim this chapter. We run into specific principal-agent models several times during the course and we then learn how to solve them. This is just an introduction to the framework.

4.3 Preliminaries

4.3.1 General assumptions

Here is the general setup:

(1) One (or more) individual, the "principal," offers another individual (or individuals), the "agent," a menu of contracts to work for him or her. Each

55

contract is a set of pairs $\{x, w(x)\}$, where x stands for the output (result) of an agent's actions and $w(x)$ is the payment to the agent associated with each output. "Offers" need not mean "designs": There is nothing to preclude the potential agent from designing the contract and informing the potential principal that this contract will be accepted if offered. Ferejohn (1999), for example, develops a model in which political representatives (agents) suggest to citizens (principals) that they are willing to keep citizens better informed about their actions if citizens give them a wider authority. What matters in this framework is that agents are the ones who generate outcomes that affect the welfare of principals. It is agents who "work" or "exert effort."

A landlord hires peasants to cultivate the land. The landlord may offer a variety of contracts. One contract may be $\{any\ x, w\}$: Whatever output the peasant produces, he receives a constant wage w. A contract may be $\{x, x/2\}$: any output will be divided in halves. Or a contract may be $\{x, x - r\}$: the peasant pays a constant rent, r, to the landlord and takes whatever is left. You may have noted immediately that the landlord is the *residual claimant* in the first contract, the peasant is the residual claimant in the last contract, while in the second contract both the landlord and the peasant are. This is important because it means that risks are differently allocated by each contract. Note that the landlord can offer the peasant a menu consisting of all three of these contracts and allow the peasant to choose one.

(2) The agent either accepts one of the contracts or rejects all contracts. If the agent rejects, the story ends.

The peasant now decides whether to accept the contract or, if he is given a choice, which one. The peasant will consider what else he can do. Suppose that by doing the best among all other alternatives, say engaging in subsistence farming or moving to a city, the peasant can obtain a *reservation utility* of $\underline{U}$ or U_0. You can guess that the peasant will accept a contract only if it generates at least the same utility. This condition is called the *participation* (or individual rationality) *constraint*.

(3) If the agent accepts, he exerts effort, e, and generates output, x. The output depends on (i) agent's effort, (ii) some exogenous random conditions, θ, and sometimes (iii) the type of the agent, which can be formalized as $f^k(.)$. Hence, agent of *type k* produces

$$x^k = f^k(e, \theta).$$

The standard assumption is that $f(e, .)$ is concave or linear, so that $f_e > 0$, $f_{ee} \leq 0$. Once the terms of the contract are set, the agent is free to choose the level of effort that maximizes his utility given the contract. You can also

Table 4.1

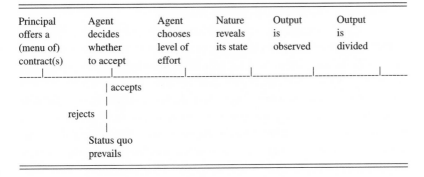

Principal offers a (menu of) contract(s)	Agent decides whether to accept	Agent chooses level of effort	Nature reveals its state	Output is observed	Output is divided
		accepts			
	rejects				
		Status quo prevails			

guess that if the peasant is given a choice he will choose the contract best for him and that, having accepted a contract, he will exert a level of effort that is best for him. This condition is called the *incentive compatibility constraint*.

Let this level of effort be $\hat{e}$. Hence, the agent will produce $x_i^k = f^k(\hat{e}, \theta_i)$, where θ_i is a particular realization of θ. Note that k varies over agents, while i varies over states of nature. A peasant who knows how deeply to plow (k represents his skill) chooses to secrete $\hat{e}$ liters of sweat to plant the seeds. Then some amount of rain, θ_i, falls and x_i^k tons of wheat is produced.

Note that the term "effort" covers all actions of the agent that benefit the principal. It is a place-holder for whatever actions that are relevant in a particular substantive context. When the agent does not do everything possible for the principal, he "shirks." This is again a generic term.

(4) Upon verifying whether the terms of the contract have been fulfilled, the agent receives w and the principal retains $x - w$. Note that observing the outcome or, more generally, verifying the terms of the contract, may be problematic. Say that the terms of contract specify that the agent gets w_i when the state of nature is i. Will the principal and the agent agree ex post which state of nature did transpire? If they do not agree, can some court determine which did? If θ represents rainfall, then perhaps the landlord and the peasant can go to court, which will hire an expert meteorologist to ascertain which value θ_i did transpire. Note that if the type of the agent and the production function is known and if θ_i can be verified, then the level of effort can be inferred. Hence, effort can be contracted. But if θ_i cannot be verified, then effort can be no longer inferred, and the only verifiable quantity is the output.

The time sequence is thus the demonstrated in Table 4.1.

This much is generic (although there are situations in which nature moves before the agent chooses effort; see the next section). But principal-agent situations differ in their informational structures:

(1) If θ_i is unknown ex ante but both the principal and the agent know and share the knowledge of the prior distribution $\theta \sim (\mu, \sigma^2)$ and if both can verify the realization of θ ex post, then information is imperfect and symmetric. This is the *benchmark* case against which outcomes in other cases will be evaluated. For example, both the landlord and the peasant may know the probability that the growing season will be sufficiently wet and they agree ex post whether it was sufficiently wet. Note that if the terms of the contract are contingent on the weather, verifying whether it has been fulfilled may be conflictive.

(2) *The actions of the agent may be hidden* from the principal, so that the principal may be unable to verify the effort by the agent, e. Information about effort is then asymmetric. The landlord may be unable or unwilling to monitor whether the peasant got out of bed with sunrise or not, whether he plowed deeply enough or not.

(3) *The type of the agent may be hidden* from the principal. The principal may not know the agent's disutility of effort or his skills at performing the task. Information about type is then asymmetric. The landlord may not be able to observe whether the particular peasant likes to work, whether he knows how to plow or not.

(4) Both actions and types may be hidden.

4.3.2   Risk postures, utility functions, and risk allocation

The utility functions of the principal and the agent are important for understanding what happens in such situations. Both can be risk neutral (or even risk prone) or risk averse.

Comment. For those of you who do not know what these terms mean, here is an explanation. A person is risk neutral if she is indifferent between a lottery with some expected value and a certain outcome with the same value. Say you are offered a chance to participate in a lottery in which the outcomes are \$200 with probability $p = 1/2$ and \$0 with probability $1 - p = 1/2$. The expected value of this lottery is $E(V) = p\$200 + (1 - p)\$0 = \$100$. A risk-neutral individual is indifferent between playing this lottery and getting \$100 for sure. A risk-averse individual prefers the sure thing. A risk-prone one takes the lottery.

U(C)

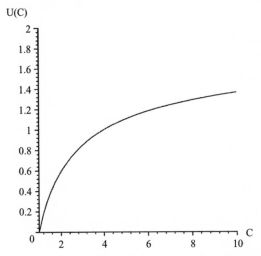

Figure 4.1. Constant relative risk aversion utility function.

A risk-averse person suffers more from losses than she benefits from gains: losing \$100 is more costly than winning an additional \$100 is beneficial. This way of thinking has a natural representation by the shape of the utility function. It means that the utility function $U(C)$ is concave, that is, $U_C > 0$, $U_{CC} < 0$, where these are the first and the second derivatives of utility with regard to consumption. Such a function looks as follows (see Figure 4.1).

One function economists routinely use to represent risk postures is

$$U(C) = \begin{matrix} \frac{C^{1-\sigma}}{1-\sigma} & \text{if } \sigma \neq 1 \\ \log C & \text{if } \sigma = 1 \end{matrix}$$

Note that $U_C = C^{-\sigma}$ and $U_{CC} = -\delta C^{-\sigma-1}$. The curvature of the utility function at any point C is thus $U_{CC}/U_C = -\sigma/C$. This expression measures the absolute risk aversion. In turn,

$$-C\frac{U_{CC}}{U_C} = \sigma$$

measures the *relative risk aversion* of an individual. Note that for this class of functions the relative risk aversion is constant, which is why such functions are called CRRA – constant relative risk aversion – utility functions. If $\sigma = 0$, then an individual is risk neutral and the utility function is $U(C) = C - 1$, linear in C. If $\sigma > 0$, an individual is risk averse. The value $\sigma = 1.5$ seems to be a ballpark number of U.S. households.

We also run into utility functions that are *additively separable*. Such functions are of the form:

$$U(x, y) = U(x) + U(y),$$

where one or both of the utilities on the right-hand side may be linear. (**End of comment**)

The utility of the principal is thus $B(x - w) = x - w$ if the principal is risk neutral, $B(x - w) < x - w$ if she is risk averse. Agents derive utility from w but they must exert effort to produce $x(e, .)$ and agents experience disutility from effort, $v(e)$, which is typically thought to be linear or convex, so that $v_e > 0, v_{ee} \geq 0$. The agent's total utility function is typically represented by an additively separable function

$$U(w, e) = U(w) - v(e),$$

with $U_w > 0, U_{ww} \leq 0$. This is because the payoff to the agent is risky but effort is not.

Note immediately that there is always some conflict of interest between the principal and the agent. Because $B_w < 0$, the principal wants low w. Because $U_w > 0$, the agent wants high w. Had there been no conflict of interests, the two could just agree what to do and the principal could *delegate* the task to the agent without worrying about incentives: The agent would want to do what the principal wants him to do out of self-interest. But even if there is some conflict of interests, the agent has mixed motives. Because $w_x \geq 0$ and $x_e > 0$, the agent will choose to exert some positive level of effort even though $v_e > 0$.

Contracts allocate not only consumption, they also allocate risk. Consider the example of landlords and peasants. The possible allocations between landlords and peasant can be characterized generally as:

$$w = \alpha + \beta x(e, \theta) - r$$
$$B = x(e, \theta) - \alpha - \beta x(e, \theta) + r.$$

Note that the particular contracts are associated with different institutional arrangements (see Table 4.2).

As we see, when the peasant is a wage worker, the landlord bears all the risk; when the peasant is a tenant, the peasant does; when the peasant is a sharecropper, they share the risk.

Table 4.2

Contract				Payments		
α	β	r	**Institution**	w	$x - w$	**Risk Bearer**
+	0	0	wage	α	$x - \alpha$	landlord
0	1	+	tenancy	$x - r$	r	peasant
0	+	0	sharecropping	βx	$(1 - \beta)x$	both

4.3.3 Questions to be answered

This is the conceptual apparatus. The questions to be answered are positive and normative. Interesting positive questions are:

(1) What contract (or a menu of contracts) will the principal offer?
(2) Will the agent accept?
(3) How much effort will the agent exert?
(4) With what results, that is, what will be the final allocation?

The normative questions are:

(1) Will the allocation $\{x, w, e\}$ be efficient? Constrained-efficient?
(2) Is there a reallocation of initial endowments (including property rights) that would improve efficiency or be superior by some other welfare criteria (compensation, utilitarian welfare function)?

Note that because contracts allocate risks, their terms will have different effects given the risk postures of the principal and the agent. Hence, we can formulate all the questions we posed above conditioning them on the risk postures. The first question thus becomes "What contract (or a menu of contracts) will the principal offer, given that she is risk neutral and the agent is risk averse?" and so on.

There is one more question, which is not frequently asked (but see Stiglitz 1994), namely, whether the property relations are socially optimal. This is the question whether if the peasant was the owner of his land and would get all of the output, x, he could compensate the landlord and still be better off.

The general line of analysis is the following. The principal will offer and the agent will accept a contract that solves the problem

$$\max_w B(x - w)$$

$$s.t.\ U(w, e) = U(w) - v(e) \geq \underline{U},$$

$$\hat{e} = \arg\max_e U(w, e).$$

The part $U(w, e) \geq \underline{U}$ is the "participation constraint," where it is usually assumed that indifference breaks in favor of participation. It says that the contract must be at least as good for the agent as the next best opportunity. The part $\hat{e} = \arg\max_e U(w, e)$ is the "incentive compatibility constraint." If the effort of the agent, e, is verifiable, then it can be included in the terms of the contract, so that the contract can be specified as $\{e, w\}$ and the principal can maximize directly with regard to e and w, as long as the terms of the contract are self-implementing, that is, the agent will want to choose $e = \hat{e}$. If effort cannot be verified, the principal must anticipate how the agent will behave in response to each contract. Finally, note that agents need not be all the same, so that the *type* of the agent may matter. Such situations are somewhat different, and we will study them later.

To solve the problem of the principal, we must first solve, therefore, the problem of the agent. The agent wants to maximize $U(w, e)$. Let us analyze the situation of the agent in the $\{e, w\}$ space (see Figure 4.2).

The agent wants to get a lot of w and to exert little e. Hence, the agent is indifferent between working hard and getting a high wage or working little and getting a low wage. The utility of the agent increases in the North-West direction. The agent would prefer to get on U' rather than on $\underline{U}$. Given a contract $\{x, w(x)\}$, the agent's problem is to

$$\max_e U[w(x(e)), (e)]\ s.t.\ x = f(e, \theta).$$

Suppose that the principal would offer the contract $\{x = f(e, \theta), w = f(e, \theta)\}$, so that $w = x$. Then the agent's solution would be given by

$$U_x \frac{dx}{de} + U_e = 0,$$

or

$$-\frac{U_e}{U_w} = -\frac{U_e}{U_x} = MRS_{we} = \frac{dx}{de}.$$

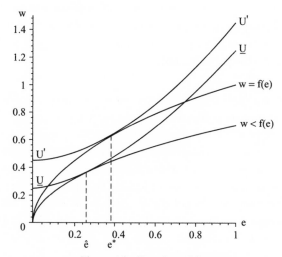

Figure 4.2. Situation of the agent.

The marginal rate of substitution of the agent between wage and effort would equal his marginal product. If the agent were the sole beneficiary of his effort, say he were the owner, the agent would exert a level of effort, e^*, which maximizes the output given his preferences over consumption and effort. But the principal would get nothing. Hence, the principal would not offer this contract.

Suppose that the principal were to offer a contract in which the output would be shared between the principal and the agent, so that $dw/dx < 1$. Now the agent's solution must satisfy

$$U_w \frac{dw}{dx} \frac{dx}{de} + U_e = 0,$$

so that

$$-\frac{U_e}{U_w} = MRS_{we} = \frac{dw}{dx} \frac{dx}{de}.$$

Hence, the agent will exert some level of effort $\hat{e} < e^*$. In any contract in which the principal and the agent share the fruits of the effort by the agent, the agent will undersupply his effort.

Comment. Suppose that the agent were to exert $\hat{e} > e^*$. Then, by the concavity of $f(e)$, $dx/d\hat{e} < dx/de^*$ and because $dw/dx < 1$, the left-hand side would have to be lower in value. But the slope of the indifference curves increases in e (the agent is willing to give up more income for little less effort when he is working hard than when he is working little). Hence, $\hat{e} > e^*$ leads to a contradiction. (**End of comment**)

Because the principal knows this, let us return to her problem of choosing the contract. Examine the problem of the principal in the same space, $\{e, w\}$. The principal does not care about agent's effort per se. She cares only about her benefit, $B[x - w(x)]$. The principal is thus indifferent between high output and high wages and low output and low wages. The principal wants the output to be high and the wage to be low. Hence, if the principal did not have to anticipate the effect of the contract on the effort by the agent, the principal would want the contract closest to the e axis: The principal's utility increases to the South-East. But the principal knows that in fact she will get $B[x(\hat{e}) - w(x(\hat{e}(w)))]$, where $\hat{e}_w > 0$: The agent's effort increases in the wage. Hence, the principal will offer a contract that maximizes $B(\hat{e})$ knowing that $\hat{e}$ depends on the terms of the contract. *To be self-implementing, the contract must be incentive compatible.*

The principal has to still worry about the agent accepting this contract. Note that the utility of the agent declines as the terms of the contract become more favorable to the principal. Hence, if the principal is making a gain, $B(\hat{e}) > 0$, when the agent is exactly indifferent between the contract and the reservation utility, $U(w, \hat{e}) = \underline{U}$, then the principal will not offer a contract that places the agent below his reservation utility. *The contract must meet the participation constraint.* But if the principal were to offer the agent any contract that would give the agent more than his reservation utility, the principal would be needlessly worse off. Hence, the participation constraint will "bite," that is, when the principal maximizes her utility, the participation constraint holds with an equality.

The optimal contract is thus determined by the point of tangency between $\underline{U}$ and B. Hence, it will be some division of x.

4.4   Analysis

4.4.1   *Imperfect, symmetric, verifiable information*

As a benchmark, let us now analyze the case of imperfect, symmetric, verifiable information.

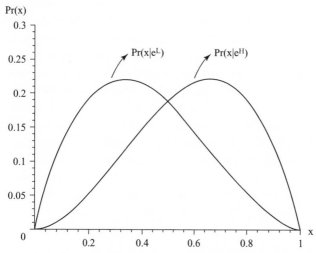

Figure 4.3. Uncertainty of outcomes given effort.

Comment. Earlier we formalized uncertainty as $x_i = f(e, \theta_i)$, where $\theta \sim \mu, \sigma^2$ is a random variable. The symbol $\sim$ stands for "distributed as," μ stands for the mean, and σ for standard deviation. Now we will think of uncertainty somewhat differently, namely, we assume that for each level of effort, e, $\Pr\{x = x_i | e\} \equiv p_i(e)$, so that p_i is the probability of x_i given e in state of nature i. For example, assume that effort can be high, $e = e^H$, or low, $e = e^L$. We then write $p_i^H \equiv \Pr\{x = x_i | e = e^H\}$ and $p_i^L \equiv \Pr\{x = x_i | e = e^L\}$. To see what is entailed, examine the Figure 4.3.

The probability that x is low is high when $e = e^L$ and low when $e = e^H$; while the probability that x is high is low when $e = e^L$ and high when $e = e^H$. But as long as $p_i > 0$ for all i and for all $e > 0$, the same outcome may emerge regardless of the level of effort, so that it may be impossible to identify effort and luck separately.

In some situations we study later, suppose that i can assume only two values, $i = 1, 2$, such that conditions are "good" when $i = 2$ and "bad" when $i = 1$. We will also represent states of nature as $\theta = \underline{\theta}$ when $i = 1$ and $\theta = \bar{\theta}$ when $i = 2$. (**End of comment**)

The problem of the principal is to

$$\max_{e, w(x_i)} \sum_{i \in n} p_i B[x_i - w(x_i)] \; s.t. \; \sum_{i \in n} p_i U(w(x_i)) - v(e) \geq \underline{U}.$$

Some features of this formulation merit a comment. It may seem strange to have the principal choosing the level of effort. After all, it is the agent who chooses how much effort to exert. But here effort is verifiable: Because the principal knows the production function and the state of nature can be verified, the principal knows how much effort the agent must have exerted for each observed level of output. Hence, effort can be contracted. The principal maximizes the expected value of her benefits: The sum in the maximand is defined over all the uncertain states of nature $i \in n$, each of which occurs with the probability p_i, yielding the outcome x_i. The agent is subject to uncertainty with regard to his wage but not with regard to his effort. Since x depends on a random variable and w is a function of x, w is also a random variable, w_i. But the agent knows how much effort he exerts.

This is again a constrained maximization problem:

$$\max_{e,w} \pounds = \sum_{i \in n} p_i B[x_i - w(x_i)] + \lambda \left[\sum_{i \in n} p_i U(w(x_i)) - v(e) - \underline{U} \right].$$

Which wage will the principal offer? Since her problem is the same for all i, this wage is given by

$$\frac{\partial \pounds}{\partial w} = p_i B'[x_i - w(x_i)](-1) + \lambda p_i U'(w) = 0,$$

where we have now written first derivatives as $dB/d[x_i - w(x_i)] \equiv B'$, $dU/dw \equiv U'$.

Let us now examine the value of the constraint facing the principal from the requirements of the agent, λ.

$$\lambda = \frac{B'[x_i - w(x_i)]}{U'(w_i)}, \text{ for all } i \in n.$$

Suppose that $\lambda = 0$. What would this mean? It would mean that the principal is not constrained by the preferences of the agent, so that the participation constraint is not binding. But because $B' > 0, U' < \infty, \lambda$ must be some positive constant. Hence, the constraint must hold with an equality sign. In other words, the principal can push the agent to his participation constraint, so that the agent will get $\underline{U}$. It makes no sense for the principal to give the agent a higher utility, because the agent accepts the contract at which $U(w, e) = \underline{U}$ and the principal would get less with any contract that gives the agent higher utility. (Note that here there is only one agent or all agents are the same.)

Now suppose there are only two states of nature, $i = 1, 2$, such that $x_1(e) < x_2(e)$ for all e, so that if the agent exerts effort at any level e, the output will be lower in the bad, $i = 1$, than in the good, $i = 2$, state of nature. Because the condition on λ must hold in both states, it must be true that

$$\frac{B'[x_1 - w(x_1)]}{U'(w_1)} = \frac{B'[x_2 - w(x_2)]}{U'(w_2)},$$

or

$$\frac{B'[x_1 - w(x_1)]}{B'[x_2 - w(x_2)]} = \frac{U'(w_2)}{U'(w_1)}.$$

Note that this condition equalizes the principal's and the agent's rate of substitution between the two states i. Because this is the condition for Pareto optimality, this contract is at least constrained efficient.

We also know that it must be true that

$$\sum_{i=1}^{i=2} p_i U(w(x_i)) - v(\hat{e}) = \underline{U}.$$

Let us now study what contract will be offered and accepted, using an Edgeworth box, the dimensions of which are x_1, x_2. Assume first that both the principal and the agent are risk averse. The agent is located at the $\{0, 0\}$ point, the principal at $\{x_1, x_2\}$, so that the agent is better off in the North-West direction and the principal in the South-East direction. When the state of nature is $i = 1$, the agent gets w_1 and the principal gets $x_1 - w_1$. When the state of nature is $i = 2$, the agent gets w_2 and the principal gets $x_2 - w_2$. The straight line with the origin at $\{0, 0\}$ represents the sure outcome – the same outcome in both states of nature – for the agent, and the line arriving at $\{x_1, x_2\}$ represents it for the principal. (See Figure 4.4.)

We know that the contract has to satisfy the conditions specified above. Suppose the contract were to lie at the agent's sure-thing line, say at point D. Then the principal could always offer the agent another contract, which would lie on the same indifference curve for the principal but that would be better for the agent. Hence, an optimal contract cannot lie on the agent's sure-thing line. Suppose the contract were to lie at the principal's sure-thing line, say at point E. Then the principal could be made better off with the agent remaining at the same indifference curve. Hence, an optimal contract must lie between the two sure-thing lines. The optimal contract is a *contingent* one: If $x = x_1$, then $w = w_1$; if $x = x_2$, then $w = w_2$. An optimal contract is thus a pair $C: \{x_1, w_1; x_2, w_2\}$. In turn, the condition that the agent must get exactly the same under the contract as he could get otherwise fixes the point to lie on the $\underline{U}$.

In the optimal contract the agent is getting a lower wage in the bad state $i = 1$ than he would be getting were his wage the same in the two states.

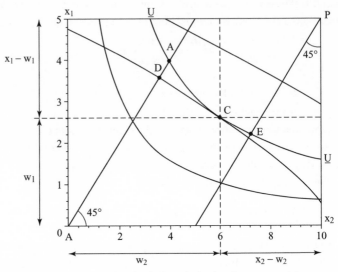

Figure 4.4. Optimal contract when both the principal and agent are risk averse.

Because any optimal contract must give the agent $\underline{U}$, if the agent were to receive the same wage in both states of nature, this wage would be at the point A where $\underline{U}$ intersects the agent's sure-thing line, $w_1 = w_2$, while under the optimal contract C, $w_1 < w_2$. Hence, the agent is not fully insured: He bears some risk. The same is true of the principal. If the principal were to be fully insured, she would get the same amount $x - w$ in both states of nature. Hence, the principal also gets less when the state of nature is bad than she would get if she were fully insured. The principal and the agent share the risk: If i is good, they both get more; if it is bad, they get less. So this is a "sharecropping" contract.

Now, let us examine the effect of other risk postures, using the condition we established earlier, namely $B'/U' = constant$. If the principal is risk neutral, then B is linear in $x_i - w_i$ and B' is a constant. This requires that $U'(w)$ must also be constant for all i. If the agent is risk averse, then the only possible way for $U'(w_1) = U'(w_2)$ is that $w_1 = w_2$. Hence, when the principal is risk neutral and the agent is risk averse, the optimal contract is that the principal bears all the risk: The agent gets the same w for all i and the principal gets the residual, $x_i - w$. (The agent is on his sure-thing line, at the point A.) Hence, now the optimal contract is a wage contract.

Consider the standard wage relation. The worker is offered a contract $\{x_i, w\}$. His marginal product varies with demand: It is $p_i f_e$. The employer gets $(p_i f_e - w)$ and bears the risk. The worker is thus insured against fluctuations of demand up to the point when $B \leq 0$ at which the employer does not offer the contract. Hence, while employment is flexible, wages are not.

Now suppose that the agent is risk neutral while the principal is risk averse. If the principal is risk averse, then $B'' < 0$. But U' is now a constant. The only way for $B'/U' = constant$ to be satisfied is that $x - w$ must be a constant. Hence, now the optimal contract is $\{x_i, x_i - r\}$: The agent pays the principal a constant rent r and bears all the risk. This is thus a "tenancy" or a "franchise" contract (point E).

When information is symmetric and verifiable, the allocation associated with the optimal contract is constrained efficient: Given this set of markets, the landlord cannot be better off without the peasant being worse off and vice versa. Is it globally efficient? The market that is missing in this story is the market for land. Hence, the question is whether a Pareto superior allocation could be reached if this market were to be opened. If the peasant were the sole owner, so that $w = x$, he would get more, $w(x(e^*)) > w(x(\hat{e}))$. This solution would be Pareto superior to landlord's ownership if the peasant could compensate the landlord, that is, if

$$U[x(e^*), e^*] - U[w(\hat{e}), \hat{e}] \geq B[x(\hat{e}) - w(\hat{e})].$$

This condition may or may not hold, depending on the utility and production functions.

Here then are the conclusions from this benchmark case. If information is imperfect (nature moves after the players do), symmetric (both know the same), and verifiable (they can determine and agree which state of nature transpired), then (1) the optimal contract depends on the risk postures of the principal and the agent, and (2) the optimal contract is constrained-Pareto efficient and may or may not be globally efficient.

4.4.2 Asymmetric information

Now suppose that the information is no longer symmetric. The agent knows something the principal does not know. This is often the very reason to hire an agent: a mechanic, a doctor, or a representative. At other times, the reason is different: The landlord just could not cultivate all the land by himself whatever the peasant knows. But even in those cases, the agent knows things the principal does not know: whether she smokes in bed, how much he dislikes working, how good she is at performing the task. Some information may be hidden from the principal.

Grossly, we can distinguish two kinds of hidden information. In some situations the **actions** of the agent are hidden from the principal: These situations are modelled as *moral hazard*. (We see later that sometimes the principal as well can be subject to moral hazard.) In other situations some **characteristics** of the agent, such as his productivity, are hidden from the principal: These situations are modelled as *adverse selection*. There are situations in which both are hidden as well.

Moral hazard. In the symmetric information case we assumed that the principal knows all the agent knows. Even if the principal could not observe e directly, if the principal observes x and θ_i and if she knows the agent's production function $x = f(e, \theta)$, she can compute e. Hence, a contract that includes e is verifiable. Suppose now that the principal knows everything she knew before but cannot observe the state i. Then the principal does not know whether the output is low because the agent *shirked* or because he had bad luck. Let $\bar{\theta}$ stand for good conditions and e^L stand for low effort; let $\underline{\theta}$ stand for bad conditions and e^H for high effort. Then it may be true that $x = f(e^L, \bar{\theta}) = f(e^H, \underline{\theta})$. The principal can verify x but not e. The agent, in turn, does not want to exert effort and he must get $U(w, e) \geq \underline{U}$.

If the principal wants the agent to exert some high level of effort (otherwise there would be no moral hazard entailed)[1] and if the agent is risk averse (otherwise the optimal contract would be of the "franchise" type), the problem of the principal is

$$\max_{w(x_i)} \sum_{i \in n} p_i^H B[x_i - w(x_i)]$$

$$s.t. \sum_{i \in n} p_i^H U(w(x_i)) - v(e^H) \geq \underline{U},$$

$$\sum_{i \in n} p_i^H U(w(x_i)) - v(e^H) \geq \sum_{i \in n} p_i^L U(w(x_i)) - v(e^L),$$

---

[1] Under communist regimes, managers of state enterprises had incentives to maximize the number of employees, rather than output. Hence, they did not care about effort. In this situation, there was no conflict of interest.

where $p_i^H = \Pr(x = x_i | e = e^H)$ and $p_i^L = \Pr(x = x_i | e = e^L)$, $p^H > p^L$ for all $i \in n$. The importance of effort not being verifiable is best seen by focusing on the second, incentive compatibility, constraint. The principal cannot now contract for effort but she wants the agent to exert a high level of effort. Hence, the incentive scheme offered by the contract must make the agent at least as well off when he exerts high effort as when he exerts low effort (indifference is broken in favor of exerting high effort).

Suppose the principal were to offer a contract

$$w = \overline{w} \quad \text{if} \quad x = \overline{x} = f(e^H, \overline{\theta})$$
$$w = 0 \quad \text{if} \quad x = \underline{x} = f(e^H, \underline{\theta})$$

with $\overline{w}$ given by $U(\overline{w}) = \underline{U} + v(e^H)$. The agent will not accept this contract. The level of effort e^H is the level the agent would choose if he were to get $\overline{w}$ for certain. The agent must be insured against the possibility that conditions are bad when he exerts a high level of effort.

On the other hand, suppose that the principal offers the contract

$$w = \overline{w} \quad \text{if} \quad x = \overline{x} = f(e^H, \overline{\theta})$$
$$w = \overline{w} \quad \text{if} \quad x = \underline{x} = f(e^H, \underline{\theta})$$

Then the agent will shirk when $\theta = \overline{\theta}$. Hence, the principal must offer the agent incentives to exert a high level of effort.

Note that we already learned the following: If the agent is not sufficiently insured, he will not accept a contract designed to make him work hard. If the agent were completely insured, he would shirk. Hence, if the principal wants the agent to accept the contract and if she wants him to work hard, the principal must offer the agent some mixture of insurance and incentives.

The participation constraint is obviously binding, by the same argument as before. The incentive compatibility constraint is also binding. The principal wants to pay the agent as little as possible for working hard. If the incentive constraint were to hold with an inequality, then the principal could pay the agent less and the agent would still work hard.

The optimal contract is constrained-Pareto inefficient, which is most easily demonstrated by returning to the Edgeworth box we used to analyze the case of symmetric information. When information is symmetric, the agent

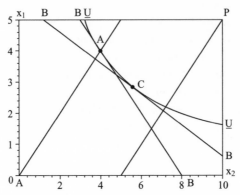

Figure 4.5. Constrained-Pareto inefficient optimal contract.

is risk averse, and the principal is risk neutral, the optimal contract is at the intersection of the agent's sure-thing line with the indifference curve that corresponds to $\underline{U}$, point A. The principal's benefit is then a straight line tangent at this point. This contract is not feasible when effort is not verifiable, because if the agent were offered complete insurance, he would shirk. With asymmetric information, the agent must be getting more in the good than in the bad state of nature and he is still getting $\underline{U}$. Hence, the solution must lie on $\underline{U}$ to the right of the agent's sure-thing line, at point C. But as long as the agent's utility is concave, the tangent to it at $w_1 = w_2$ must be closer to the principal's origin than the tangent at $w_2 > w_1$. When information is symmetric, the principal gets utility represented by the straight line tangent to the point A at the agent's $\underline{U}$; when information is asymmetric, the principal gets utility tangent to the point C at $\underline{U}$. Hence, the agent gets the same utility whether information is symmetric but the principal gets lower utility. (See Figure 4.5.)

The reason the principal's indifference curves change slopes is that for the same wage the effort level will be lower in the moral hazard case. In the symmetric information case, the effort level will be such that $v(e^S) = u(w) - \underline{U}$. In the moral hazard situation, the effort level will be such that $v(e^A) = pu(w_2) + (1 - p)u(w_1) - \underline{U}$. Assume that the expected wage in the latter case is the same as the sure wage in the former case, so that $w = pw_2 + (1 - p)w_1$. Then, by concavity of $u(.)$, $v(e^A) < v(e^S)$. Because the agent exerts lower effort and gets the same utility, the principal gets less.

Comment. Remember that if a function is concave, then any linear combination of values of this function lies below this function. Hence, if $w = pw_2 + (1 - p)w_1$, then $u(w) < pu(w_2) + (1 - p)u(w_1)$. (**End of comment**)

Adverse selection. Suppose now that before making the offer the principal does not know the *type* of the agent. We think of types as characterized either by $f(.)$ or by $v(e)$, but the idea is general. The principal may not know if a doctor is well informed about recent developments; she may not know if a politician is honest; she may not know if the mechanic has proper tools. As you see, this may be information about the utility function of the agent (honest politician), about the skills of the agent (doctor keeping up to date), or about disembodied characteristics of the agent (the tools he has). Any of these features will translate into the productivity (more generally, quality) of the agent, so we can think that there are good agents, with $f = \overline{f}$, and bad agents, $f = \underline{f}$. We can also think that there are good agents, who do not mind to work, characterized by $\underline{v}(e)$, and bad agents, who have a high disutility of effort, $\overline{v}(e)$, so that for any e, $\overline{v}(e) > \underline{v}(e)$.

What can the putative principal do now? She can offer a menu of contracts and let the agents sort themselves out, revealing their type. Suppose that she offers the same contract $\{\overline{x}, \overline{w}\}$ to all agents. If this contract is designed to meet the constraints of the good type, $\underline{v}$, the bad type $\overline{v}$ will not take this contract because he would have to work too hard to produce $\overline{x}$, given that his disutility of effort is $\overline{v}(e)$. Hence, this contract will *separate* the good from the bad types. Suppose, in turn, that the principal offers a menu of contracts, $\{\overline{x}, \underline{w}; \underline{x}, \underline{w}\}$. Now good agents would take bad agents' contract: They can exert less effort and get the same wage. Hence, the two types of agents would do the same: They would *pool*.

The principal wants to offer a menu $\{\overline{x}, \overline{w}; \underline{x}, \underline{w}\}$, such that the $\underline{v}$ types take the contract $\{\overline{x}, \overline{w}\}$ and the $\overline{v}$ types take $\{\underline{x}, \underline{w}\}$. What she wants to avoid is for the $\underline{v}$ types to take $\{\underline{x}, \underline{w}\}$. This may or may not be possible: We study a case in which *separating equilibria* do not exist when we analyze the welfare state. But if it is possible to separate the agents, the principal must make $\overline{w}$ sufficiently attractive to induce the $\underline{v}$ types to opt for the contract designed for them. Unless the principal compensates good agents for revealing their type, they will pretend they are bad. Good agents can produce $\underline{x}$ with low effort, while bad agents can produce it only with high effort. Hence, good agents have the choice of working less and getting less or working more and getting more.

Let us again write the principal's problem formally. Assume that the principal thinks that the probability that an agent is good is q. The problem is then:

$$\max_{e^G, w^G; e^B, w^B} q B(\bar{x} - w^G) + (1 - q)B(\underline{x} - w^B)$$

$$s.t. \ u(w^G) - \underline{v}(e^G) \geq \underline{U},$$

$$u(w^B) - \bar{v}(e^B) \geq \underline{U},$$

$$u(w^G) - \underline{v}(e^G) \geq u(w^B) - \underline{v}(e^B),$$

$$u(w^B) - \bar{v}(e^B) \geq u(w^G) - \bar{v}(e^G).$$

Because she is dealing with two types of agents, the principal's problem is now much more constrained. She has to worry that good agents will want to work for her, that bad agents will want to do so, that good agents will prefer their contract to one designed for bad agents, and that bad agents will prefer their contract. We run into situations in which the principal does not want bad agents to work for her at all (the regulator will want to close a bad firm), but this is the general form of the problem.

The first thing to observe about this problem is only two of these four constraints are binding. They are the participation constraint for the less efficient agent and the constraint that the more efficient agent should exert more effort. (To understand why takes simple algebra, or you can look it up.) Hence, the problem can be redefined as being subject to these two constraints.

We study solutions to this problem when we come to specific models during the course. What matters in general terms is that the principal faces in such situations a trade-off between efficiency and incentives. In the optimal contract, the best agent is induced to work efficiently and in exchange gets more than his reservation utility. In turn, the least efficient types are not paid enough to work efficiently. The reason is that the rents that must be paid to induce efficient effort by the best type must increase when the wage of the worst type increases. If the rents did not increase, then the best agent would be tempted to take the contract of a worse agent and work less.

Hence, to separate the agents, the principal must give rents (income above the marginal product) to good types. This outcome is constrained-inefficient.

4.5   Conclusion

Throughout the course, we use this apparatus to study a variety of problems, ranging from regulation to political representation to the welfare state. Hence, you will want to go back to this chapter and the readings at various occasions.

This chapter closes our abstract discussion of markets. What we have learned is that because some markets are always missing and that information is generically imperfect and asymmetric, markets do not allocate resources efficiently. Sometimes this inefficiency can be remedied by opening (or closing) markets. But there are often good reasons why some markets are missing, so that this solution may not be always available.

When some markets are missing, the existing sets of markets are generically, almost always, constrained-inefficient. What this means is that there exist allocations that are Pareto superior even without opening new markets. This possibility opens up a presumptive role for the state. If governments know how to, have the instruments to, and want to reach efficient allocations, then they can perform a positive role. But these are big "ifs." Hence, the open question is whether governments will do what they should and not do what they should not. And one can suspect that governments differ: Perhaps some do and some do not. We must study what makes governments act in which way.

Centralized mechanisms

CHAPTER 5

The state

5.1   Readings

I could find no texts that summarize the material for this class. The chapter does not follow the readings, so they should be treated as a background. The recommended readings on the structure of interests address themselves to the question whether a voting procedure can lead to a collectively rational decision when interests are in conflict.

Read:

Lane, Frederic C. 1979. "Economic Consequences of Organized Violence (1958)." In *Profits from Power: Readings in Protection Rent and Violence Controlling Enterprises*. Albany: State University of New York Press.

Coleman, Jules L. 1985. "Market Contractarianism and the Unanimity Rule." In E. Paul, D. Miller, and J. Paul (eds.), *Ethics and Economics*, 69–114. Oxford: Blackwell.

Przeworski, Adam. 1990. Chapter 2 of *The State and the Economy under Capitalism*. Char: Harwood Academic Publishers.

Background (on structure of interests):

Coleman, Jules. 1989. "Rationality and the Justification of Democracy." In Geoffrey Brennan and Loren E. Lomasky (eds.), *Politics and Process*, 194–220. New York: Cambridge University Press.

Grofman, Bernard and Scott Feld. 1989. "Rousseau's General Will: A Condorcetian Perspective." *American Political Science Review 82*: 567–576.

Estlund, David, Jeremy Waldron, Bernard Grofman, and Scott Feld. 1989. "Democratic Theory and the Public Interest: Condorcet and Rousseau Revisited." *American Political Science Review 83*: 1317–1340.

(on forms of state):

Montesquieu. 1748. Book II and III of *The Spirit of the Laws*. Any edition.

Findlay, Ronald. 1990. "The New Political Economy: Its Explanatory Power for the LDCs." *Economics and Politics 2*: 193–221.

McGuire, Martin C. and Mancur Olson Jr. 1996. "The Economics of Autocracy and Majority Rule." *Journal of Economic Literature 34*: 72–97.

5.2   Introduction

Decentralized mechanisms generate allocations by **each** individual choosing actions designed to maximize his or her objectives given the actions of other individuals. The resulting allocation is associated with a combination of actions in which no one wants to act differently given the actions of others. Hence, outcomes of decentralized mechanisms are self-enforcing. Centralized mechanisms operate by **one, some, or all** individuals deciding the allocation to all. Such allocations need not be in the best interest of everyone. Hence, their implementation may necessitate coercion. The distinguishing feature of centralized mechanisms, to which I will from now on refer to as "states," is that they can and do force individuals to do what they do not want to do and prevent them from doing what they want to do.

The state can require children to jump into icy swimming pools, it can prevent consumers from enjoying products of certain green plants, it can oblige producers to reveal which poisons they put in their products, it can prevent people from offering some services unless they are licensed to do so, it can take money from some people and give to others, and it can force human beings to shoot at other human beings. The state can keep people in jail and in some barbarian countries even kill them. Unlike any other social organization, the state is a "violence producing enterprise" (Lane 1958). It can threaten or actually use physical force to make everyone do or not do certain things. In Hobbes's words, "Covenants, without the sword, are but words."

Caveats are obvious. States never perfectly monopolize force, even organized force. They never perfectly enforce their will: At some level, the marginal cost of enforcement becomes too high, so states tolerate some noncompliance. But save for exceptional circumstances – civil war, campaign of massive disobedience, widespread corruption – these caveats are in the end minor. States do use the threat of force to organize public life.

States do this whether they are dictatorial or democratic. Coercion may be justified in different ways, it may be used for different purposes, and with different effects. But even if they do it in the best interests of a society, even if they are authorized to coerce by the expressed will of citizens, states use coercion. Bobbio's (1984, p. 93; italics supplied) parenthetical remark bares a crucial feature of the Schumpeterian definition of democracy: "by 'democratic system'," Bobbio says, "I mean one in which supreme power (*supreme in so far as it alone is authorized to use force as the last resort*) is exerted in the name of and on behalf of the people by virtue of the procedure of elections."

The demand for coercion depends on the structure of individual interests. Some interests are harmonious, which means that a collective decision is in the interest of everyone and thus is self-enforcing. But with regard to many interests, enforcing a collective decision requires a threat or an actual use of coercion. We thus begin by noting that centralized mechanisms operate differently with regard to different structures of individual interests.

The collective outcomes states generate depend on the objectives of rulers, on the means those who rule can use to promote their objectives, and on the incentives they face. Although most of the book is devoted to forms of state in which the rulers who are selected through elections cannot use their political position to accumulate private wealth, it is enlightening to consider states characterized by different property rights and different mechanisms for selecting rulers. We thus study a rudimentary framework for analyzing different forms of state.

Like markets, states can be organized in a variety of ways. Collective decisions can be made by one, some, or all individuals. One way to characterize the structure of a state is to ask whether those who make collective decisions are controlled by all those who are affected by them. In most states, moreover, those who make decisions are not the ones who implement them. Implementation is delegated to specialized bodies, to which I refer as "bureaucracies." Hence, a second way to distinguish states is by asking whether the decision makers have the incentives and the instruments to control implementation. These two topics, in reverse order, are the subject of subsequent chapters, so that at this moment they are introduced only in a preliminary way.

As you see, this chapter is just a hodgepodge of preliminaries needed to understand actions of governments.

5.3   Demand for coercion: Structures of interests and compliance

The need for coercion depends on the structure of conflicts among the interests of individuals.

(1) With regard to some issues there are no conflicts of interests in the society. These interests are harmonious: Everyone wants the same state of the world to ensue as a result of a collective decision. For example, everyone in Poland wants to avoid a foreign invasion and everyone in a Florida coastal town wants to avoid being hit by a hurricane. The same is true if the structure of interests is one of pure coordination: Individuals do not care whether they drive on the right or the left as long as they drive on the same side.

When interests are harmonious, collective decisions are self-enforcing. No coercion is needed for the collective decision to be implemented. If the decision is to evacuate the town because of an impending hurricane, everyone will trip over one another to escape it. Because everyone wants the same state of the world to prevail, a decision to bring the preferred state of the world about is voluntarily followed by each and all individuals.

Conflicts emerge in such situations only if individuals are uncertain which decision is best. For example, all members of a jury want to condemn an accused if he is guilty and to absolve him if he is innocent. The jurors have no other interest than to administer justice. Hence, if the true state of nature (guilty, innocent) were known, the decision how to act would be unanimous. Everyone is the coastal town wants to evacuate if the hurricane is to strike and not to evacuate if it will not, so that the only issue is whether it will. The collective decision process is then a search for truth. Its role is *epistemic* (Coleman 1989). If there are any disagreements, they are purely cognitive.

If all individuals are equally well informed, the truth is revealed by the verdict of the majority. The majority has a correct view of what is best for all. The minority has an erroneous view, so that the majority decision is best for all, including the mistaken minority. Once truth is revealed by the information aggregating process, the minority has no incentives to deviate from the collective decision.

When information is private, voting is the best way to reach a collective decision. In a Condorcet set up, a group of 399 voters, each of whom has a probability $p = 0.55$ of having the correct view, reaches the correct decision with the probability 0.98 by a majority vote. Hence, only if a dictator were exceptionally well informed could he do better. Things are more complex when information is costly to acquire: If information is expensive and the

Table 5.1

		j	
		yes	*not*
	yes	3, 3	1, 4
i			
	not	4, 1	2, 2

choices presented by nature are quite benevolent, then it is optimal for the deciding body to be small (Sah and Stiglitz 1988).

(2) With regard to some issues the structure of interests places individuals in a prisoner's dilemma. If individuals were to make decisions in a decentralized way, each deciding what to do, the collectivity would arrive at a state of the world that would be strictly inferior to a state that could be attained if individuals voted and the decision reached by the vote was coercively enforced. Consider the provision of public goods as a generic prisoner's dilemma situation in which individuals decide whether to contribute $(4 \succ 3 \succ 2 \succ 1)$ (see Table 5.1).

If individuals were to decide independently, they would reach an equilibrium $\{not, not\}$ with the Pareto suboptimal payoff of $(2, 2)$. Suppose now that they vote whether to cooperate and to impose sanctions against defection, effectively barring the strategy of defecting. Then the choice is only between getting a 3 or a 2, and the decision to cooperate and to punish defections is unanimous.

Note that in such situations individuals have incentives not to comply with the decision for which they have voted. Hence, there are no grounds to think that participation in decision making necessarily induces compliance: This is just a piece of wishful thinking. Even if the collective decision is to take a course of action that is collectively optimal, each individual would still be better off deviating from this decision. But if this decision is effectively enforced, in the centralized equilibrium no one defects. People have to be coerced for their own good. Voting authorizes coercion.

Distinguishing between the first and second situation is subtle and has been a subject of an interesting controversy. The issue is whether the majority verdict aggregates individual interests in a prisoner's dilemma situation. In the epistemic conception, as formalized by the Condorcet theorem, each individual has some probability, $p > 1/2$, of identifying the correct collective decision. Because the probability that the collective decision will be correct increases in the number of individuals who vote for it, the probability that the majority is correct is higher than the probability that the minority is. Voting aggregates private information. But does it aggregate interests? In a prisoner's dilemma situation, all individuals may be certain that enforcing cooperation is collectively superior to letting individuals decide independently. But this does not imply that cooperation is in individual interest: This interest is still not to cooperate if others do. Hence, voting aggregates information but not interests: At least this is the argument by Estlund (1989) and Waldron (1989) against the Condorcetian interpretation of Rousseau proposed by Grofman and Feld (1989). A counterargument, persistent in Hardin's (1991) interpretations of democracy, is that the efficiency gains derived from cooperation are so large that they dwarf the incentives to defect. If a society finds a way to cooperate, individuals fear that their deviation from any particular way of cooperating will lead to a situation that will be individually inferior. To my mind, this assumption grossly understates the importance of distributive conflicts and thus exaggerates the incentives for voluntary cooperation. But this is a matter of judgment.

(3) In the case of outright conflicts of interests, some people inevitably gain and some lose from any course of action. There is just no single interest that is shared by all, so that some individuals gain and some lose in every state of the world. Suppose citizens vote on one issue, taxes, and the majority rule equilibrium calls for a redistribution from the rich to the poor. Then interests of the minority are hurt while the interests of the majority are advanced. Note that the epistemic notion, according to which this redistribution would be also in the interest of the minority, makes no sense when interests are in conflict.[1]

While the fact that any society is a mixture of these three structures of interests appears prima facie obvious, this is a topic shrouded by ideology. Marxists have historically claimed that all, at least all important, interests are of a zero-sum nature (see Marx 1867). In turn, modern apologists for capitalism treat it as if all interests were harmonious and the democratic process were only epistemic (Buchanan and Tullock 1962; Mueller 1989).

Almost all structures of interest entail some dose of cooperation and some of conflict. Yet public decisions invariably entail distributional

---

[1] For an attempt to salvage the epistemic notion from Black's (1958) criticism, see Miller (1986).

consequences. Even the purportedly universalistic legislation differentially affects people who have different resources and different values. As Marx noted, the law that prohibits everyone from sleeping under bridges in fact concerns only those who have nowhere else to sleep. Any decision that changes relative prices – whether the licensing of nurses, reducing tariffs, regulating product safety, or protecting the environment – reduces the potential consumption of some and enhances the capabilities of others (Stigler 1975). Whether the structure of interests is one of coordination or of a prisoner's dilemma, the payoffs in the cooperation outcome are asymmetric: Someone gets more and someone gets less. Hence, in most stories encountered later, political actors have mixed motives: They want to redistribute in their favor but they do not want to give up the potential gains from cooperation.

5.4   Forms of state

With these preliminaries, let us now consider some features that may distinguish different states and let us analyze their consequences. We first consider the objectives of rulers, then technologies of rent extraction, and finally the technologies by which people can replace rulers.

5.4.1   Objectives of rulers

Let me now refer to all those who populate state institutions, that is, all those who make decisions and implement them, if need be using coercion, as "rulers," without considering the structure of the state, that is, the institutional relations among them. The first question to confront is then "What do rulers want?" Because motivations cannot be observed directly, this is a difficult question to answer.

As this question lies at the heart of methodological controversies, let us spend some time reflecting on what is entailed. The power of economic analysis derives from the fact that it is easy to make plausible assumptions about what people want when they act as economic agents. Most people prefer more consumption to less, more leisure to less, and they can make up their mind whether to work more (less) so as to consume more (less). Hence, it makes sense to assume that individuals have utility functions increasing in consumption and leisure and that they seek to maximize their utility: At least they do so when they face a new choice (otherwise they can just rely on habits or heuristics). Individuals maximize utility under constraints. Their problem, then, is to

$$\max_{a \in A} U \ s.t. \ C,$$

where $a \in A$ is the set of feasible actions and C is the set of constraints. The solution to this problem is some action a^*, which varies with the constraints. Hence, this theory implies observable "comparative statics" (or "dynamics," as the case may be), hypotheses of the form $a^* = a^*(C)$: What economic agents do depends only on the constraints they face. What makes these hypotheses testable is that U is held constant: All we vary is C and $a^*(C)$.

Consider now what happens as we move away from the economic realm. Now we have to determine what are the objectives of "rulers," whoever they may be. We see that this is not easy: Rulers may seek to do nothing else than maximize social welfare or they may be just private economic agents who happen to be dictators, elected politicians, bureaucrats, or judges. Competing politicians may want only to win election or may have policy preferences. As political actors, individuals may be selfish or altruistic. We do not know and cannot tell ex ante. But if we do not know the utility functions of political actors, then at the best we have rival models and at the worst the theory is no longer testable. The theory now predicts that $a^* = a^*(C, U)$, where we observe C but not U. Unless we can specify U, we can always invent some objective that would lead the actor to behave in the way that was observed.

The "rational choice," or as I prefer "strategic action," approach works only when we have good grounds to attribute objectives to actors. With "consumers," it is easy. We can make alternative assumptions about "regulators," "politicians," and "bureaucrats." We can also make reasonable assumptions about "capital" and "labor" or "landlords" and "peasants." But the theory works only if we can identify classes of individuals in some structure of conflict and plausibly attribute to them some objectives. To put it differently, the political economy approach works only when it is imbued with sociology. This is why it is hard to say anything about "individuals" or even "voters." They are heterogeneous: Some want one thing, some another. Some care about income, some about crime, some about moral issues, some about national defense, some about the success of the national soccer team. Unless we have grounds to say "Suppose voters care about x," we will not get very far. The assumption of "unrestricted domain" gives us only impossibility theorems, not testable hypotheses. The more sociology we can build into theories, the greater the benefit of the economic approach.

Some people make the same point by claiming that the rational choice approach works only when we know how preferences are formed. In this form, the criticism is not valid. To apply the apparatus of economic theory, all we need to know is what the preferences are, however they were acquired. Obviously, if we knew how preferences are formed, we could tell what they are. But all we need to know is what they are. As long as we make a correct guess, we can deduce the rest, and test the observable consequences.

With this methodological preliminary, let us return to rulers. Rulers may want nothing else but to advance the interests of the society (with all the caveats discussed earlier). They may thus be "public spirited." They may be motivated by "ego rents": The prestige and power accruing to ruling per se. They may pursue some ideologies or identify themselves with some special interests. Or they may just act as economic actors are assumed to do, motivated simply by consumption and leisure.

Rulers may be public spirited because all individuals are public spirited when they function in the public, as opposed to the private, realm. Even if as economic actors individuals promote their own interests, once they enter into the public realm they dedicate themselves to the pursuit of the public interest. This view, however, entails a schizophrenic perspective of individual psychology: The same individuals have different motives depending on the sphere of life in which they function. Another way to think is that individuals self-select to the public service: There are some individuals who are motivated by self-interest and others who are motivated by the public interest, and only the latter seek to enter the public service. Finally, we can think that individuals are heterogeneous and states differ in a way they select for the public service. For example, someone whose principal objective is to become rich will not seek public service in a state that has a well-designed system of checks and balances, so that only those who are willing to serve under the constraint of transparency of their actions and of potential sanctions for transgressing the public interest would seek public service. Note that in the last view the motivations of rulers are endogenous to the ways in which the states are organized, specifically, democratic rulers are more public spirited than those in various forms of dictatorships.

The assumption that, for any of the above reasons, rulers are public spirited cannot be rejected out of hand. But there are several reasons to think that this is not a plausible general assumption. First, we have widespread evidence that some public officials pursue their private economic interests while in power, in democracies as well as under dictatorships. Second, we have widespread evidence that rulers act so as to perpetuate their tenure in power. Third, the only way to accede to public offices in many states, some democracies included, is to indebt oneself to some special interests.

Clearly, the most plausible way to think is that different rulers have different motivations. But we cannot tell ex ante who is who: Why is it that President Park Chun Hee of South Korea was a developmentalist leader and President Joseph Mobutu of Zaire just a thief? When we enter the realm of politics, it is no longer equally obvious what the arguments of the utility functions are. All we can do is to commit ourselves to assumptions and study their consequences.

Several models of states assume that rulers are self-interested (Findlay 1990; Olson 1991), specifically that they seek to maximize expected economic rents of their tenure in power, where *rents* are any benefits they derive at the cost of the public. Note that if a person with a high income potential in the private realm becomes a public official and acts in a publicly spirited way, her rents may be negative. If this person uses the public office to enrich himself, however, these rents are positive. Rents are a generic term that may cover all kinds of benefits, including the "perks" of office, that is, socially costly consumption by public officials. "Ego rents," however, are not economic rents in the sense defined above, because the private enjoyment of prestige or power is not costly to the society as long as it does not lead to a misallocation of resources. (We discuss rents again later.)

In these models rulers maximize expected rents, that is, rents over their tenure in office, the duration of which is uncertain. You can easily guess that if the hazard rate – the marginal probability that a ruler will leave office during the next moment given the duration of his tenure up to the moment – increases in rents, then rulers must trade at the margin extracting larger rents and extending their tenure.

Just to get a flavor of such models, I develop a particular story of "predatory state," that is, a story based on the assumption that rulers maximize expected rents subject to a variety of constraints.

5.4.2   Technologies of rent extraction

Rulers can extract rents in a number of ways, to which I refer as technologies of rent extraction.

The most obvious technology is *theft*: Rulers can simply steal from the society. Note, however, that theft need not have a legal meaning in this formulation. Historically, there have been forms of state, which Weber (1968) called "patrimonial," in which rulers had a legally qualified right to appropriate privately societal output. To get a label for states in which rulers can steal, whether this action is legally qualified, I extend Weber's, term to cover "crony capitalism," that is, states, such as Ferdinand Marcos's Philippines, Suharto's Indonesia, Anastazio Somoza's Nicaragua, or Rafael Trujillo's Dominican Republic, in which this extraction was illegal but widespread.

The second technology of rent extraction is *usufruct*. Rulers may be legally or factually unable to privately appropriate the fiscal residuum but they may be able to enjoy perks by virtue of holding office. Specifically, rulers cannot acquire legal property titles but can enjoy goods and services in excess of their next best opportunity. This technology of rent extraction was characteristic of communist and some other institutionalized dictatorships, such as Mexico. Communist leaders lived in *dachas* but they did not hold the legal title to them and could not sell them or bequeath them to their offsprings. Indeed, in the aftermath of the democratic transition in the Soviet Union, it turned out that the Soviet Communist Party did not hold a legal title to its central headquarters in Moscow. The head of the Polish television in the 1980s entertained scantily clothed young women in a villa in Kenya, but he held the villa "only to make films for the state." And attempts to privately appropriate public property did cause scandals: A Polish communist prime minister was forced to retire quietly when his son was discovered to hold a Swiss bank account. Let me refer to states in which rulers benefit from using public property but do not appropriate it privately as "bureaucracies."

Assume now that total output, Y, is produced by private capital (or labor, as in Findlay 1990), P, and public capital (or currently financed public capital expenditures), G. The production function is then

$$Y = F(P, G),$$

where the total amount of capital at a particular moment is

$$K = P + G.$$

Note that, given K, the total output is maximized when[2]

$$F_G = F_P.$$

---

[2] First-order condition for a maximum with regard to G is

$$\frac{dY}{dG} = F_P \frac{dP}{dG} + F_G \frac{dG}{dG} = 0,$$

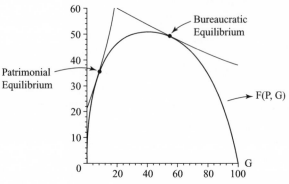

Figure 5.1. The size of the public sector under different forms of the state.

If rulers maximize expected rents, then their utility function in a patrimonial state is $U(Y, G)$, with $U_Y > 0$, $U_G < 0$, the latter derivative negative because in a state in which rulers can privately appropriate the net output, G is a cost for the state. This is what the state must pay (to the private sector if output is privately produced or to its own firms) for the output Y. In turn, in a bureaucratic state, the utility function of rulers is $U(Y, G)$, $U_Y > 0$, $U_G > 0$. The assumption here is that the larger the state sector (whether in terms of public ownership or purchases from the private sector), the greater are the opportunities for usufruct by the rulers.

What centralized allocations we would expect in these two forms of state? The possibility frontier – the most that can be produced by any combination of public and private inputs – is given by the production function. The output increases in G when G is low (so that F_G is high and F_P is low) up to the point when output is maximized, that is, where $F_P = F_G$. If the public sector gets larger than the relative size associated with the maximum output, then output declines (see Figure 5.1).

Now, rulers of a patrimonial state are indifferent between a large output and a large public sector and a small output and a small public sector. Their utility increases to the North-West, that is, they are better off getting a higher

where, given that $P = K - G$, $\frac{dP}{dG} = -1$, while $\frac{dG}{dG} = 1$. Substituting yields

$$-F_P + F_G = 0,$$

or

$$F_G = F_P.$$

output at each size of the public sector or having a smaller public sector at each level of output. The patrimonial equilibrium occurs at the point where their indifference curve is tangent to the possibility frontier. Hence, patrimonial state will undersupply the public inputs into production. To see it algebraically, substitute the production function and the condition $G = K - P$ into the maximand of rulers. Their problem is to

$$\max_G U(Y, G) = U[F(P, G), G] = U[F(K - G, G), G],$$

implying that

$$F_G = F_P - \frac{U_G}{U_Y}.$$

Because for patrimonial rulers $U_G < 0$, the last term on the right-hand side is positive, which implies that the marginal product of the public sector is larger than the marginal product of the private sector, so that output can be increased by making the public sector larger and the private one smaller. Patrimonial rulers undersupply public inputs into production because they have to pay someone, whether private or public firms, for supplying public capital inputs. They care only about the excess of output above the cost of public productive inputs. But the society, whether private or public firms, benefits from the income it derives by supplying productive inputs.[3] Hence, social welfare is at the maximum when the output is at the maximum but private welfare of rulers is maximized when the total output is short of the maximum.

Consider now a bureaucratic state. Bureaucrats are indifferent between a large output and a small public sector and a small output and a large public sector. They are better off to the North-East, that is, they are better off getting a larger output at each size of the public sector and having a larger public sector at each level of output. Hence, bureaucratic state will oversupply the public inputs into production. The problem of bureaucrats is the same as of patrimonial rulers, but for bureaucrats $U_G > 0$. Hence, they will choose the size of the public sector for which $F_G < F_P$, that is, they oversupply. The reason is that they benefit from a large size of the public sector.

---

[3] Be careful when reading Olson (1991) or McGuire and Olson (1996), because in their model taxes collected by the state mysteriously disappear from the social welfare function, rather than be paid to someone in exchange for the services they provide to the state. Social welfare should be seen as $W = (Y - G) + G$, where the part in parentheses goes to rulers and G is the payment to whoever supplies this input into production. Only deadweight losses, λG, if there are any, disappear.

Patrimonial states undersupply and bureaucratic states oversupply the public inputs into production. What then about democracy? If democratic rulers do not steal and do not benefit from usufruct, then they are indifferent about the size of the public sector at all and just maximize total output. Hence, democracy leads to productive efficiency, setting $F_G = F_P$. But this is an idealized view of democracy. McGuire and Olson (1996), on the one hand, thought that democracies in which interests of the ruling coalition are not "encompassing" are similar to what they called "autocracies," our patrimonial states. Niskanen (1971), on the other hand, held that bureaucrats under democracy behave exactly in the same way as our rulers in the stylized bureaucracy. We leave democracy for later.

5.4.3   Technologies for replacing rulers

You may have noticed that there was one assumption in this model that was not introduced explicitly. Why do patrimonial or bureaucratic rulers derive positive utility from the total output? Why did we write the utility functions as $U(Y, G)$ and not just as $U(R)$, where the potential rents are $R = Y - G$ for the patrimonial state and $R = G$ for the bureaucratic one?

I presented the story in this way to smuggle in an assumption about intertemporal preferences of rulers. Suppose that rulers decide how much rent to extract, seeking to maximize the utility of the current rents and of the rents they will be able to extract in the future. But to be able to extract rents in the future, they have to remain as rulers. What I hid under Y is the assumption that the probability that the incumbents remain in power, p, increases in the output that is generated as a result of their decision about the size of the public sector and thus about their current rents. Hence, Y matters for rulers because $p = p(Y)$, $p_Y > 0$, does. Suppose that the present value of being in power during the next period for the rulers is V. Then their problem is to

$$\max_G U[G, p(Y)V].$$

First-order conditions are

$$U_G + U_F p_Y(-F_P + F_G)V = 0,$$

so that

$$F_G = F_P - \frac{U_G}{U_F V} \frac{1}{p_Y},$$

where U_F is the marginal utility of future rents. Note again that for the patrimonial rulers $U_G < 0$, so that the patrimonial state undersupplies public inputs to production. But the rate under which it undersupplies them, and the rents it extracts, depend on p_Y. If p_Y is very high, then the last term vanishes, and the allocation by the patrimonial state converges to the efficient allocation. It is similar for bureaucrats, for whom U_G is positive. (The way to see it graphically in Figure 5.1 is to think that the indifference curves of rulers become flatter as p_Y increases.)

What is the function $p(Y)$? This function maps the outcomes generated by rulers on the sanctions inflicted on rulers by the society. If Y is high (given the technological possibilities and the total capital stock), then the society retains the rulers. If Y is low, then the society throws them out. We refer to such functions – those that relate sanctions to performance – as *accountability functions* and to the mechanisms by which "the society" (to be differentiated later) effectuates these sanctions as *accountability mechanisms*.

One can think of numerous technologies by which a society can throw rulers out. Elections are the easiest and the least costly among them. All they take is for some qualified proportion of voters to cast their votes against the incumbent. You should not conclude from this statement that democratic rulers leave office only as a result of elections: In fact, many prime ministers are replaced by other politicians (losing the confidence of their party or of coalition partners) and most presidents leave because of term limits. Conversely, in some democracies – Italy and Japan were the prime examples – it is next to impossible to vote out of office the incumbent party or politicians. But elections are a technology for replacing rulers at a very low cost to society. Other ways of throwing rulers out are more costly, where the cost sometimes entails lives. To throw out the Shah of Iran, thousands of people marched repeatedly against machine guns. Revolution, insurrection, coup, and palace putsch are among the technologies by which rulers are replaced.

We do not continue further, because our purpose was just to identify the pieces that are necessary to analyze the behavior of states, rather than to develop a particular model. These pieces include motivations of rulers, technologies of production, technologies of rent extraction (with the associated deadweight losses), and technologies of accountability. Rulers maximize utility subject to the constraints imposed by these three technologies and their participation constraint. There are thus good reasons to think that governments will pursue different policies under the same economic conditions, depending on the way in which they can extract rents and the way in which they can thrown out of power.

5.5   The structure of the state

5.5.1   *Collective decision making*

To distinguish among centralized mechanisms we need to ask who makes the collective decision. Two distinctions are obvious. The first one is whether the decision is made by a single individual (a *dictator*) or a *committee* composed of many individuals. The second distinction is whether *all* or only *some* of those who are affected by the decision participate in making it. Cicero's principle – according to which all those who are affected by a decision have the right to participate in making it – is seen by some (Kelsen 1929) as the criterion of democracy. Note, however, that we are now speaking only of those decisions that grant to someone the authority of enforcing it coercively, not generally about emission of externalities.

Decisions by committees are the subject of social choice theory, initiated by Arrow (1954) and Black (1958). It is important to realize that committee decision procedures can be different, as can be the decision rules. In the first chapter, for example, we considered a procedure in which all proposals, even those that were previously defeated, could be offered again and the decision rule was one of pairwise majority. Many committees, however, use a procedure in which a defeated proposal cannot be offered again. In turn, decision rules other than simple majority are also frequent (see Mueller 1989 for their discussion). Both the procedures by which proposals are offered and the decision rules have consequences for the outcomes of collective decision making. Hence, to analyze the collective decision-making process, we must describe how it is organized.

As we have seen in the first chapter, the first question to be asked about collective decision making is whether it is *decisive*, that is, whether it picks a single alternative from the set of all possibilities. The answer to this question depends on the distribution of individual preferences, on the voting procedure, and on the decision rule. We discuss this topic later, in the context of party competition.

The second distinction is whether collective decisions are made by some or by all for all. When they are made only by some, the question arises whether those who make collective decisions are *representative*. This is not an obvious concept (Pitkin 1967). One way to think about it is that if all were to participate the decision would be the same as when only some do. According to Lord Brougham (cited by Pitkin 1967, p. 150), "the essence of Representation is that the power of the people should be parted with, and given over . . . to the deputy chosen by the people, and that he should perform that part in the government which, but for this transfer, would have been performed by the people themselves." But typically decision making is delegated to agents because they have privileged knowledge of the issues or it is delegated so that someone would specialize and acquire privileged knowledge. Under such conditions, Lord Brougham's criterion no longer works: If all were to participate, the decision would be different because some of the participants would be less well informed.

Another way to think about representation is to say that decision makers are representative if they act in the best interest of the represented. But whether this is a meaningful criterion depends on the structure of interests that are subject to representation. When individual interests are harmonious, the government can represent individuals interests, because the common interest is nothing but their sum. When they constitute a prisoner's dilemma, the government cannot represent individual interests: These are to not to cooperate if others did. Yet the government can represent an interest that is collective in the sense that everyone is better off under the centralized decision than they would have been had they all pursued individual interests. Finally, when interests are in conflict, there is no general interest to represent: The government can at most represent the interests of a majority against a minority. Note as well that this entire discussion assumes that individuals know what their interests are, an assumption that economists are more willing to make than political scientists (Pitkin 1967).

Since political representation is the subject of a separate chapter, these preliminary observations suffice at this moment.

5.5.2 Delegation and implementation

The people who make collective decisions, whoever they are, are not the ones who implement them. In all states, implementation is delegated to specialized organizations. I refer to such organizations generically as "bureaucracies." The people who populate these organizations, public functionaries or "bureaucrats," may have interests of their own, interests that diverge both from the interests of decision makers and from private individuals (who may or may not be the same). Hence, *implementation* is generically problematic: The centralized allocation that is implemented need not be the same as the one that is collectively decided. This is why the structure of the state – the particular manner of organizing the relation between the decision makers and the implementing organizations (*"oversight"*) and between the implementing organizations and private agents (*"regulation"*) – matters for the outcomes of the centralized mechanisms. These relations are the subject of the three subsequent chapters.

Last but not least, except for military dictatorships, rulers delegate the use of force to specialized agencies – the police, the army, the tax authority. One of the most puzzling, and poorly understood questions, is "Why do people who have guns obey people who do not have them?"

Many political processes have the following structure. The decision maker, whoever it is, chooses the policy that maximizes some objective, subject to the constraints that those who implement this decision will do whatever is best for them and that private agents maximize their utility. Given the policy, the implementors maximize their objective, subject to the constraint that private agents maximize their utility. Finally, given the policy and its implementation, private agents maximize utility subject to technological and budget constraints. The resulting outcome is a combination of the collective decision, its implementation, and actions of each individual facing the threat of coercion, such that everyone does what is best for them, given their beliefs and given what others are doing. Associated with this political-economic equilibrium is an allocation of resources to uses and a distribution of consumption among individuals.

Consider just one example, which was already introduced. Suppose that the political regime is democratic, that is, decision makers are selected through elections. Political parties propose tax-transfer rates and individuals choose among them by voting. Some decision concerning taxes and transfers is made. The implementation of this decision is delegated to various bureaucracies, some of which tax and others of which transfer incomes. These bureaucracies regulate the behavior of individuals as market agents. The final outcome depends on the decision, its implementation, and actions of market agents, where the final outcome consists of an allocation of resources to alternative uses and the distribution of consumption among the decision makers, bureaucrats, and private agents.

To solve for such equilibria, we must work backward. We must first ask about the effects of regulation on individual actions, then about the effects of decisions on the actions of those who implement them, and finally about the collective decisions. For every implementation, there exists a course of action that is best for private agents given their constraints. The bureaucrats know this (perhaps imperfectly or incompletely), so that they can choose an implementation that is best for them given private agents' reactions. The decision makers know this, so that they can choose the decision that gets them the best implementation.

Comment. Such asymmetric Nash equilibria are called *Stackelberg* equilibria. With just two actors, the idea is the following. One actor "moves first": We examine in a moment what this means. Call this actor "the leader." The leader's problem is to $\max_l L$ subject to the fact that the second actor, called "the follower," which solves the problem $\max_{f|l} F$. Let the solution of the follower be $f^*(l)$. This is a function of l: For every action of the leader, there exists some action of the follower that constitutes the "best reply." Because the leader knows this, the leader chooses $l^{**}(f^*(l))$, which solves the maximizing problem.

Say one centralized and encompassing union federation uses its market power to choose the labor share of value added, m, so as to maximize the present and future income of union members, W. Given each decision of the union, small homogenous firms choose how much to invest, s. For every m, there exists some $s^*(m)$, which maximizes the present value of profits, P. Knowing this, the union can pick the best combination of labor share and investment, $m^{**}(s^*(m))$.

In this story, the union is the leader and the (identical, small) firms are the followers. This is because the firms respond to decisions of the union but the union does not respond to the decision of the firms. Suppose that if firms were not to invest at s^*, the union would deviate from m^{**}: It would respond. Then the union would no longer be the leader and the appropriate equilibrium concept would be some kind of a symmetric Nash equilibrium.

So what is it that makes the union "move first?" The asymmetry comes from the assumption that the union can *commit* itself not to deviate from m^{**}. This is a controversial matter: There was a debate in the 1970s whether workers or firms are better at solving their collective action problems. The assumption here is that firms cannot commit themselves to some fixed rate of investment because they use investment as a strategy of competition. In turn, centralized, encompassing unions can commit themselves. Hence, to be a leader means to be able to commit. If the state were to change the tax rate as a function of labor supply by households, it would no longer be the leader.

The methodological question, therefore, is whether all political-economic equilibria are Stackelberg equilibria. Many probably are, but not all. We study, for example, "endogenous regulation," where the decisions of the bureaucrats or even of the decision makers are a result of a bargain with the private actors. Hence, the appropriate analytical tool depends on the situation that is being analyzed. (**End of comment**)

To characterize the structure of the state, we must examine therefore at least three relations. The first one is between all who are subject to the collective decisions and those who make these decisions. The questions to be asked about this relation are whether the decision makers *represent* the best interests of others. The second relation is between decision makers and the populated agencies that implement decisions. What is at stake here is whether the decision makers have the incentives and the instruments to *oversee* the implementing agencies. Finally, the third relation is between the implementing agencies and the economic agents: individuals, households, and firms. The question is whether *regulation* constitutes an implementation of decisions made by the decision makers or deviates from them as a consequence of discretionary actions by the implementing agencies.

All these relations are principal-agent relations. The decision makers are agents of all the individuals or at least those who enjoy political rights. But they are a special kind of agents, because they can order the principals what to do or not to do. The implementors are agents of the decision makers. And the same individuals (at least if political rights are coextensive with economic activity) who are principals of decision makers are agents of regulators. Hence, individuals appear in this perspective simultaneously as political actors, in which role they are principals, and as economic actors, and in which role they are agents.

CHAPTER 6

Governments and private agents: Regulation

6.1   Readings

Study:

Laffont, Jean-Jacques and Jean Tirole. 1994. Introduction (you can skip Section 3) and Sections 1.1, 1.2, 1.3, and 1.5 from Chapter 1, Section 9.1, Sections 16.1, 16.2, 16.4, and 16.5 of *A Theory of Incentives in Procurement and Regulation.* Cambridge, MA: MIT Press. (Macho-Stadler and Pérez-Castrillo 1997 will be helpful in reading Laffont and Tirole.)

Read:

Peltzman, Sam. 1976. "Toward a More General Theory of Regulation." With "Comments" by Jack Hirschleifer and Gary Becker. *Journal of Law and Economics 19*: 211–248.

Spiller, Pablo T. 1995. "Regulatory Commitments and Utilities' Privatization: Implications for Future Comparative Research." In Jeffrey S. Banks and Eric A. Hanushek (eds.), *Modern Political Economy*, 63–79. Cambridge: Cambridge University Press.

Recommended (on regulation in practice):

Baron, David T. 1995. "The Economics and Politics of Regulation: Perspectives, Agenda, and Approaches." In Jeffrey S. Banks and Eric A. Hanushek (eds.), *Modern Political Economy*, 10–63. Cambridge: Cambridge University Press.

Majone, Giandomenico. 1997. "From the Positive to the Regulatory State: Causes and Consequences of Changes in the Mode of Governance." Working Paper 93. Madrid: Instituto Juan March de Estudios e Investigaciones.

(on time inconsistency and commitment):

Drazen, Allan. 2000. Chapter 4 of *Political Economy in Macroeconomics*. Princeton: Princeton University Press.

Chari, V. V., Patrick J. Kehoe, and Edward C. Prescott. 1989. Pages 265–282 of "Time Inconsistency and Policy." In Robert J. Barro (ed.), *Modern Business Cycle Theory*. Cambridge: Harvard University Press.

Sanchez Cuenca, Ignacio. 1997. "Institutional Commitments and Democracy." *Archives Européennes de Sociologie 39*: 78–109.

Background ("Chicago school"):

Stigler, George. 1975. Chapters 7 and 8 of *The Citizen and the State. Essays on Regulation*. Chicago: University of Chicago Press.

Posner, Richard A. 1987. "The Constitution as an Economic Document." *The George Washington Law Review 56*: 4–38.

("Virginia school"):

Tollison, Robert D. 1982. "Rent Seeking: A Survey." *Kyklos 35*: 575–602.

6.2 Introduction

We now study the relation between the state, seen here as a "regulator," and private agents. Regulation is taken here as encompassing all actions by the state designed to cause some specific actions on the part of individuals or some specific allocations of goods and services. The state is regulating when it forces children to attend school, when it taxes cigarettes, when it licences nurses, when it subsidizes exports, and so on; the list is endless. The state regulates promulgating laws and other legal acts, taxing or subsidizing, or offering goods and services that it produces or purchases from the private sector. The choice of regulatory methods is a subject that will not be discussed here, but you can guess that some objectives can be pursued by alternative means. For example, if the state wants factories not to pollute rivers, it can tax pollution, subsidize clean technologies, or order firms to place their water intake below the water output (as did the Czechoslovak government at some time in the 1980s). Note that regulation includes what used to be referred to as "intervention" of the state into the economy: I prefer "regulation" because this term better connotes the intuition that markets are always subject to some rules, rather than that they exist "of themselves" and are "intervened."

We begin with "optimal regulation," assuming that all the regulator wants is to maximize social welfare and asking how well it accomplishs this goal when some features of the entities to be regulated are hidden. The regulator has the legal authority to issue regulations, including setting relative prices.

Typically, however, the entity to be regulated knows something relevant that the regulator does not observe, say the price elasticity of cigarette consumption or the cost schedule of a monopoly firm. Hence, the regulator must regulate under uncertainty. The regulator's difficulty is that the incentives created by regulation may be socially beneficial under some conditions or with regard to some agents but not under other conditions or with regard to other agents. It turns out that generically the regulator faces a trade-off between inducing the agents to behave in the desired ways and offering them some socially costly rewards, rents. Hence, even if the regulator is a benevolent, utilitarian maximizer of social welfare, optimal regulation at best generates only second-best allocations. Moreover, often the regulator would want to reneg on the promises it makes once the regulated agents do what the regulator wants them to do. And if the agents know this, then regulation is not credible, the agents do not respond to incentives, and the regulator is impotent. This much is generally, although not invariably, true of regulation.

To illustrate the generic problems of regulation, we use a framework developed by Laffont and Tirole (1994), who study the relation between a regulatory authority and a monopoly firm. I chose this framework because it will be useful in clarifying what happens when regulation is endogenous but also because much of the regulation in which governments engage has this structure. Because some of the math is tedious, although it should not be difficult once you have studied the principal-agent framework, I present only the general setup and the central conclusions. You should, however, study the Appendix, where the argument is developed in full detail.

Once we understand what second-best optimal regulation would look like, we have to ask what we should expect in real life. Any form of regulation has distributional consequences: Someone gains and someone loses. One should thus expect that different groups will seek to influence the government to regulate in their favor. And if the government, or some specific authorities, are vulnerable to these efforts, regulation is endogenous. A positive theory of regulation, therefore, must begin with competing interests, must analyze the structure of the state, and must derive predictions about the regulation we would expect to find in practice. Hence, we will ask what happens when the targets of regulation seek to affect the regulations and their implementation. In particular, we study under what conditions and with what consequences the regulating agency colludes with the entity it regulates, a phenomenon often referred to as "regulatory capture." Hence, we consider regulation as an outcome of the political process, as endogenous with regard to its potential effects.

6.3   A general model of regulation

Suppose that a government authority regulates the actions of a private firm. The authority is here the principal, which issues regulation, and the private firm is the agent.

The firm produces goods or services positively valued by consumers at a cost that is a function of the technology of the firm and the effort of the managers to keep the costs down:

$$C = C(\beta, e, \ldots) + \varepsilon,$$

where β is the technology of the firm, defined in such a way that $C_\beta > 0$, e stands for effort exerted by managers to reduce costs, so that $C_e < 0$ (and $C_{ee} \geq 0$), and ε is a random variable.

Regulation assumes here the following form. The state offers the firm to purchase its output reimbursing its cost, C, and giving it a net transfer of t. (Alternatively the state subsidizes consumer purchases, fixing the price in such a way that the firm gets the same.) The state collects revenues by distortionary taxes, so that each \$1 spent by the government costs the society \$$(1 + \lambda)$, where λ is the *shadow cost of public funds*. What this means is that when the state collects \$$(1 + \lambda)$, the amount λ disappears, presumably because taxes reduce the supply of labor, or of savings, or distort private allocations in some other ways. The ballpark number used by Laffont and Tirole (1994) is $\lambda = 0.3$, but the distortionary cost of taxation is a complex and controversial matter.

The firm can refuse to produce. U is the expected utility of the firm. $U^o = 0$ is the reservation utility, so that any $U > 0$ represents rents to the firm.

Both the regulator and the firm are risk neutral. The firm cares about its income and effort. The utility function of the firm is additively separable:

$$U(t, e) = t - \Psi(e),$$

where $\Psi(e)$ measures (in money terms) managers' disutility of effort, with $\Psi' \equiv \Psi_e > 0$, $\Psi'' \equiv \Psi_{ee} > 0$.

Consider now different contracts that a regulator can offer to the firm. The class of *linear contracts* $\{C, t\}$ is defined by

$$t = a - bC.$$

Now, consider two extreme contracts (see Table 6.1).

Under the fixed-price contract, the firm's problem is to $\max_e \{a - C(e) - \Psi(e)\}$, with first-order condition $dC/de = -\Psi'(e)$. Because the firm is the

Table 6.1

Contract	b	Effort Inducement	Rent Extraction
Fixed price	1	high	none
Cost-plus	0	none	high

residual claimant to its cost savings, managers equalize the marginal cost saving to the marginal disutility of their effort. But because they appropriate all the cost savings, they keep all the rents, and the regulator does not expropriate them. Under the cost-plus contract, the firm's problem is $\max_e\{a - \Psi(e)\}$, so that managers have no incentive to reduce costs. Hence, the regulator necessarily faces a trade-off between cost reduction and rent extraction. The parameter b represents the *power of incentives* and contracts in which $0 < b < 1$ are referred to as *incentive contracts*.

Consider now a benchmark model, in which the regulator can observe β and e. Assume that a single firm can realize an indivisible project. Let the, observable, cost function be

$$C = \beta - e.$$

The firm will agree to undertake the project if

$$U(t, e) = t - \Psi(e) \geq U^o = 0.$$

Net surplus to the consumers is

$$S - (1 + \lambda)(C + t) = S - (1 + \lambda)(\beta - e + t).$$

A utilitarian regulator maximizes social welfare, which includes consumer surplus and the utility of the firm:

$$W = S - (1 + \lambda)(\beta - e + t) + t - \Psi(e)$$
$$= S - (1 + \lambda)(\beta - e + \Psi(e)) - \lambda U.[1]$$

The value of the project is S. The total cost of the project to the society is $(1 + \lambda)(C + \Psi(e))$ plus the shadow price of rents accruing to the firm. Note that the rents are not a cost to the society: The firm is a part of the society,

---

[1] Some algebraic tricks are entailed. The steps are:
$S - (1 + \lambda)(t + \beta - e) + t - \Psi(e) = S - (1 + \lambda)(\beta - e) - (1 + \lambda)t + U = $ [add and subtract λU] $= S - (1 + \lambda)(\beta - e) - (1 + \lambda)t + (1 + \lambda)U - \lambda U = S - (1 + \lambda)(\beta - e) - (1 + \lambda)$ $(t - U) - \lambda U = $ [because $t - U = \Psi(e)$] $= S - (1 + \lambda)(\beta - e + \Psi(e)) - \lambda U.$

so that whatever the firm gets increases social welfare. But the shadow cost of rents is just lost to everyone.

The regulator chooses a contract that maximizes social welfare under the constraint that the firm maximizes its utility. Under complete information, knowing β and observing e, the regulator would solve

$$\max_{U,e} W = S - (1 + \lambda)(\beta - e + \Psi(e)) - \lambda U \; s.t. \; U \geq 0.$$

Because $\partial W / \partial U < 0$, the regulator would place the firm at $U = 0$, extracting all the rents. Hence, the first conclusion of this simple model is that **a benevolent, utilitarian, regulator will want to minimize private rents**. In turn, the first-order condition with regard to e implies that $\Psi'(e) = 1$, so that the firm would exert an efficient amount of effort, $e = e^*$.

What contract would implement this program? Say the contract is a fixed-price contract $\{C, t(C)\}$, such that $t(C) = a - (C - C^*)$, where $a \equiv \Psi(e^*)$, $C^* = \beta - e^*$. The firm is then the residual claimant to its cost savings. Its problem is to

$$\max_e \{t - \Psi(e)\} = a - (C - C^*) - \Psi(e) = a - (\beta - e - C^*) - \Psi(e).$$

The first-order condition implies $\Psi'(e) = 1$, or $e = e^*$, and the condition $a = \Psi(e^*)$ implies $U = 0$. Hence, the allocation reached by this fixed-price contract would be efficient.

Now consider the case of incomplete information. The regulator does not know whether the firm has a high or a low cost. For the high cost, inefficient, firm, $\beta = \overline{\beta}$; for the low cost, efficient one, $\beta = \underline{\beta}$. Suppose the regulator were to insist that the inefficient firm operate at the efficient level, $\overline{e} = e^*$. But then the efficient firm could generate the same output while working below its capacity. If the regulator wants the efficient firm to exert the optimal amount of effort, it has to give sufficient rents to this firm, so that the firm would not want to behave as if it were inefficient. The regulator thus faces a trade-off between the effort level of the inefficient firm and the rents it must give to the efficient one: The higher the level of effort required of the inefficient firm, the higher the rents the regulator must give to the efficient one. It turns out (study the Appendix!) that **the regulator will want the efficient firm to exert the efficient level of effort** and will allow the inefficient firm to shirk. This result, sometimes called, "efficiency at the top," is generic for this kind of problem and you will find it useful to remember it. Moreover, to induce the efficient firm to operate efficiently, the regulator will have to leave some rents in its hands. This is a crucial conclusion, because it means that **with incomplete information first-best optimal regulation is not possible**.

Because we began with a very broad conception of regulation and ended up with a specific example, we need to put it back into a general context. The most important thing we learned from this example is that a utilitarian welfare maximizing regulator faces a trade-off between the effort by the less efficient agents and the rents of the more efficient agents. To maximize utilitarian social welfare, that is, the sum of individual utilities (measured in money equivalent throughout these examples), the benevolent regulator generates an allocation in which the agents who happen to be efficient are induced to exert an efficient amount of effort and get rents above the next best opportunity, while the agents who happen to be less efficient are not induced to work hard and receive no rents.

Note the distributional consequence of optimal regulation: Efficient agents are overrewarded, while the inefficient ones are allowed not to work hard and get little. In the context where the agents are firms, this implication may not be particularly disturbing, in particular because the technology of a firm at any time is a consequence of its previous decisions. But suppose that we apply this framework to education, specifically the distribution of scholarships. The second-best optimal regulation of education will be to give high scholarships to talented students, so that they would exert an efficient amount of effort in exchange for rents, and just barely maintain in school the less talented ones. If you think that this policy is unjust or otherwise undesirable, then you will not want the regulator to pursue the utilitarian maximand, at least in money terms. Hence, we are back to the question we raised at the beginning of the course: What are the proper criteria for evaluating allocations or, what are the proper maximands of the government? We return to this question when we discuss the distributive role of the government.

6.4   Moral hazard of the principal

This entire analysis was based on the implicit assumption that the regulator delivers on the terms of the contract: It is a Stackelberg leader. Suppose that during period $\tau = 1$ the regulator offers the firm a contract stating that if the firm produces at cost C it will receive during period $\tau = 2$ a net transfer of $t(C)$. But what is the maximand of the utilitarian regulator once the project has been produced and the costs have already been reduced? It will be $W_2 = t - (1 + \lambda)t$: t will be the benefit of the firm, a part of social welfare, and $(1 + \lambda)t$ will be the cost of this transfer. Because $\lambda > 0$, the regulator will maximize social welfare by not executing the promised transfer to the firm. The optimal strategy of the regulator is *time-inconsistent*: It is to promise the firm a compensation for its cost reduction at $\tau = 1$ and not to compensate the firm at $\tau = 2$.

Suppose the regulator is free to renege on its promises. Then the promise by the regulator to pay the firm $t(C)$ is not *credible*: The firm knows that once it reduces its costs, it will not be in the best interest of the regulator to compensate it. Knowing this, the firm will not accept the contract or will accept it and exert no effort to reduce the cost. And because we have already seen that social welfare is maximized when the firm reduces its costs, the outcome will be inefficient.

The paradox of regulation (Spiller) is the following. In political systems in which laws are difficult to pass – say a proportional representation electoral formula induces the creation of multiparty coalitions, so that several parties must agree for a piece of legislation to be adopted – laws are difficult to adopt but also difficult to change. In such systems regulation is likely to be limited, vague, and credible. In turn, in political systems where laws are easy to pass – say in those that promote legislative majorities – laws are easy to adopt but also easy to change. Hence, regulation is likely to be extensive, detailed, and not credible.

The regulator would want to *commit* itself to fulfilling its promise. But how can the state commit itself to anything? Pace Olson (1991), this question is not specific to dictatorships. True, a dictator is not bound by law. But even if a democratic government is bound by existing laws, it can change them. Once the firm exerts effort, a benevolent, representative, democratic government will want to change laws so as not to pay the firm. And even if the contracting government would for some reason not want to do it, what prevents the people from electing at $\tau = 2$ a government that would?

One could think that the institutional device that generates commitments under democracy is the constitution. Constitutions are not iron-clad, but they are hard to change. Yet the mere fact that they are hard to change does not mean that they commit anyone to any specific course of action. One has to be careful here: It is one thing to say that the constitution is a commitment and another that it allows commitments (Sanchez-Cuenca). Suppose a paragraph in the constitution were to say that profits due to cost savings cannot be taxed. This would be a commitment not to undertake a specific course of action. But, except for guarantees of rights, such commitments to specific policies are rare. In general, constitutions do not permit the current governments to bind future governments. There are some clauses, such as Article I, Section 8 of the U.S. Constitution, which give the Congress the power "to promote the progress of science and useful arts, by securing for limited times to authors and inventors the exclusive right to their respective writings and discoveries." But, in general, current governments can change the status quo established by previous governments.

As in all problems that entail commitment, one should also worry about its costs. To anticipate the topic to which we are about to move, suppose that the current government promises to pay a firm for reducing its costs even though it knows that the firm has an efficient technology and does not need to reduce its costs, splitting the rents with the firm. If this government can commit future governments not to expropriate the payment to the firm, then the society will have given rents to the firm for no good purpose and yet it will be unable to recuperate these rents. There are good commitments and bad commitments, and it is not always obvious which is which.

Consider briefly the example discussed by Laffont and Tirole (1994) in Chapter 16. The setup is the following. Firms are efficient or inefficient, as above. Government subsidy to an inefficient firm increases social welfare but a subsidy to an already efficient term is pure rent. A good regulatory policy is thus to subsidize the firm if it is inefficient and not to subsidize it if it is efficient. A bad regulatory policy is not to subsidize an inefficient firm and to subsidize an efficient firm. Consider now two constitutions. In one, "no-commitment constitution," the current government cannot commit future governments not to expropriate the profits the firm will gain by reducing its costs. In the second, "commitment constitution," the current government can write long-term contracts that do commit future governments: This constitution contains clauses such as Article I, Section 8 of the U.S. Constitution. Under no-commitment, the inefficient firm will not invest in cost reduction and the public will lose. Under commitment constitution, a dishonest government will subsidize an efficient firm and future governments will be unable to recuperate the rents, so the public will lose again.

Which constitution is better depends, therefore, on the probability that the current government is "honest." Hence, if you were a "founding father" (they were all "fathers"), you would want to write a commitment constitution if you expected that future governments will tend to be honest and a non-commitment one if you feared that they are likely to be dishonest. The U.S. Constitution, for example, bears a distinctive mark of Madison's belief that men are not angels. It allows one government to commit future governments only in rare cases: foreign treaties and patents and copyrights. One objective of a constitution is to promote long-term actions but another objective is to permit citizens to control governments. If we knew that all governments will be honest, we could focus exclusively on the first goal; if we fear they may not be, we want to emphasize the second.

6.5   Endogenous regulation

We have ended by considering the possibility that the regulator may collude with the firm. Indeed, the main thrust of some views of regulation is that such collusion is to be expected. If the regulator has the capacity to affect the welfare of private economic agents, these agents have incentives to influence decisions of the regulator. And if the regulator can obtain some private benefits in exchange for regulation favorable to private agents, then it will regulate in the interest of those regulated, rather than of the public. In this argument, regulation is thus always endogenous: It is supplied in response to the demand by those regulated. For example, if truckers are politically more powerful than railroads, the state regulates transport to promote the interests of truckers (Stigler 1975). Note that this analysis cuts across the ideological spectrum: Habermas (1975), Skidelsky (1977), and Stigler (1975) all argued that when the state can affect the welfare of private agents, these agents seek to influence the decisions of the state. The result is, in one language, "regulatory capture": The state becomes permeated by private interests, most of its actions consist of income transfers from the politically powerless to the politically powerful, and public policy loses any internal cohesion. Because the more the state regulates, the more is at stake, and because the more is at stake, the more everyone wants to influence the state, the state is either completely ineffectual and autonomous or it is highly interventionist but subservient to special interests.

This picture is grossly exaggerated. To begin with, it is based on dubious economic assumptions. And it leaves a number of basic questions unanswered. The foremost among them is how do the regulators hide their actions from the public?

Here is the essence of Peltzman's (1976) model of regulation, which he presents as "an extension and generalization of his [Stigler's] pioneering work" (p. 211). Think of the economy as composed of producers, consumers, and the regulator. Producers derive utility from profits, π, consumers care

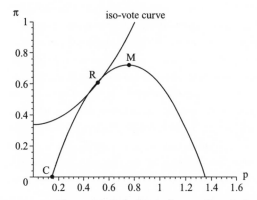

Figure 6.1. Peltzman's theory of regulation.

about prices, p, and the regulator wants to maximize votes. The profit-price possibility frontier, given by $\pi = f(p)$, has the shape of a hill shown in Figure 6.1.

When price is at the competitive level, profits are zero, and the allocation is efficient. This situation is portrayed by point C. As price increases from its competitive level, profit increases. But as price increases, demand falls, so that profits are maximized when the marginal increase of price equals the marginal decline in demand. This is point of full monopoly, M. If price were to increase above this level, profits would decline, so that no one wants to be on the declining slope of the hill.

The votes for the regulator are cast by producers and consumers. Producers vote for the regulator when profits are high; consumers vote for the regulator when prices are low. Hence, the regulator is indifferent between low profits and low prices and high profits and high prices. The total vote for the regulator increases to the North-West. The solution is thus at the point of tangency between the profit-price frontier and the iso-vote curves, at point R.

In industries that are naturally competitive, regulation is thus a transfer from consumers to producers: Producers are better off under regulation than under competition because profits are higher, and consumers are worse off because prices are higher. Moreover, the society incurs a loss of consumer surplus. In industries that are naturally monopolistic, regulation is a transfer from producers to consumers and it increases the consumer surplus. Note, however, that the general conclusion of the Chicago school of regulation

(Stigler 1975; Peltzman 1976; Becker 1983; but not Posner 1987) is that "the producer interests tends to prevail over the consumer interest" (Peltzman 1976, p. 212). Regulation is a form of "producer protection."

As an economic model, this is not a persuasive story, for all the reasons we discussed. Perfect markets are just not a useful benchmark for evaluating allocations: Markets are always incomplete, information is imperfect and asymmetric, and so on. Thus, let us concentrate on the political aspects of this model. Note immediately that the shape of the iso-vote curves is based on some implicit assumptions about the way in which votes are produced. Suppose that voters are fully informed about the costs of regulation and that they base their vote on the observed profits and prices. Because in any society there are more voters who are consumers than voters who are producers, regulators would maximize votes by keeping prices at the competitive level: They would never regulate naturally competitive industries, only natural monopolies, and the allocation would be efficient. (The iso-vote curves would be vertical.) Hence, the iso-vote curves can assume the shape postulated by Peltzman (1976) only if consumers are not fully informed or somehow misled.

Indeed, echoing Downs (1957), Stigler (1975) assumed that voters are "rationally ignorant." The argument is that consumers do not want to acquire costly information about matters of little importance to them. The benefits of regulation are concentrated among a few producers; the costs of regulation are diffused among many consumers. If the government regulates toothpaste industry, transferring a million dollars to a firm in an economy composed of one million consumers, then the cost of regulation to each consumer is one dollar. If a consumer has to spend more than one dollar to learn the cost of regulation, she will not do it. Hence, when benefits are concentrated and costs are diffuse, consumers are rationally ignorant. A transfer from consumers to producers increases the vote of the producers without equally reducing the vote of the consumers, so that iso-vote curves are flat, and the regulation equilibrium occurs at some level close to monopoly. But note that rational ignorance may at most explain regulation that is not too costly for consumers. If it is costly, then someone will have the incentive to inform consumers that they are being hurt by regulation. If the government protects the automobile industry at the cost of $100 to each consumer, a consumer group will form, investigate the automobile policy, and sell the information for $99.

Peltzman does not rely on rational ignorance. In his general model, the regulator maximizes a majority of votes,[2] M, which is a function of prices and profits, so that

$$M = M(p, \pi),$$

subject to a constraint on total wealth, which is equivalent to

$$\pi = f(p).$$

An increase in prices reduces the majority; an increase in profits increases it; so that there is some maximum at a tangent to the increasing slope of the possibility frontier. But the question is how prices and profits become transformed into votes, formally, and what are the functions M_p and M_π? In the general model, they are just taken for granted. But they are spelled out in a more detailed model, where the probability that a loser from regulation will vote for the regulator depends on something that is strangely referred to as "voter education expenditures" (p. 216). The story is that special interests contribute money to the regulator, who sells regulation to them, and uses this money to "educate" losers to vote for the regulator. The higher these expenditures per loser, the less likely a loser is to vote against the regulator who takes money from her. This is not just "rational" but subsidized ignorance.

Becker (1983) extended this model to competition among several interest groups for regulation in their favor. Each group contributes money to influence the regulator. In the Nash equilibrium, the level of contributions is such that no group wants to contribute a different amount given the contributions by other groups. The regulation reflects the relative balance among the contributions: Opposing influences cancel one another. Regulation is always inefficient because regulatory policies have shadow costs. Becker's contribution to this line of analysis is to show that among all the methods of regulation, the regulator will choose the least costly one in terms of consumer surplus. If the regulator were to choose a method that is inefficient, it would have been possible to make some group better off while maintaining constant the wealth of other groups. Hence, in a political-economic equilibrium, the least inefficient method of regulation will be chosen. But in his model as

---

[2] This is a strange maximand for a (re)election-seeking politician, but because Peltzman (1976) does not consider party competition, it has no qualitative consequences in the present context.

well, groups collect contributions and the effect of money is to dissuade the losers from turning against the regulator who hurts them.

In the end, even if one swallows the economic assumptions of the Chicago school of regulation, one is left with a political black box. Why would money buy votes?

Another variant of the theory of endogenous regulation, the "Virginia school," differs from the Chicago version in that it sees the regulator not as seeking votes but as seeking private benefits. Governments can create rents; indeed, most government actions, whether tariffs, licensing of nurses, or subsidies to sugar industry, create them (Krueger 1974). Hence, private actors have reasons to try to influence public officials to award rents to them. Suppose two pharmaceutical companies produce medicaments that are close substitutes in treating a particular disease. If one of them could somehow persuade the regulator that the other product is ineffective or harmful, it would capture monopoly rents. Hence, the theory goes, these firms will spend resources to influence the government. And if government officials seek private benefits, they will be susceptible to this influence. The result is not only that the government introduces socially costly distortions in the economy but that resources are wasted in pursuit of this distortion. The latter aspect is the specific twist of the rent-seeking theory. In the extreme case, when the political process awards the prize to the highest bidder, the bidders are risk neutral, and their valuation of the prize is symmetric. Rents will be totally dissipated, that is, the contestants will spend the amount equal to the expected value of the prize.

This theory encounters several difficulties:

(1) It is not quite clear why governments respond to the rent-seeking activities by offering the rents that are being sought. We could tell some kind of a story, for example, one that follows, but in no plausible model will the government be just bought by the highest bidder. One possible outcome, indeed, is that the government would take the contributions of the groups competing for influence and would continue to pursue a nondistortionary policy. Grossman and Helpman (2001, Section 8.4) develop a model of trade policy, in which all members of society are represented either by a producers' association or by a union. They show that competition for influence results in a stalemate, in which tariffs equal export subsidies, and the resulting allocation is the same as under free trade. The competing groups must make political contributions, because

if one of them did not, the policy would shift in favor of the other. Hence, the government collects contributions but the final allocation generates no loss of social welfare. According to Grossman and Helpman (2001) "This outcome is typical of situations in which the policymaker cares about aggregate welfare and all members of society are represented by some interest group or another" (p. 274).

(2) What rents are is never clearly defined in this theory. While Tollison (1982, pp. 575–576; italics supplied) observes that rents are normally defined in economics as "a return in excess of resource owner's opportunity cost," the theory of rent seeking "involves the study of how people compete for *artificially contrived transfers.*" I have no idea what this means. If the starting point is the first-best equilibrium of the competitive economy, then rents are simple to define. But if we begin from a second-best, the concept of rents becomes fuzzy, and it is not always true that creating new rents must reduce social welfare (Baghwati and Srinivasan 1980).

(3) Finally, it is not quite clear why rent-seeking activities would be socially costly: Rents may be, but why would expenditures to obtain them additionally reduce social welfare? Obviously, these activities are costly to the rent seekers, but one could think that whatever the rent seekers give, someone gets, so that utilitarian social welfare remains the same. To justify the claim that the pursuit of rents is socially injurious, the rent-seeking theory assumes that if they were not spent in this way, the same resources would have been used productively to increase social welfare. This assumption is again far from obvious: Would the pharmaceutical companies spend more on research or would they just increase the salary of their CEOs?

To my taste, this is just not a persuasive theory.

6.6   Regulatory capture

To get a better intuition of endogenous regulation, we now study the model presented in Chapter 11 of Laffont and Tirole (1994). The general setup and the notation is the same as before, except that instead of a unit project, the cost of the firm now depends on the quantity it produces, q, so that

$$C(q) = (\beta - e)q.$$

The generic "regulator," however, is now structured as two bodies: the regulatory agency (to which I refer alternatively as the "regulator" or the "agency") and the Congress. Here the Congress is the principal, the regulator is a bureaucracy, a "supervisor," and the firm is the agent. Note that this is the setup with which we began the analysis of the state.

The regulator receives from the Congress income s and derives utility $V(s - s^*) = s - s^*$ from this income, where s^* is the reservation income of the agency, including salaries and costs of acquiring information. The agency seeks information $\sigma \in \{\beta, \emptyset\}$ about the firm's technology. With probability ζ, the agency learns the truth ($\sigma = \beta$); with probability $1 - \zeta$, the agency learns nothing ($\sigma = \emptyset$). The regulator thinks that the firm is efficient with probability v and inefficient with $1 - v$. There are thus four states of nature: (1) with probability ζv, the true technology is β and the signal is informative; (2) with probability $(1 - \zeta)v$, the technology is $\underline{\beta}$ but the regulator does not know it, so the agency does not modify its prior belief v; (3) with probability $\zeta(1 - v)$, the technology is $\overline{\beta}$ and the regulator is so informed; and (4) with probability $(1 - \zeta)(1 - v)$, the technology is $\overline{\beta}$ and the regulator is not informed.

The agency reports to Congress. If the regulator has learned nothing, $\sigma = \emptyset$, it can only say so. If it has learned the truth, $\sigma = \beta$, it can either report it or say it does not know. The firm knows what the regulator has learned.

The maximizer of utilitarian social welfare is no longer the regulator but the Congress. Note that we are pushing the analysis one step further. In the previous section, the regulator was a benevolent maximizer; now the regulator has an interest of its own (in income), but the Congress, the principal, is a benevolent maximizer. Social welfare is given by

$$W = U + V + S(q) - P(q)q - (1 + \lambda)[s + t + (\beta - e)q - P(q)q],$$

which can be rewritten as

$$W = [S(q) + \lambda P(q)q] - (1 + \lambda)(s^* + (\beta - e)q + \Psi(e)) - \lambda U - \lambda V.$$

The first expression says that social benefits from producing the quantity q consist of the utility of the firm, U, the utility of the agency, V, and the utility of consumers, $S(q)$. The social costs include those paid by the consumers for the output of the firm, $P(q)q$, and the tax financed, distortionary (because $\lambda > 0$) payments by Congress to the regulator, s, and to the firm, which are $t + (\beta - e)q - P(q)q$. (This is because the firm gets a transfer t and is reimbursed by the amount by which the costs were not covered by the revenue from sales.) Note from the second expression that the principal does not want leave to rents in the hands of the firm, which was also true before, and in the hands of the intermediary, the regulator.

Congress observes neither β nor σ. It bases its decision on observing C, q (or $p = P(q)$) and the report it gets from the agency, which is $r \in \{\sigma, \emptyset\}$. The contract is now an incentive scheme for the regulator, $s(C, q, r)$, and for the firm, $t(C, q, r)$. Hence, a contract is a triple $\{C, q, r; s; t\}$. The optimal contract maximizes expected social welfare over the four possible states of nature.

The benchmark model here is one in which the firm cannot influence the regulator, so that regulation is exogenous. Then the Congress offers the regulator a constant income equal to its reservation income s^*. The agency always tells the truth, so that Congress knows all the agency knows. Because by now you should be able to read Laffont and Tirole (1994) on your own – something I strongly recommend because their book is a treasure of enlightening stories – we not follow the algebra but only the intuitions.[3]

Because the agency cannot collude with the firm, it reports what it knows. If it knows $\sigma = \beta$, it so informs the Congress. If it does not discover the technology of the firm, $\sigma = \emptyset$, it says so. You can immediately guess that in the first case, because the Congress is now fully informed, it extracts all the rents from the firm, whether the firm is efficient or inefficient, and demands from the firm the efficient level of effort. Hence, under full information

---

[3] The only tricks are in deriving equation 11.7 in Chapter 11 of Laffont and Tirole (1994). Here are the steps:

$$\frac{dW}{dq} = 0 = \frac{dS}{dq} + \lambda \frac{dP}{dq} q + \lambda p - (1 + \lambda)(\beta - e).$$

Now add and subtract p:

$$\frac{dS}{dq} + \lambda \frac{dP}{dq} q + (1 + \lambda)[p - (\beta - e)] - p = 0.$$

But $\frac{dS}{dq} = p$, so that we have

$$(1 + \lambda)[p - (\beta - e)] = -\lambda \frac{dP}{dq} q.$$

Now multiply both sides by the elasticity of demand with regard to price, $\eta(p) = -\frac{dq}{dp} \frac{p}{q}$, to get

$$\eta(p)(1 + \lambda)[p - (\beta - e)] = \lambda p.$$

optimal contract generates $U(\beta) = U^o$ and $e(\beta) = e^*(\beta)$ for all β. In the second case, when the agency does not learn the type of the firm, the Congress is in the situation the regulator was when it faced imperfect information. We know that it will offer the second-best optimal contract, which will yield $\underline{U} = U^o + \Phi(\overline{e}), \overline{U} = U^o, \underline{e} = \underline{e}^*, \overline{e} < \overline{e}^*$. The only difference is that the Congress must now pay the agency s^* for the information it provides, at the cost of $(1 + \lambda)s^*$.

You may wonder whether the Congress will want to establish a regulatory agency. Without one, the Congress has to operate on its prior belief, $v = \Pr\{\beta = \underline{\beta}\}$, and design an asymmetric information contract. With the agency, the Congress will be fully informed with the probability ζ and not be informed with the probability $(1 - \zeta)$ but it will have to bear the cost $(1 + \lambda)s^*$. You can do the algebra to find when the Congress will want to run a regulatory agency. Clearly, the more likely is the agency to discover the type of the firm, the more valuable it is to the Congress.

This is just to set the benchmark model of no collusion. Now let us examine the effect of the possibility of collusion between the firm and the regulator. Suppose the firm can give a transfer of $\widetilde{s}$ to the regulator, so that the agency can get an income $s + \widetilde{s}$. This bribe costs the firm $(1 + \lambda_f)\widetilde{s}$, where λ_f is the shadow cost to the firm of transferring $\widetilde{s}$. This cost includes the possibility that the firm will be sanctioned if it is caught bribing the regulator. Let $\underline{s}_1$ stand for the agency's income when it reports $r = \underline{\beta}$, let $\overline{s}_1$ be the income of the agency when it reports $r = \overline{\beta}$, and let s_0 be its income when it reports $r = \emptyset$.

Collusion occurs when the regulator hides its information from the Congress. Now note that if the firm is inefficient, $\beta = \overline{\beta}$, it has no incentives to bribe the regulator, because it will get no rents whether the regulator reports $\overline{\beta}$ or $\emptyset$. (Remember that under imperfect information, the inefficient firm gets no rents in the optimal contract.) Hence, the possibility of collusion arises only if the firm is efficient. If the regulator were to report $r = \underline{\beta}$, the firm would get no rents. But if the regulator reports $r = \emptyset$, the efficient firm gets rents $\Phi(\overline{e})$, where $\overline{e}$ is the effort level of the inefficient firm under asymmetric information. Hence, if the firm is not to bribe the regulator, the rent to the agency from reporting $r = \emptyset$ rather than $r = \underline{\beta}$ must be at least as large as the gain of the firm from getting an imperfect information contract. Hence, it must be true that

$$(1 + \lambda_f)(\underline{s}_1 - s_0) \geq \Phi(\overline{e}).$$

Because the Congress will pay the agency its reservation income, s^*, when the agency says it does not know, the agency gets

$$\underline{s}_1 = s^* + \frac{\Phi(\overline{e})}{1 + \lambda_f},$$

where the last fraction represents the rent to the agency.

Now it is the Congress that is in the situation in which we earlier found the regulator. If the Congress increases the effort level of the inefficient firm, it will have to increase the rents of the efficient firm. But, in addition, as the rents of the efficient firm go up, its incentive to bribe the regulator increases. If Congress is to prevent collusion, it will thus have to pay a higher rent to the regulator as well. The trade-off the Congress faces is now not just between the effort level of the inefficient firm and the rents of the efficient one, but also the rents of the agency. In the optimal contract the inefficient firm has to work at a lower effort level than when collusion is not possible and the agency must get some rents. The output is lower, prices are higher, and social welfare is lower than under no collusion. You may want to investigate again whether the Congress would want to keep the agency that can collude or would prefer to just punt in the dark.

6.7   Competing interests

What happens when there are competing special interests? The example of Laffont and Tirole (1994) involves a firm that pollutes and an environmental group that wants to reduce pollution. Both interests want to bribe the regulator: The firm wants a high level of output, the environmentalists want a low level. The social value of the project is now its value to the consumers minus the cost of pollution. The Congress does not want the regulator to collude with either group. The most interesting result is that the effects of lobbying by two opposed interests do not cancel out (as in Becker's 1983 model) but add up. The explanation goes as follows. The environmentalists have the incentive to bribe the regulator to reduce output, which occurs if the regulator reports that it does not know the technology of the firm, while in fact it knows that the firm is inefficient. (If the regulator reports that the firm is inefficient, then the Congress sets $e = \overline{e}^*$ and the output is higher.) To reduce this incentive, the Congress must increase $\overline{e}$. But if the Congress increases $\overline{e}$, then it must also increase $\Phi(\overline{e})$. Hence, the effect of competition among interest groups for political influence is that rents of the efficient firm are higher than they would have been if the firm were the only lobbyist.

One aspect of this model calls for attention. In the Laffont and Tirole (1994) story, each group attempts to influence the regulator separately. But suppose that the Congress sets up a public hearing to listen to messages from the two opposing interests. Assume that both the environmentalists and the firm know the technology of the firm. Suppose that the firm is inefficient. The environmentalists would want the Congress to believe that the firm is efficient, so that the Congress would minimize $\Phi(\overline{e})$, hence $\overline{e}$, and hence the output of the inefficient firm. The inefficient firm would not care, because it would get no rent whatever the Congress thinks. Hence, the Congress would hear $r\left(\overline{\beta}\right) = \{\underline{\beta}, \emptyset\}$, where the first part of the message is by environmentalists and the second by the firm. Suppose, in turn, that the firm is efficient. Now the environmentalists would not care what the Congress thinks, because the Congress will want the efficient firm to exert an efficient amount of effort in either case. But the firm would want the Congress to believe that it is inefficient, to get $\Phi(\overline{e}^*) > \Phi(\overline{e})$. Hence, the Congress would hear $r(\underline{\beta}) = \{\emptyset, \overline{\beta}\}$. And because the Congress would learn different things under different states of nature, it could extract information from the messages it receives. Adversary democratic deliberation would thus improve information as to the best course of action.[4] And, indeed, some regulatory agencies are required by law to hold public hearings. Hence, the Laffont and Tirole (1994) setup may unduly exaggerate the informational deficit of politicians.

Another way of understanding what happens when interests compete has been offered by Grossman and Helpman (2001). Their setup differs from Laffont's and Tirole's in that the policymakers do not have any source of information other than that originating from lobbies of special interest groups. There are no specialized government agencies charged with producing information for policymakers. In the Grossman and Helpman story, a legislator (or legislature) chooses a policy p from some continuous closed interval. The optimal policy depends on some state of affairs, θ, unobserved by the decision maker but known to special interests. The utility function of the policymaker is such that the optimal policy is simply $p^* = \theta$. The special

---

[4] Most stories about democratic deliberation bark up the wrong tree. These are stories about people persuading each other to act in a just way. The value of democratic deliberation is that when it is adversarial, it generates information.

interest groups are characterized by their policy biases, such that the ideal policy of group i is $p_i = \theta + \delta_i$, where the bias δ can be positive or negative. Given that the decision maker knows that groups are biased, she must distrust their information. The question is whether the special interests will be able to convey to the policymaker information in which they policymaker will believe and act on.

If there is only one lobby and only two states of the world are possible, so that $\theta \in \{\theta_L, \theta_H\}, \theta_H > \theta_L$, the special interest can convey the truth and the policymaker will believe it on the condition that its bias is not too large, specifically, $\delta \leq (\theta_H - \theta_L)/2$. When the states of the world are continuously distributed in $(\theta_{min}, \theta_{max})$, the special interest group cannot convey the exact information but, again if its bias is not too large, the lobbyist can credibly make a coarse report, such as "θ is small (medium, large)." Let n be the number of distinct messages a lobbyist may communicate. Then any of the n different reports is believed by the policymaker if $\delta < (\theta_{min} - \theta_{max})/2n(n - 1)$. The intuition is this: Suppose that a group with a positive bias observes a small value of θ. If it reported a large value, the decision maker, knowing that the group would want a large policy, would not believe it and would just continue thinking that θ may be anywhere in the full range of its possible values. But the special interest does not want the policy to diverge from the true state of affairs by more than δ. Hence, there is some maximum value $\theta_1 > \theta_{min}$, such that the special interest would prefer the decision maker to believe that the truth lies in (θ_{min}, θ_1), rather than in the full range. Thus, the lobby informs the decision maker that θ is "low," that is, in (θ_{min}, θ_1), and the decision maker is willing to believe this message.

Let us now get back to the situation in which there are two special interests with opposing biases, so that $\delta_1 > 0$ and $\delta_2 < 0$. Group 1 would want production to be high; group 2 would want pollution, hence production, to be low. The state of affairs $1/\theta$ is then the amount of pollutants emitted per a unit of output. In general, an equilibrium with "partial revelation" exists whenever both lobbies are "nonextreme," meaning that they do not wish the decision maker to believe that the state of the world is θ_{min} or θ_{max} regardless of the truth. Partial revelation means in turn that the policymaker is able to infer that the true state of the world lies in some interval smaller than the full range of feasible values. Hence, some truth is conveyed by adversary lobbying. Moreover, partial revelation yields higher ex ante welfare to the policymaker and to both special interests than does any equilibrium with lobbying by a single group. Hence, the regulator benefits from conflicting interests.

6.8   Money and politics

As we have seen, the story of regulation has two parts: motivations of the elected politicians, who are the decision makers, and the incentives for the specialized bureaucracies that implement regulations. In the Laffont–Tirole (1994) model politicians were assumed to maximize social welfare. But the Chicago school is right that politicians may want to win (re)election and the Virginia school is right that at least some politicians seek private benefits. To make the analysis tractable, let us now shortcut the regulator and ask what will happen if politicians regulate directly. What will they do?

Consider two questions: (1) Does money buy policies, that is, do politicians sell regulation in exchange for contributions from special interests? (2) Does money buy votes, that is, are those who lose from regulation less likely to vote against politicians who regulate against them if politicians spend more money in electoral campaigns?

The Chicago answer to both these questions is positive: Regulators sell policies for money and they use the money to buy their offices. Voters are gullible.

If money were to buy policies but not votes, regulators would face being voted out of office if they sold policies to special interests. If they are exclusively (re)election oriented, they would not do it. If they seek private benefits, they may decide to go for them and be thrown out. Hence, either policies would not be sold and we would get second-best optimal regulation or we would observe frequent defeats of incumbents, which is a rare event anywhere.

If money buys votes but not policies, the following may be true. Candidates have different preferences with regard to policies: Either they have different ideological positions or different "technical beliefs" about effects of policies. Special interests can guess who is who. They contribute to the candidate whose position would lead her to adopt policies favorable to their interests. While in office, the elected candidate pursues policies that she prefers, thus advancing the interests of some special interests and uses the contributions to dissuade those hurt by these policies from voting against her. Hence, an observed correlation between contributions and policies does not resolve the question of direction of causality: In equilibrium it may be true that money buys policies but it may also be true that money follows policies.

It turns out that we can say more than this. But not much more: As I see it, the central puzzle remains. Grossman and Helpman (2001) develop a model in which there are elected politicians (individuals or parties), voters, and special interest groups. Parties maximize the probability of winning a majority of seats, while special interest groups maximize the welfare of their members. Voters, note, come in two kinds: **strategic** voters maximize expected utility, while **impressionable** voters are favorably influenced by campaign advertising. Special interests can make campaign contributions, politicians choose policies, and voters vote; not necessarily in this sequence, because contributions can play a twofold role. They can be used early in the campaign to induce parties to announce platforms that are to the liking of special interests or they can be used once the platforms have been announced to sway voters to vote for the party closer to the special interest.

If there is only one interest group, the conclusions are that: (1) To influence their platforms, the group contributes to both parties, giving more to the party that is the ex ante favorite to win; (2.1) If the resulting platforms are the same, the special interest is indifferent as to which party would win and contributes no more; (2.2) If the resulting platforms differ, the group contributes additional funds to tilt the election in favor of the front-runner. "Overall," Grossman and Helpman (2001) conclude, "the contributions bias the policy outcome away from the public interest both by influencing the parties' positions and perhaps by tilting the election odds" (p. 339). The electoral motive – contributions designed to tilt elections in favor of the party whose announced position is more to the liking of the special interest – is even weaker when several interest groups compete for influence. With sufficiently many special interests, the electoral motive vanishes entirely, while special interests continue to contribute in order to influence the platforms. The reason multiple groups are unlikely to make electorally motivated contributions is the opportunity to ride free on the contributions of other groups.

In the end, platforms reflect contributions and deviate from the welfare of the average voter. Parties act as if they were maximizing a weighted average of campaign contributions and of the aggregate welfare of strategic voters. Moreover, parties sell policies rather than special interests supporting parties closer to them independently of contributions.

None of it, however, elucidates the puzzle: Why would, at least some, voters be more likely to vote for parties that sell themselves to special interests? Grossman and Helpman stipulate it as an assumption and cite some evidence. But think as follows. You are a voter whose interests are not those of a special interest group that made a contribution to the party. You know that these contributions were made to influence the party platform in favor of the special interest and that the party that accepted these contributions places a higher weight on the special interest than on your interest. Would this information not sway you away from this party? The impressionable voters of Grossman and Helpman are not anymore rational than those of Peltzman, with whom we began. Hence, the question remains: Why would money buy votes?

All we can say is that whether regulation is exogenous or endogenous hinges on whether voters can and want to control representatives. This is the topic of Chapter 8.

6.9   Appendix: Optimal regulation under incomplete information

This Appendix is an explanation of some steps in Laffont and Tirole (1944). Here is their story.

The regulator does not know whether the firm has a high cost, $\beta = \overline{\beta}$, or a low cost, $\beta = \underline{\beta}$. Let $\overline{\beta} - \underline{\beta} \equiv \Delta\beta$. The regulator observes C but not β or e. A contract (or a menu of contracts) is now $\{C(\underline{\beta}), t(\underline{\beta})\}$ for type $\underline{\beta}$ and $\{C(\overline{\beta}), t(\overline{\beta})\}$ for type $\overline{\beta}$. Let $U(\beta) \equiv t(\beta) - \Psi(\beta - C(\beta))$ denote the utility of rent for type β. This is because $\beta - C(\beta) = e$ is the cost reduction of type β. Then

$$\underline{U} \equiv \underline{t} - \Psi(\underline{\beta} - \underline{C}),$$
$$\overline{U} \equiv \overline{t} - \Psi(\overline{\beta} - \overline{C}),$$

where all the $\underline{X}$ quantities refer to the low cost ("efficient") type and all the $\overline{X}$ refer to the high cost ("inefficient") one. The regulator offers a menu of contracts and the firm picks the one it prefers. The incentive compatibility constraint (IC) facing the regulator is that the contract designed for type β must be the one preferred by this type in the menu of cost-transfer pairs. Because $e = \beta - C$, IC amounts to

$$\underline{t} - \Psi(\underline{\beta} - \underline{C}) \geq \overline{t} - \Psi(\underline{\beta} - \overline{C}),$$
$$\overline{t} - \Psi(\overline{\beta} - \overline{C}) \geq \underline{t} - \Psi(\overline{\beta} - \underline{C}).$$

The first of these (in)equalities says that the efficient firm, the firm with low costs, must prefer to get the transfer designed for it and produced at low cost to obtaining the transfer designed for the high-cost firm and producing at high cost. The second refers to the inefficient firm. It can be shown (this step is tricky because it entails double integration) that if $\Psi(e)$ is convex, then $\overline{C} > \underline{C}$, that is, the firm that has higher costs to begin with, $\overline{\beta} > \underline{\beta}$, will end up producing at higher costs. Incentive compatibility, therefore, implies that under the optimal contract $dC/d\beta \geq 0$.

The participation constraint or, as Laffont and Tirole (1994) prefer to call it, the individual rationality (IR) constraint, requires in turn that for each type

$$\underline{U} \geq 0,$$
$$\overline{U} \geq 0.$$

As we have learned earlier in a more general case, some of these constraints are redundant. It is sufficient that the contract satisfies the incentive compatibility constraint for the efficient type $\underline{\beta}$ and the individual rationality constraint for the inefficient type $\overline{\beta}$. Any contract that gives $\overline{U} \geq 0$ to the inefficient type will also give $\underline{U} \geq 0$ to the efficient one. The efficient type can always work less and get $\overline{U}$. To see it, note that IC for the $\underline{\beta}$ type, $\underline{U} \geq \overline{t} - \Psi(\underline{\beta} - \overline{C})$, and IR for the $\overline{\beta}$ type, $\overline{U} \geq 0$, respectively imply

$$\overline{t} \leq \underline{U} + \Psi(\underline{\beta} - \overline{C})$$
$$\overline{t} \geq \Psi(\overline{\beta} - \overline{C}).$$

Hence, it must be true that

$$\underline{U} + \Psi(\underline{\beta} - \overline{C}) \geq \Psi(\overline{\beta} - \overline{C}),$$

or

$$\underline{U} \geq \Psi(\overline{\beta} - \overline{C}) - \Psi(\underline{\beta} - \overline{C}).$$

But $\overline{\beta} - \overline{C} > \underline{\beta} - \overline{C}$ and $\Psi'(e) > 0$. Hence,

$$\underline{U} \geq 0.$$

The IR for the efficient type never bites. If the inefficient type decides to produce, then the efficient type will produce as well.

Let us now return to the utilitarian regulator. We already know that ex-post social welfare when the firm is of type β is

$$W(\beta) = S - (1 + \lambda)[C(\beta) + \Psi(\beta - C(\beta))] - \lambda U(\beta).$$

A utilitarian regulator maximizes expected social welfare, knowing only that the firm is efficient with probability v and inefficient with probability

$(1 - v)$. His problem is then

$$\max W = vW(\underline{\beta}) + (1 - v)W(\overline{\beta})$$

$s..t$

$$\underline{t} - \Psi(\underline{\beta} - \underline{C}) \geq \overline{t} - \Psi(\underline{\beta} - \overline{C}),$$

$$\overline{U} \geq 0.$$

For the moment, we will ignore the IC for the inefficient firm, checking it later. The IC for the efficient type can be rewritten as

$$\underline{U} \geq \overline{t} - \Psi(\underline{\beta} - \overline{C}) \geq \overline{U} + \Phi(\overline{e}),$$

where

$$\Phi(e) \equiv \Psi(e) - \Psi(e - \Delta\beta) = \Psi(e) - \Psi(e - (\overline{\beta} - \underline{\beta})).$$

The function $\Phi(e)$ determines the rent of the efficient type relative to the rent of the inefficient type. It is the difference in the disutility of effort of the efficient type, $\Psi(e)$, and of the inefficient type, $\Psi(e - \Delta\beta)$, for any effort e. To see why this is true, let $e = \overline{e} = \overline{\beta} - \overline{C}$. Then

$$\Phi(\overline{e}) = \Psi(\overline{\beta} - \overline{C}) - \Psi(\overline{\beta} - \overline{C} - \Delta\beta)$$
$$= \Psi(\overline{\beta} - \overline{C}) - \Psi(\overline{\beta} - \overline{C} - \overline{\beta} + \underline{\beta}) = \Psi(\overline{\beta} - \overline{C}) - \Psi(\underline{\beta} - \overline{C}).$$

Hence, $\Phi(\overline{e})$ measures the difference in the disutility of effort in producing at high cost, $\overline{C}$, between the high-cost type and the low-cost type. It tells how much the efficient type can shirk to produce at $\overline{C}$. Now, at any fixed $\overline{C}$, $\Phi(e) = \Phi(\overline{e})$, $\underline{U} \geq \overline{t} - \Psi(\underline{\beta} - \overline{C})$. But $\Psi(\underline{\beta} - \overline{C}) = \Psi(\overline{\beta} - \overline{C}) - \Phi(\overline{e})$. Hence, $\underline{U} \geq \overline{t} - \Psi(\overline{\beta} - \overline{C}) + \Phi(\overline{e}) = \overline{U} + \Phi(\overline{e})$.

Let us now use this form of the constraint to return to the problem of the regulator. His final problem is to

$$\max_{\underline{C}, \overline{C}; \underline{U}, \overline{U}} v[S - (1 + \lambda)(\underline{C} + \Psi(\underline{\beta} - \underline{C})) - \lambda\underline{U}]$$
$$+ (1 - v)[S - (1 + \lambda)(\overline{C} + \Psi(\overline{\beta} - \overline{C})) - \lambda\overline{U}],$$

$s.t.$

$$\underline{U} \geq \overline{U} + \Phi(\overline{e}),$$

$$\overline{U} \geq 0.$$

Because rents are costly, $\overline{U} = 0$: The participation constraint of the inefficient type bites. Thus, $\underline{U} = \Phi(\overline{\beta} - \overline{C})$. Substituting back into the regulator's maximand yields

$$W = v[S - (1 + \lambda)(\underline{C} + \Psi(\underline{\beta} - \underline{C})) - \lambda\Phi(\overline{\beta} - \overline{C})]$$
$$+ (1 - v)[S - (1 + \lambda)(\overline{C} + \Psi(\overline{\beta} - \overline{C}))].$$

For the efficient firm, the regulator will choose the cost that satisfies

$$\frac{\partial W}{\partial \underline{C}} = 0 = v(1 + \lambda)\left(1 + \Psi'(\underline{e})\frac{de}{d\underline{C}}\right) = v(1 + \lambda)(1 - \Psi'(\underline{e})),$$

implying that

$$\Psi'(\underline{e}) = 1$$

and

$$\underline{e} = e^*.$$

Hence the regulator will want the efficient firm to exert the efficient level of effort.

For the inefficient firm, the regulator will choose the cost that satisfies

$$\frac{\partial W}{\partial \overline{C}} = 0 = -v\lambda\Phi'(\overline{e})\frac{de}{d\overline{C}} - (1 - v)(1 + \lambda)\left(1 + \Psi'(\overline{e})\frac{de}{d\overline{C}}\right)$$
$$= v\lambda\Phi'(\overline{e}) - (1 - v)(1 + \lambda)(1 - \Psi'(\overline{e})),$$

or

$$(1 - v)(1 + \lambda)(1 - \Psi'(\overline{e})) = v\lambda\Phi'(\overline{e}),$$

implying that

$$\Psi'(\overline{e}) = 1 - \frac{\lambda}{1 + \lambda}\frac{v}{1 - v}\Phi'(\overline{e}).$$

Because the last term on the right-hand side is positive, $\Psi'(\overline{e}) < 1$ and $\overline{e} < e^*$. Hence, the regulator will want the inefficient firm to exert less than the efficient level of effort. I will leave it to you to check that the incentive compatibility constraint for the inefficient type is satisfied.

Here then are the main conclusions. For S large enough, *optimal regulation* under incomplete information is characterized by $\underline{e} = e^*$ and $\overline{e} < e^*$. The efficient firm exerts an efficient level of effort and gets a rent $\Phi(\overline{e}) > 0$. The inefficient firm exerts less than the efficient level of effort and gets no rent, $\overline{U} = 0$. If the regulator wants to realize the project even if the firm is inefficient – this is what "sufficiently large S" means – then it must give a

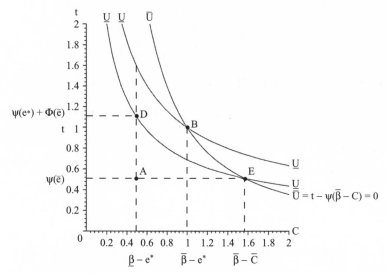

Figure 6.2. Trade-off between effort of inefficient type and rents of efficient type.

rent to the efficient type. This rent, $\Phi(\overline{e})$, is a function of the effort level required from the inefficient type.

If the regulator were to insist on first-best level of effort from the inefficient type, so that $\overline{C} = \overline{\beta} - e^*$, the cost would be a higher rent for the efficient type, $\Phi(e^*) > \Phi(\overline{e} < e^*)$. Hence, the regulator faces a trade-off between the effort of the inefficient type and the rents of the efficient type: As the inefficient type increases effort, the efficient type gets higher rents when he works at the efficient level. Figure 6.2 provides intuition for this conclusion. Think of utilities of the two types in the $\{C, t\}$ space.

The indifference curves of the efficient type are flatter in this space, because this type can reduce costs exerting less effort. Note first that if the regulator were to offer the contract A to the $\underline{\beta}$ type and the contract E to the $\overline{\beta}$ type, the efficient type would take the contract designed for the inefficient one. In turn, if the regulator were to offer any contract to the right of the point E, the inefficient type would take the contract designed for the efficient one. The optimal contract is located at point D for the efficient type and point E for the inefficient one. At the point D, $C = \underline{C} = \underline{\beta} - e^*$ and $t = \Psi(e^*) + \Phi(\overline{e})$. Hence, under D, the efficient type exerts a high effort and gets a high rent. At the point E, $C = \overline{C} = \overline{\beta} - \overline{e}$ and $t = \Psi(\overline{e})$. Under E the inefficient type is exerting an inefficient amount of effort and is getting no rents. The incentive compatibility for the efficient type is exactly satisfied, because its indifference curve passes through the point E. Suppose now that the regulator were to require an efficient level of effort from the $\overline{\beta}$ type, setting the contract at the point B, where $C = \overline{\beta} - e^*$. To keep the $\underline{\beta}$ type from taking the contract B, the regulator would then have to increase the rents to the efficient type, setting the contract for the efficient type at G. Hence, the regulator faces a trade-off between the effort required of the inefficient type and the rents that must accrue to the efficient one.

CHAPTER 7

Politicians and bureaucrats: Oversight

7.1 Readings

Bendor, Jonathan. 1988. "Review Article: Formal Models of Bureaucracy." *British Journal of Political Science 18*: 353–395.

Kiewiet, D. Roderick and Matthew D. McCubbins. 1991. Chapter 2 of *The Logic of Delegation: Congressional Parties and the Appropriation Process.* Chicago: University of Chicago Press.

Moe, Terry M. 1990. "Political Institutions: The Neglected Side of the Story." *Journal of Law, Economics, and Organization 6*: 213–253.

Recommended:

McCubbins, Matthew and Thomas Schwartz. 1984. "Congressional Oversight Overlooked: Police Patrols versus Fire Alarms." *American Journal of Political Science 28*: 165–179.

7.2 Introduction

The relation between decision makers and the populated agencies to which decision makers delegate the implementation of their decisions is among the least well understood topics of political theory. I consider this question in the context of democracy, where the decision makers are elected. Hence, the topic of this chapter is the relation between elected politicians, appointed bureaucrats, and citizens who at the same time elect the politicians and receive services of bureaucrats.

The central puzzle of this relation is, in my view, the following. The state derives its claim to authority from universalism, from its status as the organization of the entire political community. Yet under democracy those who command the state are recruited in partisan elections. How can those who are elected by a part rule on behalf of all?

Politicians may have universalistic, partisan, and personal goals. They may want their country to progress; they may want to stay in office, and may have their own ambitions. Universalistic interests are shared across the political spectrum, but partisan interests oppose teams of like-minded politicians seeking to win and retain public office. Personal ambitions lead politicians to compete with their partisan colleagues. They are advanced if politicians loyally serve the party and if the party wins elections: Hence, politicians are disciplined to prioritize partisan interests.

The conflict between universalistic and partisan goals is a source of tension between politics and administration. The people who are elected to make decisions on behalf of the political community are not the ones who implement them. In all states, implementation is delegated to specialized organizations, "bureaucracies." Delegation is inevitable. As Kiewiet and McCubbins (1991) observe, "desired outcomes can be achieved only by delegating authority to others" (p. 3).

The bureaucracy is supposed to implement decisions made by the elected politicians. It is not supposed to be autonomous. Yet democratic decision makers want to use the bureaucracy for partisan purposes. This situation exposes bureaucracies to conflicting pressures. If a bureaucracy implements decisions of governing politicians, then it will be, to some extent at least, an instrument for consolidating partisan advantage. In turn, if bureaucracy is autonomous, then it is not an instrument of the public. Ideally, one would want a bureaucracy that implements those decisions by politicians that are in the general interest of the public without becoming an instrument of those interests that are merely partisan. But this first-best solution may be unfeasible.

Political uses of public power constitute a phenomenon often referred to as "clientelism," "nepotism," "prebendalism," "patrimonialism," or, in a language we already know, "endogenous regulation." But these are vague terms and the phenomenon is not always easy to identify. Almost all public decisions entail distributional consequences. Because political parties are organizations whose goal is to attain and maintain control over the government, it would be naive to think that governments would be oblivious to these consequences when they make decisions. Yet, whereas the line may be fuzzy, the difference between universalistic uses and partisan abuses of public power is often apparent.

Our system of representative government, however, is not based on a pure majority rule (Manin 1997). It contains several mechanisms designed to temper the current majority. A system of checks and balances is intended to protect the bureaucracy from partisan control while at the same time not allowing it to become autonomous. Another solution relies on contramajoritarian institutions, in the form of independent, nonelected authorities. The law, as implemented by the courts, is the principal instrument for preventing discretionary abuses of public power by governments. In the extreme, some policy realms may be removed from partisan control altogether.

The plan of this chapter is the following. First, we discuss generic problems of oversight, assuming that the elected politicians who exercise it are social welfare maximizers. Then we ask what to expect when the elected politicians seek to use the bureaucracy to advance their partisan interests. These questions lead us to examine systems of checks and balances among elected and nonelected authorities.

7.3   Generic problems of oversight

In a democracy, the authority of the state to regulate the life of the society is derived from elections. Yet many functions of the state and all of the services the state supplies to citizens are delegated by the elected representatives to someone else, specifically to the public bureaucracy.

Delegation raises principal-agent problems. Because it is impossible to write legislation that would fully specify the actions of agents under all contingencies, the executive and administrative agencies are left with a significant degree of discretion. But the objectives of bureaucrats need not be the same as those of citizens or even of the elected politicians who represent them. Bureaucrats may seek autonomy or security of employment; they may want to render clientilistic favors to friends and allies, shirk their duties, aggrandize their budgets, or simply get rich – all at the expense of the public. Again, they have private information and undertake actions that can be monitored only at a cost or only inferred from outcomes. Hence, delegation must inevitably give rise to agency costs. Indeed, given the discretion bureaucracies must enjoy, the question is how to avoid a regime of "policy without law," as Lowi (1979, p. 92) described the U.S. political system.

Some of the agency costs inherent in managing the public bureaucracy are not different from those confronted by private firms. Yet the principal-agent relation is not the same in the public and the private sectors. The main reason is that in the private sector, the principals get free information about the performance of their agents from the market. A private firm has owners and a bureaucracy, which is an agent of the former. It offers products to the public, which does or does not buy the goods or services offered by the firm at a price. By revealing its demand for the firm's products, the public sanctions the firm; it generates profit or loss for the owners. Hence, the principals, the owners, get free information from the public about the performance of the agents, the bureaucracy. The owners read the bottom line, compare it with the performance of similar firms, and reward or punish the bureaucracy.

The performance of public agencies does not generate the same information. One reason is that when a public bureaucracy is a monopoly, citizens cannot vote with their feet. I can get annoyed that it takes the U.S. Passport Office three weeks to issue a new passport. But I cannot go somewhere else to get it faster. I can be upset that teachers are frequently absent from school but in most countries I cannot take my children out of the assigned public school. In some countries wealthier people do leave a public system for a private one, even if the former is tax-financed and thus free: The Italian health service or the Brazilian secondary education are good examples. But typically my consumption of public services does not provide the politicians with the same information as the consumption of private goods and services. Moreover, because public agencies provide several services, evaluating them is not easy. There is no "bottom line." Financial performance is certainly not a good yardstick. Finally, even if individual citizens express their dissatisfaction (or satisfaction) with a performance of a bureaucracy, our institutional framework does not include mechanisms by which such expressions can be aggregated and communicated to the putative principals, the elected politicians. Our political institutions were designed when there was almost no bureaucracy to speak of and until today our institutional frameworks bear the trace of their origins.

Consider the difficulties in evaluating the performance of the public sector:

(1) What are the criteria by which not only individual agents, but also teams of them, can be evaluated? Suppose that local clinics are charged with "maintaining the health of the population." This is obviously a vague standard but such standards are often vague. Tirole (1994) points out that, for example, the task given to the U.S. Department of State is "promoting the long-range security and well-being of the United States,"

while the Department of Labor is charged with "fostering, promoting, and developing the welfare of wage earners in the United States" (p. 4).

(2) Such tasks can be translated into specific targets. Say that local clinics are told to or contracted to take care of the sick, pursue preventative programs, and minimize costs. Assessing their performance will still be difficult, because the multidimensionality of the tasks may render these assessments ambivalent. Say one clinic received 100 sick people, vaccinated 50 children, and spent 120 pesos, while another received 200 sick people, vaccinated no children, and spent 150 pesos: Which one performed better? Private firms also perform multiple tasks, but to the extent to which they face a market constraint, their performance can be measured by financial criteria: There is a single bottom line. Public agencies have no such unique criterion by which different aspects of their performance can be weighted.

(3) Another difficulty stems from the fact that public agencies are frequently monopolies, which in turn implies that there are no comparative yardsticks by which their performance can be evaluated. The performance of the management at Banque Nationale de Paris (which is private in spite of its name) can be compared with that of Crédit Lyonnais, but the performance of the Banque de France can be at most compared to that of central banks in other countries. Yardstick evaluation of public agencies is not available when they constitute monopolies.

Faced with these difficulties, politicians are prone to control bureaucrats by relying on conformity with rules rather than on incentives. The first form of control is often referred to as "bureaucratic," while the latter as "managerial."

"Bureaucratic" control relies on rules. It consists of an ex ante control of processes, as opposed to an a posteriori control of results. Tirole (1994) observes that "the central feature of a bureaucracy is that its members are not trusted to make use of information that affects members other than themselves, and that decisions are therefore based on rigid rules" (p. 14). These rules are intended to structure activities of bureaucrats and to prevent shirking. They may say that a public employee must be in the office from nine to five, should not take more than two coffee breaks, should not spend more than twenty minutes on an individual client, and should write a quarterly report about her activities. Individuals are judged by whether they are observed to conform to such rules and by what they report. Sanctions are applied to deviations from the rules, so that an employee who posts the third piece of paper "Went for coffee" during the same day will not be promoted if caught. Needless to say, this is not a very effective mode of control: Not only is it costly (the principal bears the cost of monitoring and of the time agents spend on filling reports), but it does not establish any direct relation between outcomes and sanctions. Nevertheless, this is the way most public bureaucracies operate, and perhaps it is for good reason: We see that the alternative mode of control has problems of its own.

Ex post or "managerial" control relies on contracts, that is, sets a relation between performance and incentives. Now we are back to the principal-agent framework. But the relation between politicians and bureaucrats is not a typical principal-agent relation. Suppose you, a citizen, go to a public post office and find a note on the window, saying "Went for coffee. Will be back." As a citizen, you are in some sense a principal of the shirking bureaucrat. But you cannot individually sanction the bureaucrat. The body that can are your representatives. Hence, you are at most a principal of the representatives, who are principals of the bureaucracy of which you are a client. Your principal-agent relation with the bureaucracy is mediated by your relation to the representative body, by the relation between this body and the specialized agency, and by the hierarchical structure of this agency. Moreover, as a principal-agent relation it is a strange one, because you, the ultimate principal, are better informed about the actions of the bureaucrats than your agent, the representative body that oversees the bureaucracy. You go to the post office, not your representatives. You are the one who knows if teachers turn up in school, if police takes bribes, if social security checks arrive on time, and so on.

Hence, while citizens, as clients of the public agencies, are best informed about their performance, they do not have instruments either to sanction them directly or even to inform politicians. Suppose you find the note in one post office, someone else has the same experience in another post office, and so on. The problem is how to aggregate this information and convey it to the principals of public functionaries, the elected politicians. If citizens have some mechanisms for revealing and aggregating their information, then politicians, as principals, can rely on the information provided by the affected parties to control bureaucrats. This is, in the terminology of McCubbins and Schwartz (1984), "fire alarm" oversight. This form of oversight has two virtues: (1) it allows the principals to acquire information at a lower cost than that of "police patrol" (bureaucratic, ex ante) oversight, and (2) it provides better information, particularly about the most egregious actions of the agents. Even though the legal authority rests with the elected politicians, fire alarm oversight is a mechanism that generates accountability of the bureaucracy to citizens. As Haggard (1995) argues, "The ultimate check on government must come through institutionalized forms of participation" (pp. 41–42).

Yet even if this form of oversight would enhance accountability and even if in many countries there is widespread political demand for some forms of public control over bureaucracies, experiments with institutions that would enable such control appear to have been unsuccessful. Corporatist arrangements have often led to "regulatory capture." Experiments with direct participation of citizens in the supervision of service delivery agencies meet with public apathy. Monitoring by nongovernmental organizations privileges those interests that can mobilize organizational and financial resources. While such experiments are ongoing, particularly in Latin America (Cunill Grau 1997), the institutional design of public oversight is not obvious.

7.4   Political uses of public power

Is social welfare is maximized when politicians control bureaucracies? A positive answer may seem intuitively obvious, but things are not that simple. The reason was mentioned in the Introduction. Governments are partisan: Either they have interests of their own or they favor the interests of some segment of the population. Indeed, whenever interests are in conflict, party governments pursue their own interests by favoring the interests of their constituencies.

The role of political parties requires a clarification. According to democratic theory, or at least parts of this theory that recognize the existence of political parties at all, parties are supposed to be vehicles by which citizens are represented in the public realm. But public bureaucracy is supposed to be nonpartisan, in the sense of not favoring supporters of one or another party. Parties are expected to advocate and implement different policies but partisan governments are expected to treat all citizens equally. But the pressure of electoral competition (move about this following) pushes parties to adopt similar policies and to pursue clientilistic policies while in office.

Some years ago, when I was living in Chicago, the tires of my car froze into the ice created by the overnight cold. I called the city government and nothing happened. After a wait of some days – ice never melts in Chicago – my wife, who knew better, called the Democratic precinct captain. He was at our door in a few minutes, pointing out that we had not voted in the last municipal election. We assured him that we were registered Democrats, promised that we would vote in the next election, and one hour later the ice was chipped away by a city crew. Guided by partisan interest, the public bureaucracy was buying our votes by selectively providing public services, while voters in the Republican precincts of the city could only swear at the municipal government, regardless of the urgency of their, as opposed to my, needs.

The story will be immediately recognized by citizens in many democracies, under the terms of "clientilism," "nepotism," "prebendalism," "patrimonialism," and the like. But it is not always obvious whether a particular public decision was made to promote public or partisan interests.

Consider a decision to build schools. Even if this is what the country needs, schools have to be located somewhere, which means that some communities will have new schools while others will not. A road has to go through somewhere, which implies again that some people benefit when it is built while some others will be hurt. Someone has to direct the local post office, so that one candidate for this position benefits, while others are disappointed. I will not go on, because we can all think of innumerable examples.

How would a truly universalistic government behave? Let us think with the aid of an example. Suppose the government decides how many primary schools to build during a particular year. The budget is obviously limited, so the number of schools must be limited as well. The government uses some universalistic criterion to allocate its resources and discovers that it should build 100 schools. Now the question becomes where to locate them. Some universalistic criterion is employed again: need, productive consequences, demand from parents. For example, the government decides to locate schools in those 100 communities where children are most distant from the existing schools. Once the schools are built, the government must appoint principals. Again, it announces a public competition and hires the 100 most qualified candidates. This is rational administration: Universalistic criteria are used to make decisions.

I am sure that this image will be received with a sneer: This is just not the way things work. "If he only knew" is the likely response of those who have seen how this process in fact operates. It starts at the political level, where the minister of education fights for resources with the minister of health, and they both fight against the minister of finance. The minister of education claims that schools produce more votes than health clinics; both argue with the minister of finance that austerity is the best way to be voted out of office. The prime minister or the president arbitrates these conflicts and decides that 100 schools should be budgeted. Once the funds are appropriated, the minister of education chooses where to locate the schools and it turns out that they are built in the electorally marginal districts. A representative from a particular district where a school is built then lobbies the minister or the political secretary of the chief executive to appoint his nephew as the principal.

With these intuitions, let us now pose the problem analytically. If the maximand of the government in making all the decisions is universalistic, we may conclude that the government is behaving in the best public interest: Say the government chooses the number of schools, their location, and their principals to maximize the present value of the utility of the representative household. But if the government makes these decisions to maximize the chances of reelection, or some other partisan criterion, then it follows its political interest.

Yet in many situations it is difficult to tell whether actions of the government are publicly or politically motivated. Just imagine that building schools is both best for the country and electorally advantageous for the government, that districts that most need schools are also electorally marginal, and that the nephew of the local representative is the most qualified candidate for the principal. Then the two motivations lead to the same decisions. In other situations, universalistic criteria are not sufficiently discriminating: There may be 200 districts that equally need new schools or two equally well-qualified candidates for the principal. The government may still locate the schools in the electorally marginal districts or appoint a nephew, but these decisions, even if politically motivated, will not be socially costly.

Consider vote buying. If a government is using public funds to buy votes, it is obviously acting in its partisan interest. But if buying votes is just a form of redistributing incomes, without any consequences for total welfare, then it is not socially costly: Whatever some people lose, other people gain. Motivation is not sufficient to conclude that the government is sacrificing the public interest for its political goals: *A government is abusing its power only if its decisions are collectively suboptimal by some criterion of social welfare.*

Political parties are organizations whose goal is to attain and retain public office. To achieve this goal, they do not need the support of everyone: All they have to obtain and maintain is the support of a majority, or some other qualified number, of voters. Even if political parties want to attain office only because they want to be able to do what is best for the country, to implement their policies they have to first reach and then maintain control over the government, and to win elections they have to obtain the support of marginal voters. This much is inherent in any democracy. Almost all public decisions have distributional consequences and it is just naive to think that governments would be oblivious to the political consequences of their decisions. Hence, there is every reason to expect that governments would promote the interests of some groups at the expense of other groups.

7.5   Checks and balances

This situation raises issues of institutional design of government. The institutional bet of the founders of the institution of representative government was that governments can be structured in such a way that while it would not be the task of any particular body to maximize general welfare, their interaction would generate this effect (Manin 1994). Although the traditional theory of separation of powers and of checks and balances was developed when the functions of governments were much more limited than they are today and bureaucracies were miniscule, this hypothesis – which is what it is – suggests a number of principles for the design of governments. The first one is that adversary procedures should be built into the governmental decision making, by creating multiple principals or multiple agents with dissonant objectives. The second principle is that horizontal institutional checks should be built into the delegation process. Kiewiet and McCubbins (1991) point out that "agents are often in a position to do more harm to the principal than to simply withdraw effort: embezzlement, insider trading, official corruption, abuse of authority, and coups d'etat are all testaments to this fact. Whenever an agent can take actions that might seriously jeopardize the principal's interests, the principal needs to thwart the agent's ability to pursue such courses of action unilaterally" (p. 33). Their solution is "institutional checks [that] require that when authority has been delegated to an agent, there is at least one other agent with the authority to veto or to block the actions of that agent" (p. 33).

Checks and balances come in two varieties: They can be multipartisan or contramajoritarian. By multipartisan, I mean situations in which no single party controls all the elected agencies of the government, so that partisan interest of each party is checked by other party or parties. By contramajoritarian, I mean the oversight of the elected by nonelected authorities.

7.5.1   Multipartisan control

When the system of government allows for multiple independently elected powers, it creates the possibility that partisan control will be divided among them. It is useful to think in terms of Tsebelis's (1995) "veto players." These veto players may include the chief executive, the parties that join in a government coalition, and two houses of the legislature. When the institutional system allows for an independently elected president and a bicameral legislature or when the electoral system promotes coalition governments, it is then for the voters to decide whether they want all the parts of the government to be in the hands of a single party or for control to be shared among parties.

Note that the rule of single-party majorities is not the dominant pattern among modern democracies. Having examined the patterns of government formation is almost all democracies that existed between 1946 and 1999, Cheibub, Przeworski, and Saiegh (2002) discovered that a party of the chief executive controlled an absolute majority of the lower house of the legislature in 43.2 percent of cases under parliamentarism and in 45.0 percent under presidentialism. When the party of the chief executive did not hold a legislative majority, the government consisted of a minority of a single party, a minority coalition, or a majority coalition.

The essence of multipartisan control is that different parties must agree before a policy can be determined and different parties have the power to observe how it is implemented. Contrary to Weber (1994, p. 185), who thought that multipartisan control can be exercised by granting the minority a constitutional right to investigate the bureaucracy, legal provisions are not sufficient. But when a government, either of a single party or a coalition, is a minority, it can legislate only with the agreement of some part of the opposition. When a government is a majority coalition of different parties, it requires again the consent of all the partners of the coalition. Because the government cannot act without the support of multiple parties, the power of any single party to instrumentalize the state is diluted.

The presence of veto players imposes, therefore, restrictions on the partisan use of public power. Multipartisan mechanisms can fail, however, for a variety of reasons.

One is that the parties may collude. The infamous Chilean system of what was called the *quoteo* is a case in point: The government of Unidad Popular simply divided all the public posts and the perks of office proportionately to the strength of the parties within the government coalition. The joke was that if the driver of a public bus was a Socialist, the conductor had to be a Communist. One may even suspect that minority governments are more prone to use the spoils of power as an instrument for buying votes, so as to reach a legislative majority.

The second reason is that many government decisions are not subject to control by the legislature. The executive, as the superior of the bureaucracy, has ample prerogatives in making all kind of decisions that escape legislative scrutiny: decree powers, executive orders, appointment powers, and the like. The U.S. tax bureaucracy, the Internal Revenue Service, for example, sent to millions of taxpayers a letter telling each how much their taxes were reduced because of President Bush's initiative.

Finally, control over the legislature by multiple parties promotes the autonomy of the bureaucracy by allowing the emergence of what is called "implementation coalitions" (Bendor 1788). Note that bureaucratic discretion may arise not only because it is impossible to specify exactly the actions that the bureaucracy should undertake but also because the legislature is a collective body. Suppose that the legislature consists of three representatives, who ideal points in some multidimensional policy space are X, Y, Z. Suppose that simple majority voting generates an instruction to the bureaucracy, B, which is closer in this space to X and Y than to Z. Suppose, however, that the bureaucracy prefers some course of action B', which is closer to Y and Z and further away from X. Then the bureaucracy can do B' and the legislature will not vote to punish the bureaucracy for deviating from B. The "implementation coalition," composed of the legislators whose ideal points are $\{Y, Z\}$ and the bureaucrats, will be different than the legislative coalition, $\{X, Y\}$, which issued the original instruction. If the policy space is multidimensional, the bureaucracy is in a perverse way the agenda setter and (by McKelvey 1976, theorem) can lead the legislature to the outcome it desires. This form of bureaucratic discretion is attenuated when the legislature allocates the oversight to specialized committees, thus reducing the dimensionality of the policy space. But implementation coalitions are possible, even when legislators have perfect information.

To summarize, when political power is shared by multiple parties, the ability of any single party to use the bureaucracy for partisan purposes is restricted. But the bureaucracy can be still instrumentalized if these parties collude or if the chief executive enjoys decisional latitude independently of the partisan composition of the government. Finally, even if the presence of multiple veto players may restrict the partisan utilization of public power, it may in turn promote bureaucratic autonomy.

7.5.2   Contramajoritarian control

In fact, most of the control over partisan behavior is exercised by public authorities, which are not subject to election and reelection, mainly courts but also independent oversight agencies. These bodies are independent in the sense that they are not subject to partisan control of the current majority. Independence is accomplished by appointment and removal procedures: Members of such bodies either are appointed for life, or for long, fixed terms, not coinciding with electoral periods, or are removable only with nonpartisan consent. Such agencies differ greatly in their power. In the extreme case, such as of the Canadian Human Rights Commission, they have direct enforcement power. Weaker powers, such as those of the Canadian Information Commissioner, include investigation leading to judicial proceedings. Still weaker are powers to investigate and report to the legislature: This is the case of the Canadian Security Intelligence Review Committee. Finally, the weakest are those of agencies that can only hear complaints and suggest remedial actions, such as the Canadian Police Public Complaints Commission (based on D'Arcy Finn 1993). Indeed, according to Sutherland (1993, p. 24), at one time there were 650 such independent review bodies in Canada. Other examples of independent oversight agencies include the *Ministerio Publico* in Brazil, the Chilean *Controlaria*, or the French *Cour des Comptes*.

The most important institution that is supposed to prevent abuses of public power for partisan purposes is the judicial system. The rule of law is a limitation on the rule of majority. According to Raz (1994), "Legislatures because of their preoccupation with current problems, and their felt need to secure re-election by a public all too susceptible to the influences of the short term, are only too liable to violent swings and panic measures" (p. 260) and "The rule of law functions in modern democracies to ensure a fine balance between the power of a democratic legislature and the force of tradition-based doctrine" (1994, p. 361). Dworkin (1986) goes even further: "Any competent interpretation of the Constitution as a whole must therefore recognize ... that some constitutional rights are designed exactly to prevent majorities from following their own conviction about what justice requires" (p. 376). In such views, as Guarnieri (2003) observes, "Submitting the performance of public functions to the scrutiny of independent judges becomes an effective and essential check on the exercise of political power, ensures the supremacy of the law and guarantees citizens' rights."

The opposition of democracy and the rule of law is typically posed in conceptual, almost logical terms, as a conflict between abstract principles of popular sovereignty and of justice. But what are the grounds to juxtapose intemperate legislators to oracles of "the law," "tradition," or even "justice"? Are we asked to believe that judges have no interests other than to implement "the law," that their decision power is nondiscretionary, that independence guarantees impartiality of decisions? Because the legitimacy of nonelected authorities rests on their impartiality, the courts have an institutional self-interest in appearing to be impartial, at least nonpartisan. But there are no grounds to think – indeed, as both Guarnieri (2003) and Maravall (2003) evidence, there are reasons to doubt – that independent judges always act in nondiscretionary, impartial manners. The rule of judges need not be the rule of law. And, to cite Guarnieri (2003), "If the interpretation of the laws becomes the exclusive domain of self-appointed bureaucrats, the risk for democracy is evident" (p. 240).

The relation between democracy, understood in this context as the rule of majority, and the rule of law is always and everywhere a concrete relation between two populated institutions: the legislatures and the courts. "Where legal institutions successfully claim broad authority to regulate and structure social interaction," Ferejohn and Pasquino (2003) observe, "democratic rule seems somewhat restricted. And the converse seems true as well: Where parliament claims sovereign authority to make whatever law it chooses, judicial institutions are relegated to a subservient status – judges become, at best, agents of the legislature and interpreters of its commands". Legislatures, courts, the executive, the regulatory and the investigative authorities may or may not be in conflict. The legislature may find that its action is deemed by a court contrary to the constitution and may desist from pursuing it further. But it may push through a constitutional amendment or simply change the rules by which the courts are regulated. The courts will have it in the first case; the legislature in the second. This is what the relation between democracy and the rule of law is about. No more than that: a world of populated institutions in which actors may have conflicting interests and different powers behind them.

Constitutional courts and governments may come into conflict over ideological issues. But even when they are not divided by ideology, both politicians and judges desire to expand their institutional authority. Each of these conflicts, as Ferejohn and Pasquino see them, is "political in the sense that it is rooted in desires to maintain or increase authority and is not necessarily connected to norms of legality themselves" (2002).

The general consensus is that during recent times the victors in these conflicts have been the courts. This trend is being generally described as a "judicialization" of politics. Yet it is necessary to distinguish the enhanced judicial authority over legislation – "constitutionalization" – from judicial actions against politicians, "criminalization."

Ferejohn and Pasquino (2002) describe the trend toward the displacement of the political by the juridical, of elective and accountable organs by nonaccountable courts. They argue that courts acquire extensive authority over legislation whenever the political system is fragmented, indecisive, or gridlocked. In the Kelsenian model, specialized tribunals acquire direct legislative prerogatives, because constitutional adjudication is a positive legislative function. But even in the United States, where judges are limited to applying laws to particular controversies and cannot repeal statutes, they render decisions of the legislature invalid when they decide not to apply them on constitutional grounds.

Maravall (2003) argues that criminalization of politics is a response to collusion among politicians. When politicians collude, successfully hiding their actions from the public, electoral as well as parliamentary accountability mechanisms fail. This is when groups in the civil society, whether business, unions, or media, with interests of their own, seek to activate judicial action. For example, a revolt against what was in effect an illegal tax imposed by different political parties to finance their activities led business groups in Italy, France, and several other countries to seek judicial intervention. In the end, the courts prevailed.

But the lines of conflict do not necessarily juxtapose legislatures and courts. Courts can be used by politicians as instruments in partisan struggles. Even if the courts are independent, they need not be impartial. When the partisan opposition sees no chance to win elections, it may seek to undermine the government by provoking judicial actions against incumbent politicians. To consolidate its partisan advantage, the incumbent government may use friendly judges to harass the opponents. Courts are instruments in this conflict. The rule of law means simply compliance with judicial decisions. And, as Maravall (2003) observes, losers may comply not because they recognize the decision as legal or just but only because they do not want to threaten the institutions.

The conflict between rule of majority and rule of law is just a conflict between political actors who use votes and actors who use laws as their instruments. Whether legislatures or courts prevail in particular situations is a matter of politics.

7.6   Insulated bureaucracies

Under some conditions politicians may not want to control a particular bureaucracy. One story developed in a general form by Moe (1990) and popular in explaining the origins of independence of central banks goes as follows. Suppose that the incumbent, partisan government has some ideal point on a policy line. Let the government be right-wing, with an ideal point at R. While this government is in office, it wants to control the bureaucracy, so that the bureaucracy would implement policies as close as possible to R. But suppose that this government fears that in the forthcoming election it will lose office to a party with the ideal point at L. If the incumbent government knows that the ideal point of the bureaucracy, say B, is closer to R than to L, then it will use its current majority to make this bureaucracy independent from political oversight, knowing that the bureaucracy will implement B. Hence, at least under some conditions, politicians have incentives to abdicate rather than delegate their control over bureaucracies.

As an explanation of the origins of independent agencies, this story does not fare well in empirical analyses. What does seem to be true, at least in the United States, is that the Congress spends little time and effort overseeing agencies or attempting to influence policy implementation. Yet even this fact is not telling: It may be that the Congress does not care what the bureaucracies do or that they do what the Congress wants, so that little oversight is necessary. Because these two equilibria are observationally equivalent, we do not know which holds.

Another reason for insulating bureaucracies emerges when political control is suboptimal for everyone. Recently we have seen the emergence of public authorities that are independent of elected politicians, primarily central banks, but also semi-independent regulatory agencies. These authorities are empowered to pursue specific objectives, whether monetary stability or the regulation of natural monopolies. Their personnel are appointed by the elected politicians. But these agencies are supposed to act independently and their personnel cannot be removed for policy reasons.

The justification for the existence of such bodies consists of two steps. One argument is that there are some combinations of policies that should not be made by the same decision maker, whoever it might be, because of time inconsistency. No single body should pass laws and adjudicate particular cases, no single body should make fiscal and monetary policy, no single body should fix prices of monopolies and tax them. If the same agency fixed prices and taxes, it would be tempted to subsidize them to induce investment and then to tax away their rents. If the same body chose fiscal and monetary policy, it would be tempted to adopt expansionary policies before an election and then accommodate with monetary policy.

The second argument is that in some decisional realms there exist policies that are uniquely optimal for everyone. If money supply should increase at the rate of economic growth or if natural monopolies should earn the competitive rate of return, then the only problem is implementing a rule. The issue is then one of "rules versus discretion," and the public interest is best served by the optimal rule. The only role of the relevant bureaucracies is then technical, to correctly apply the rule.

Both of these assumptions are controversial. If no unique best rule exists – say that the public has preferences over the rate of inflation[1] – then the issue is no longer of rule versus discretion but of discretion of independent agencies versus discretion of elected ones. And, as Minford (1995) observed, nothing does guarantee that independent agencies will pursue policies preferred by citizens. Directors of the central bank may pursue policy objectives that are preferred by citizens but they may also have objectives that differ from those of the public, and citizens have no instruments to induce central banks to act according to their interests. Independent regulatory agencies can be captured by the interests they are supposed to regulate and, again, the public will have no way to control them. By making some bureaucracies independent of government control, we make a bet that independent authorities would act in the best interest of the public. But nothing guarantees that independent agencies would act in this way.

The argument that some agencies should be independent of the government does not imply that they should be independent of voters: In principle

---

[1] It is ironic that Kydland and Prescott (1977) in their classical article first claim that "A change in administration . . . reflects a change in the relative costs society assigns to unemployment and inflation" (p. 478) and then go on to assume that there exists some uniquely optimal rate of inflation (p. 480).

we could elect the body that controls the fiscal policy (the government) and the body that controls the monetary policy. Bureaucratic insulation is an extreme remedy for preventing partisan abuses. By removing policy realms from voters' control, it undermines the democratic process. After all, we have elections so as to select governments that would implement the will of the majority and the bureaucracy is a necessary instrument of governmental actions.

7.7   Conclusion: Politics and administration

Partisan abuse of governmental power is a widespread phenomenon, intuitively recognized by citizens of most democracies. Given that the goal of political parties is to win and retain public office, it is only natural that governments would use the powers they have to promote their partisan interests. The ideal of "rational administration in the public interest" is the first best, but it is not a realistic yardstick for evaluating the performance of democratic governments. One cannot eliminate politics from public administration: This is a project with authoritarian overtones. One can only control its forms and moderate its magnitude.

Some forms of control are institutional. When power is shared by multiple parties, the system of checks and balances reduces the discretion of the government. Even when governmental power is controlled by a single party, the judiciary and other oversight agencies can prevent some abuses of this power. In the extreme case, some policy realms can be removed from partisan control altogether and delegated to independent authorities. None of these mechanisms can guarantee that governments would not abuse their power but together they can prevent the most flagrant abuses.

Ultimately, the power to prevent such abuses is in the hands of voters. Voters can prevent the incumbent from acting arbitrarily by posing the threat of voting her out if she were to abuse power. Governments must anticipate retrospective sanctions of voters (Manin 1997; Przeworski, Manin, and Stokes 1999). When voters agree about what constitutes major transgressions and when they coordinate their actions, they can sanction the government. And when the government anticipates that voters may, it does not transgress (Weingast 1997). Even if voters do not sanction many transgressions, democratic rulers must anticipate that they might. Moreover, in our times, sanctions by voters come not only at the time of elections: When a democratic chief executive loses popularity, as expressed by the polls, his or her capacity to govern declines. Either the executive's party, fearing a defeat during the forthcoming election, turns against the prime minister, or the legislature raises its head against an embattled president.

Yet for electoral accountability to operate, citizens must desist from pursuing their short-term interests: Some voters must be willing to sanction governments even if they benefit from their actions. They must act against the perpetuation of the system in which partisan control is a source of spoils for the victors, whether they are the current beneficiaries or the victims of this system. This is perhaps an unrealistic expectation, but under democracy the power to prevent partisan abuses ultimately rests with voters.

As we see, the optimal structure of the state is far from obvious. Moreover, we have never asked "Optimal for what?" And this question raises yet another conundrum. Presumably, when the structure of government includes a well-designed system of checks and balances, citizens are protected from the state. The liberal argument, put forth most eloquently by Holmes (1995), is that "liberalism is a necessary, though not sufficient condition for some measure of democracy in any modern state" (p. 6). Liberty, protection from arbitrary encroachments by the state, is necessary for citizens to be able to exercise their positive political rights, to express their opinions, to formulate the collective will, and to choose good governments.

Yet although such a system of checks and balances may be effective in protecting citizens from the state, citizens do not just want to be protected from the government. They need and want to be served by it. Such a system may prevent governments from taking actions injurious to citizens, but at the same time makes it more difficult for the government to act at all. In the extreme, with checks and balances at every step, the government can do almost nothing.

Clearly, what one takes to be the proper balance between protecting people from the government and enabling the government to act depends on what one thinks governments should be doing. If the only role of the state is to protect people from killing one another, then the primary concern is that the "horizontal danger" does not become transformed into a "vertical" one (Dunn 1999), that is, that the state does not abuse its powers. But if one thinks that there are many things that the state can do to enhance social welfare – promote growth, redistribute incomes, insure individuals against bad luck – then one would want the state to have the power to act.

CHAPTER 8

Citizens and politicians: Representation

8.1   Readings

Read:

Manin, Bernard, Adam Przeworski, and Susan C. Stokes. 1999. Introduction and Chapter 1 of *Democracy, Accountability, and Representation.* New York: Cambridge University Press.

Fearon, James. 1999. "Electoral Accountability and the Control of Politicians: Selecting Good Types versus Sanctioning Poor Performance." In Adam Przeworski, Susan C. Stokes, and Bernard Manin (eds.), *Democracy, Accountability, and Representation*, 55–97. New York: Cambridge University Press.

Ferejohn, John A. 1995. "The Spatial Model and Elections." In Bernard Grofman (ed.), *Information, Participation, and Choice*, 107–124. Ann Arbor: University of Michigan Press.

Persson, Torsten, Gérard Roland, and Guido Tabelini. 1997. "Separation of Powers and Accountability." *Quarterly Journal of Economics 112*: 1163–1202.

Recommended:

Cheibub, José Antonio and Adam Przeworski. 1999. "Democracy, Elections, and Accountability for Economic Outcomes." In Adam Przeworski, Susan C. Stokes, and Bernard Manin (eds.), *Democracy, Accountability, and Representation*, 222–250. New York: Cambridge University Press.

Background:

Ferejohn, John A. 1986. "Incumbent Performance and Electoral Control." *Public Choice 50*: 5–25.

8.2   Introduction

The claim connecting democracy and representation is that under democracy governments are representative because they are elected: If elections are freely contested, if participation is widespread, and if citizens enjoy political liberties, then governments will act in the best interest of the people. Yet note that this is again just a hypothesis. It states that if we have a particular set of institutions, we will observe a particular kind of outcome. The topic of this chapter is whether and under what conditions this hypothesis is true.

There are four generic reasons why governments may act in the best interests of the people:

(1) Only those persons who are public spirited offer themselves for the public service, and they remain uncorrupted by power while in office.

Many persons who seek public office want to serve the public interest, and some remain dedicated to the public service while in office. Yet this possibility is not distinctive of democracy, a system in which rulers are selected by elections and subjected to being thrown out of office in the same way. Dictators can also be representative: If they know and if they seek to do what people want, nothing prevents them from doing it. But under dictatorship, this is just a matter of luck. A central claim of democratic theory is that elections systematically cause governments to act in a representative manner (Dahl 1971; Riker 1965).

(2) While individuals who offer themselves for public office differ in their interests, motivations, and competence, citizens effectively use their instrument of control, the vote, to select either those candidates whose interests are identical to their own or those who are and remain devoted to the public service while in office.

(3) While anyone who holds office may want to pursue some interests or values different from and costly to the people, citizens use their vote effectively to threaten those who would stray away from the path of virtue with being thrown out of office.

(4) Separate powers of government check and balance each other in such a way that, together, they end up acting in people's best interest.

A preliminary clarification is needed. The entire following discussion assumes that voters know what is best for them. If they do, then they have two ways to make politicians act in their best interest, that is, to represent: They can choose politicians who are more likely to act in that way or they can threaten to throw out politicians who do not. Pitkin (1967) argued, however, that representation can be still thought to occur when individuals do not know what they want, as long as the government acts "in the best interest" of the represented.

Consider the following situation, in which voters have time-inconsistent preferences. Say that the electoral term is divided into two periods, Early (E) and Late (L), and that ex ante all voters have a utility

$$U^{EXANTE} = E + \delta L,$$

while ex post they have a utility

$$U^{EXPOST} = \delta E + L,$$

where $0 < \delta < 1$ is the rate of time preference. Then voters elect a government that promises to give them U^{EXANTE} but reelect a government that gives them U^{EXPOST}. Who is then to say which of the two governments – the one that pursues the ex-ante or the ex-post preferences – acts in the best interest of voters? If voters' preferences cannot be used as a criterion to evaluate actions of politicians, then the judgment as to whether the government acts in the best interest of the represented can still be made by someone else. But I do not think that the term applies. Are parents "representatives" of their children? Or are they "custodians" of their welfare? Clearly, definitions are arbitrary, but in my view if interests cannot be read from preferences, then representation is not a meaningful criterion for assessing the relation between citizens and politicians.

To highlight what is entailed in political representation, I first present a very simple model of the principal-agent relation between a single voter and a politician, designed to capture the main intuitions of Ferejohn (1986) and Fearon (1999). Then I revisit the assumptions of this model.

8.3   A simple model of electoral accountability

Take a single decisive voter (or homogeneous voters), to whom we also refer as "the electorate." Assume that this voter cares about the change of her welfare during an electoral term, $\triangle W$.

The change of welfare during the term is produced by the incumbent with the technology:

$$\triangle W = \beta - r, r \leq \mu$$

where β stands for the exogenous conditions prevailing during the term and r stands for rents the incumbent extracts. By "rents" I mean something very broad: Rents may consist of shirking on the job or of simple theft but they may mean only that the government is doing in good faith something people see as diminishing their welfare. Rents here are whatever governments do or fail to do that **all** voters finds injurious. The highest amount of rents politicians can extract without risking going to jail is $r = \mu$: Above that amount accountability becomes legal rather than electoral. Hence, μ represents the effectiveness on nonelectoral mechanisms of accountability.

Assume there are only two terms. During the first term, the incumbent gets utility only from rents $u(r) = r$. If reelected, during the second term the incumbent gets an exogenously determined utility with the present value R, which may include ego rents as well as economic rents. R is thus the continuation value. If defeated, the incumbent gets a utility of 0.

The total utility of the incumbent is thus

$$U(r, R) = r + p(\triangle W(r))R,$$

where $p(\triangle W)$ is the probability that the incumbent is reelected having generated $\triangle W$ for the electorate – an "accountability function," as it was defined in Chapter 5. For the moment, politicians are the same, so that potential challengers have the same utility function as the current incumbent.

The voter's problem is decide how to vote so as to maximize $\triangle W$. The optimal rule of the voter under such conditions (Ferejohn 1986) is to choose and announce to the politician at the beginning of the period some criterion of welfare, k, such that

$$\text{if } \triangle W \geq k, \text{ then } p = 1,$$
$$\text{if } \triangle W < k, \text{ then } p = 0.$$

If the incumbent performed at or above some threshold level, the electorate retains the incumbent. If the incumbent performs below this level, the electorate is certain to vote against the incumbent. The politician hears the announcement of the voter, observes β and chooses r. This is the basic setup.

As always, we begin with a benchmark model in which the voter observes β and knows R. Since the incumbent can always extract μ during the current period and go down to defeat, the voter knows that the incumbent will want to be reelected if

$$\beta - k + R \geq \mu.$$

Hence, the voter knows that the best reply function of the incumbent is

$$r^*(k) = \begin{cases} \beta - k & \text{if } \beta \geq k + \mu - R \\ \mu & \text{otherwise} \end{cases}$$

Because the voter maximizes her welfare by minimizing incumbent's rents, she sets $k^*(\beta) = \beta - \mu + R$. The incumbent gets $r^* = \beta - k^* = \mu - R$, while the voter gets $\triangle W = k^* = \beta - \mu + R > \beta - \mu$.

Even this extremely simple model generates two interesting results. One is that the less the voters can rely on the operation of legal controls on the incumbent (the higher the μ), the higher the rents they must tolerate as voters. Electoral and legal accountability thus serve as substitutes in controlling politicians. The second aspect, to which we return later, is that voters want to have politicians who care about being reelected. Whether politicians want to occupy elected office because they are devoted to the public service or because they are egomaniacs, voters are better off when politicians want to win elections.

Having the benchmark, we can now consider asymmetric information. Incumbents know lots of things voters do not know. For example, only the government knows whether the negotiating stand of the IMF is tough or soft. Voters are not present during these negotiations and there is no way for them to ascertain these conditions independently. Voters could calculate the demand for the exports of a country abroad, but it is too costly for them to do so, and they have to rely again on second-hand information.

We assume throughout that β can have only two values: $\beta = \beta^G$ when conditions are good and $\beta = \beta^B$ when they are bad, with $\triangle \beta \equiv \beta^G - \beta^B > 0$. Suppose that voters know only that $pr\{\beta = \beta^G\} = q$. Now they are in a quandary. If they set $k^G = k^*(\beta^G) = \beta^G - \mu + R$ and the conditions are in fact bad, $\beta = \beta^B$, the incumbent will opt for extracting μ and give up on reelection. If the voter sets $k^B = k^*(\beta^B)$, she will get $\triangle W = \beta^B - \mu + R$ regardless of the actual conditions, because the incumbent facing $\beta = \beta^G$ can extract $r = \mu - R + \triangle \beta$ and be reelected.

This is the only choice voters have: Any k strictly between β^G and β^B would be worse than one of the extreme values. Hence, voters face the choice of taking the risk and expecting to get $[qk^G + (1 - q)(\beta^B - \mu)]$ or going for a certain k^B. This is the same trade-off we have seen before. If voters want the government to act efficiently when conditions are bad, they will allow it to shirk (extract additional rents of $\triangle \beta$) when conditions are good. If they opt to make the government act well when the conditions are good, they have to be prepared that the government would shirk ($r = \mu$) when they are bad. If their prior belief that conditions are good is sufficiently high, voters choose $k = k^G$; otherwise they choose $k = k^B$. But in either case, they must expect to give some rents to the incumbent. Hence, **voters' control of the incumbent is imperfect**.

Thus far we have assumed that a voter chooses some k and announces the voting rule specified earlier. Is this announcement credible, that is, can the incumbent believe that the voter will vote for the incumbent with the probability $p = 1$ if her welfare improves by $\triangle W \geq k$? Let us go back to the full information case, where the voter gets exactly k. Suppose that a challenger appears claiming that under the same circumstances he would have produced more. Now voters' beliefs about politicians come into play. If the voter believes that all politicians are the same, then she has no reason to deviate from the announced rule. But suppose that the voter believes that politicians come in types. They may differ in their competence, that is, the ability to produce voters' welfare out of β. Alternatively, they may differ in the value they attach to being reelected, R. The logic is the same, so suppose that they differ in R. Precisely, voters have a prior belief that R is a random variable, R^j, varying across politicians. Let R^I stand for the value of the incumbent and R^C of the challenger. The incumbent meets her incentive compatibility constraint when

$$r^I + pR^I \geq \mu,$$

while the challenger exerts effort as long as

$$r^C + pR^C \geq \mu.$$

If $R^C > R^I$, then the challenger will be better in the sense that he will be induced to extract lower rents by any rule that meets the incentive compatibility constraint. Suppose now that the voter observes $\triangle W^I$. Given the voters' prior belief about the distribution of politicians, the voter now thinks that the challenger is better with the probability

$$\Pr\{\triangle W^C > \triangle W^I\} = \Pr\{R^C > R^I\}$$
$$= 1 - \int_0^{R^I} f(R)dR = 1 - F(R^I) \equiv \alpha(R^I).$$

If voters observe an incumbent who generated $\triangle W^I$, then knowing β they can infer R^I, and they will vote for the incumbent with the probability $p = 1 - \alpha(R^I)$.

The equilibrium is then as follows. The voter sets k at $k^I = \beta - \mu + (1 - \alpha)R^I$, the incumbent gets $r^I = \mu - (1 - \alpha)R^I$, and the voter votes for the incumbent with the probability $p = 1 - \alpha$. To see that this is an equilibrium, suppose that voters set their criterion at $k^* = \beta - \mu + R^I$. Because voters will vote for the incumbent who delivers $\triangle W = k$ with $p = 1 - \alpha$, the incumbent will extract $\beta - \mu$. In turn, if voters set their criterion at some $k < \beta - \mu + (1 - \alpha)R^I$, the incumbent can extract rents above r^I and be reelected. Finally, if voters set $k = k^I = \beta - \mu + (1 - \alpha)R^I$, the incumbent will extract r^I and be reelected with $p = 1 - \alpha$.

Note that $k^I = \beta - \mu + (1 - \alpha)R^I < k^* = \beta - \mu + R^I$. Hence, **when voters use their vote to elect a better politician as well as to provide incentives for the incumbent, they must reduce the power of incentives for the incumbent.** Voters have only one instrument – the vote – to reach two goals: retrospectively sanction the incumbent and prospectively choose a better candidate. If they care about both, they must trade these goals against one another.

We have learned two things from this model. The first one is that if voters do not know something politicians know, they can control politicians only imperfectly. The second is that if voters want to use their vote to select good politicians prospectively and to sanction the incumbents retrospectively, they must pay higher rents to the incumbent.

8.4   Voters' control over politicians

The model set up above can be criticized on a number of grounds. Several aspects of this model give still an excessively rosy picture of the extent to which voters can control politicians. For one, voters should care not only about the change of their welfare during a particular term but also about the prospects for future welfare at the end of the term. Suppose that the incumbent generated a large increase in the income of the voter by cutting down half of the trees in the country. Then voters will have lived on champaign during the term but few trees will be left for the future. Hence, voters' objective should be

$$\triangle W + T,$$

where T is the present value of their future prospects at the end of the term. The difficulty is that while $\triangle W$ can be easily observed, T cannot be. Hence, voters can easily condition their vote on $\triangle W$ but not on T.

Ferejohn (1986) raises another difficulty. Note that we have not specified above whether $\triangle W$ refers to the welfare of the particular voter, so it is $\triangle W_i, i \in N$, and voters vote their "pocket book," or $\triangle W$ refers to the aggregate or the average, so that voters are *sociotropic*, coordinating their votes. If voters look only at their own welfare, then the politician can manipulate them, in the limit extracting all the μ. Suppose that all politicians are the same and the incumbent government gives different groups of voters, indexed by the subscript, $\triangle W_1 < \triangle W_2 < \cdots < \triangle W_N$. Groups 1 through K vote against the incumbent, groups $K + 1$ through N vote for it, and the incumbent is reelected. Now members of group 1 say to the government "We will vote for you if you give us $\triangle W_N - \varepsilon$." The government can then give $\triangle W_1$ to the $N - th$ group, $\triangle W_N - \varepsilon$. to the $1st$ group, and still be reelected. Such bidding can go on and on, until everyone gets ε and the government extracts all the rents.

Whether voters are in fact guided by their own welfare or vote sociotropically is a matter of an extensive empirical controversy. But even if voters were all sociotropic, that is, if they all set the same criterion, a more profound obstacle to their control is that $\triangle W$ is in fact multidimensional. It may include change of disposable income, the inflation rate, the unemployment rate, the crime rate, peace, and so on. An average Western European parliament passes several hundreds pieces of legislation during its term; the U.S. Congress about 2,000. But voters have at most three instruments (in presidential systems with a bicameral legislation) to control the entire multidimensional performance of politicians. One cannot control hundreds of targets with three instruments. Hence, even if voters were perfectly informed and even if they perfectly coordinated their voting decisions, they might have to vote for a government that produces bad outcomes in some realms. And because voters have to trade-off different aspects of politicians' performance, politicians can always get away working hard on some aspects and shirking with regard to other aspects. If politicians know that voters care about peace at the cost of economic performance, they can get reelected even if they shirk on the economy; if they know voters care utmost about the economy, they can get reelected even if they pay little attention to national security, and so on. As I am writing, President Bush enjoys enormous popularity because of the "war on terrorism," although most people say that his administration is beholden to special interests.

Suppose that a government makes ten decisions during one term, the incumbent makes all decisions against the interest of the majority, and the challenger offers to make one decision right. Then citizens will elect a government that will make nine decisions wrong. Obviously, the question is why would some other challenger not offer to make two right decisions, or three, or four, up to ten? One answer is the barriers to entry: Partisan politics is the most protected industry in the United States. But if there were no barriers to entry, then parties would have an incentive to form, to promise to make all ten decisions right, make none right, get out, and reappear under different labels. If entrance into the electoral system entails fixed costs, competition will be limited; if it is free, then parties will not suffer when they lose. So we may get either highly collusive party systems, such as in the United States, or completely ephemeral systems, such as in Ecuador, where there is a new party system at each election.

This is just the way things are: This is the cost of representative government. If voters could vote on each dimension separately – say on each minister – then they could exert more control.[1] But their information costs would be much greater. Moreover, the cohesion of public policy would be threatened: If voters voted out the social spending minister who does not spend enough and the taxing minister who taxes too much, the government could not govern. One reason to have a representative system is for the government to work out such trade-offs.

In turn, one can also find arguments to the effect that voters' control over politicians may be more effective than the above model would suggest. First, the accountability model presented earlier applies the principal-agent model rather naively. The voter is a principal, the politician is the agent. The principal announces a contract $\{k, p\}$ and the politician decides how hard to work for the voter knowing the contract. But voters announce no such contracts. They could: Instead of just casting ballots, each voter could cast a contract, saying that if income increases by 4 percent and if the crime rate declines by 3 percent, she will vote for the politician. But they do not. In fact, even if they set such contracts in their mind, voters keep politicians in the dark. Hence, politicians must decide how much to work not knowing what the k is. It may be k^B but it may be k^G, so that a politician who observes $\beta = \beta^G$ does not know whether he can get away with generating $\triangle W = k^B$. Information is asymmetric on both sides: The voter does not observe β but the politician does not know k. Under such conditions, if the politician thinks that it is quite likely that voters set $k = k^G$, she will be more likely to work

---

[1] Suppose that in a multiparty system voters vote anticipating which coalitions will be formed in the parliament, where a coalition, a là Laver and Shepsle (1996), is an allocation of ministerial portfolios to parties, each of which then controls a specific policy realm. Then voters would be in effect voting on ministers.

hard when $\beta = \beta^G$ and less likely to do so when $\beta = \beta^B$ (because she cannot get reelected even if she were to generate k^B). Whether keeping politicians in the dark induces them to work harder than letting them know what the terms of the contract are cannot be determined in general: It depends on voters' prior beliefs about β and on politicians prior beliefs about k.

The second argument invokes separation of powers. Persson, Roland, and Tabelini (1997) developed an interesting model, in which voters perfectly control politicians even if they are not informed. In their setup, there is one power – the legislature – that announces to voters whether conditions are good or bad (β in the model above). Then the second power – the executive – makes a take-it-or-leave-it budget proposal to the legislature and the legislature votes whether to accept or to reject the budget proposal. In equilibrium, no rents are extracted and both the executive and the legislature are reelected. This is not a plausible story, because the absence of political parties in their model makes it impossible for the two powers to collude. But it shows that institutional arrangements do affect voters' ability to control politicians.

The relation between citizens and elected politicians differs from the standard principal-agent model in yet a different way. As lawmakers, the principal can order the agents what to do and what not to do. Moreover, while this aspect is not inherent to democracy, laws also regulate the production of and the access to information. Citizens can base their decisions only on what they are allowed to know: At one time, for example, the British government barred the access of nongovernment researchers to tissues extracted from cows suffering from the "mad cow" disease.

Yet voters have two agents, not one: the government and the opposition. Indeed, any reasonable understanding of representative government must include the opposition. The opposition is an agent of voters because it wants to win office and, in order to win office, it must also anticipate the retrospective judgments of the voters. Anticipating these judgments, the opposition has incentives to monitor the government and to inform (truthfully or not) voters about the performance of the incumbent. Whether this information is useful to voters depends on whether parties care only about being elected, which puts them in a situation of pure conflict, or whether they also care about public welfare, which induces some cooperation. If the government always says that what it does is right and the opposition always says that it is wrong, there is nothing that voters can learn: Speech that can be predicted from interests is not credible. But if the government sometimes admits mistakes and the opposition sometimes praises the government, there is some information voters can extract.

The media, the role of which is emphasized by Arnold (1993), thus have a particular role to play. Unless they have clearly partisan interests, they are more credible than either the government or the opposition. More generally, the emphasis on the scarcity of information may be exaggerated. In fact, voters are barraged with information: from the political contestants, from the media, and from various nonpartisan groups. True, much of this information is strategic – intended to mislead – and navigating in this sea is not easy. But information is not scarce.

Hence, my view is the following. Information is not scarce; in fact, it is abundant. But extracting a signal – the true state of affairs – is difficult. The dimensionality problem is even more serious. It can be mitigated in two ways. One is by setting barriers to entry into the party system in such a way that parties emphasizing different issues can enter but the entry is sufficiently costly to prevent irresponsible entries. Another is by allocating to parties the responsibility for different portfolios, so that when voters vote for or against parties, they have some control over the different dimensions of the issue space. But this space will be always too large for voters to be able to control the government in all realms.

Because much of this literature is reviewed in Manin, Przeworski, and Stokes (1999), I leave the matter here.

8.5   Conclusion

This chapter closes our analysis of the state as a centralized mechanism of allocation. We have made a full circle: We began with ways in which bureaucracies affect the actions and the welfare of private actors, we made a step back to inquire how decision makers structure the actions and the outcomes of bureaucrats, and we returned to private actors, now in their role as citizens, asking how they can control the decision makers. I hope to have persuaded you that states can be organized in a variety of ways and that there are good reasons to think that these ways matter for the allocative and distributive decisions. Yet, given that none of the principals in all the relations that structure the government are completely informed and given the multidimensionality of government policies, it is clear that first-best government is not possible. In this sense, governments fail just as markets do. But this entire discussion was excessively abstract, for we never asked what it is that governments might do. This is the topic of the last section of the book.

The state and the economy

The state has a role to play in the economy if it can do something, for better or worse, that markets cannot do. We already know what it is: The state can compel. It can force a particular agent to use resources in a different way than she wants. It can take money from agents who want to use it in one way and give it to some other agents who would want to use it in a different way. It can take resources from private agents and use them or consume them. It can condition what agents get on what they do. These are powerful instruments, for they can be applied to cause an allocation of resources or a distribution of income different than those that can be reached by markets.

We study the application of such instruments in three realms of policy, asking what governments can do to promote economic growth, to redistribute, and to insure. These are three generic "functions of the state." We ask throughout whether there is something governments can do, what it is that they should do, and how to evaluate what they do. We also raise throughout the question whether the governments have the capacity and the incentives to do what they should and not do what they should not.

CHAPTER 9

Government and economic growth

9.1 Readings

Read:

Cheibub, José Antonio and Adam Przeworski. 1997. "Government Spending and Economic Growth under Democracy and Dictatorship." In Albert Breton et al. (eds.), *Understanding Democracy: Economic and Political Perspectives*, 107–124. Cambridge: Cambridge University Press.

Grossman, Gene M. 1990. "Promoting New Industrial Activities: A Survey of Recent Arguments and Evidence." *OECD Economic Studies 14* (Spring).

Study:

Barro, Robert J. 1990. "Government Spending in a Simple Model of Endogenous Growth." *Journal of Political Economy 98*: S103–S126.

Bénabou, Roland. 1996. "Inequality and Growth." In Ben Bernanke and Julio J. Rotemberg (eds.), *NBER Macro-Economics Annual 1996*. Cambridge, MA: MIT Press.

Recommended (If you read it, you will be amused by comparing Krueger's recommendations with Westphal's explanation of Korean success):

Sen, Amartya, Nicholas Stern, and Joseph Stiglitz. 1990. "Development Strategies: The Roles of the State and the Private Sector." *Proceedings of the World Bank Annual Conference on Development Economics*: 421–435.

Krueger, Ann O. 1990. "Government Failures in Development." *Journal of Economic Perspectives 4*: 9–25.

Westphal, Larry E. 1990. "Industrial Policy in an-Export-Propelled Economy: Lessons from South Korea's Experience." *Journal of Economic Perspectives 4*: 41–60.

9.2   Mechanics of growth

First, we have to understand the mechanics of economic growth. Suppose the output y is produced at each time t by some technology f using a storable stock of some input(s) x, so that

$$y_t = f_t(x_t),$$

with $f(x)$ increasing in x. The output y can be consumed or stored as x. Let the part of the output that is consumed be c_t.

We want to know how much output the economy will produce during the next period, given x_t. It matters somewhat how we will think about time. We can conceive of it in discrete units, such as years, so that $t = 0, 1, \ldots$ measures (equally spaced) time periods. Or we can think of time in continuous terms, so that "next period" is $t + dt, dt \to 0$. Because the first way is more intuitive, let us begin this way, asking what the output will be at $t + 1$.

First, we have to know how much will be consumed and how much will be invested (stored) at t. Suppose that technology does not change. If consumption at t is c_t, then the amount of productive resources will increase by

$$x_{t+1} - x_t \equiv \Delta x_t = f(x_t) - c_t.$$

This is sufficient to deduce the output at $t + 1$, which will be

$$y_{t+1} = f(x_t + y_t - c_t).$$

Hence, the change of output will be

$$y_{t+1} - y_t \equiv \Delta y_t = f(x_t + y_t - c_t) - f(x_t).$$

The rate of growth of this economy will be then

$$\gamma_t = \frac{\Delta y_t}{y_t} = \frac{f(x_t + y_t - c_t) - f(x_t)}{f(x_t)} = \frac{f(x_t + y_t - c_t)}{f(x_t)} - 1.$$

Hence, if $c_t < y_t$, so that the entire output is not consumed, the economy will grow; otherwise it will stagnate or decline. Consumption at t determines the output at $t + 1$ and thus the growth of the economy between t and $t + 1$.

As an example, consider a simple case in which the technology is linear, so that

$$y_t = v x_t$$

for all t, and consumption is always a constant share of output,

$$c_t = (1 - s)y_t,$$

where s is the saving (and investment) rate. Then

$$\Delta x_t = y_t - c_t = sy_t,$$
$$y_{t+1} = v(x_t + sy_t) = y_t + vsy_t,$$

so that

$$\Delta y_t = vsy_t,$$

and

$$\gamma = vs,$$

for all t. As you see, in an economy in which the production function is linear and the rate of savings is constant, output will grow at a constant rate. Given the initial output $y(0) = vx(0)$, the economy will thus grow (or decline) according to

$$y(t) = (1 + \gamma)^t y(0).$$

Moreover, note that

$$\frac{\Delta x_t}{x_t} = \frac{sy_t}{x_t} = sv = \gamma$$

and

$$\frac{\Delta c_t}{c_t} = \frac{(1 - s)y_{t+1} - (1 - s)y_t}{(1 - s)y_t} = \gamma,$$

so that output, the stock of inputs, and consumption grow at the same rate.

We learned, therefore, that all we need to know to deduce the rate of growth is how the economy transforms inputs into outputs (the production function) and how much the agents invest (or consume) at each time (the investment function).

Thinking in continuous terms changes only the notation and the appropriate mathematical tools, but not the logic. We still need a description of how the economy produces and an investment equation, which now becomes

$$\frac{dx}{dt} \equiv \dot{x} = f(x) - c.$$

To determine the change in output over dt, we can differentiate y with regard to time, to get

$$\dot{y} \equiv \frac{df(x_t)}{dt} = \frac{df}{dx}\frac{dx}{dt} \equiv f_x\dot{x}.$$

Substituting the investment equation yields

$$\dot{y} = f_x(y - c),$$

so that the rate of growth of this economy is

$$\gamma = \frac{\dot{y}}{y} = f_x\left(1 - \frac{c}{y}\right).$$

Note that if the production function is linear and the saving rate is constant, so that $f_x = v$ and $1 - \frac{c}{y} = s$, the rate of growth is $\gamma = vs$, as before.

9.3   Optimal growth

With apologies to those mathematically minded among you, let me introduce the basic idea of optimal growth. Suppose now that given the technology and the stock of x, which we will now take to represent capital stock per worker, k, you want to maximize the utility of consumption at the present and in the future, attaching at each t a weight $0 < \beta < 1$, to next period consumption. Your problem then is to decide how much to consume during each period so as to

$$\max_{\{c_0, c_1, \ldots\}} \sum_{t=0}^{t=\infty} \beta^t U(c_t)$$

$$s.t.$$

$$y_t = f(k_t),$$

$$\Delta k_t = y_t - c_t.$$

$$c_t > 0 \,\forall\, t.$$

Now, note that your consumption at $t + 1$ is

$$c_{t+1} = -k_{t+2} + k_{t+1} + y_{t+1} = -k_{t+2} + k_t + y_t - c_t + y_{t+1}.$$

while your consumption beyond $t + 1$ no longer depends on c_t but only on the choices you will be making in the future. (As long as you will want to do at $t + 1$ what you had planned to at t, so that your optimal plan is time consistent, it makes no difference whether you plan the entire time path of

c_t at $t = 0$ or decide independently at each time.) Hence, we can solve this problem as if you cared only about the present and the next period, so that your problem would be

$$\max_{c_t}[\beta^t U(c_t) + \beta^{t+1} U(c_{t+1})].$$

The first-order condition is then

$$U'(c_t) + \beta U'(c_{t+1})\frac{dc_{t+1}}{dc_t} = 0.$$

Because

$$\frac{dc_{t+1}}{dc_t} = -1 + \frac{df(k_{t+1})}{dk_{t+1}}\frac{dk_{t+1}}{dc_t} = -1 - \frac{df(k_{t+1})}{dk_{t+1}},$$

one can rewrite the first-order condition as

$$\frac{U'(c_t)}{U'(c_{t+1})} = \beta(1 + f_{k_{t+1}}).$$

If the utility function is of a class we already know, namely, $U(c) = C^{1-\sigma}/(1 - \sigma)$, $\sigma \neq 1$, then the expression on the left-hand side can be rewritten as

$$\left(\frac{c_{t+1}}{c_t}\right)^\sigma = \left(1 + \frac{\Delta c_t}{c_t}\right)^\sigma = \beta(1 + f_{k_{t+1}}),$$

so that

$$\frac{\Delta c_t}{c_t} = [\beta(1 + f_{k_{t+1}})]^{1/\sigma} - 1,$$

where k_{t+1} is given by

$$\Delta k_t = y_t - c_t.$$

This pair of equations gives the condition that must be satisfied by any path of consumption that is optimal in the sense of solving the original problem.

To see what you should do, consider an economy in which the production function is concave in k, so that $f_k > 0$, $f_{kk} < 0$, and in addition, $\lim_{k\to\infty} f_k = 0$. The feasible paths of this economy are portrayed in the *phase-space* $\{k, c\}$. (See Figure 9.1). Note first that if at any value of the capital stock you were to choose $c > f(k)$, the capital stock would decline; if you were to choose $c < f(k)$, it would increase. Hence, $c = f(k)$ is the locus of points at which $\Delta k = 0$. Now consider the value of $k = k^*$ such that $\beta(1 + f_{k^*}) = 1$ or $f_{k^*} = 1/\beta - 1$. You know that if your consumption

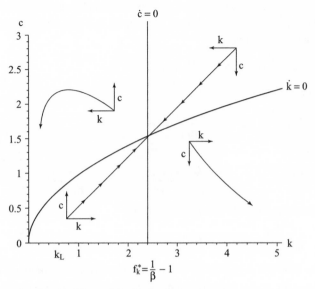

Figure 9.1. Optimal growth paths.

path is to be optimal, it must be true that you will be increasing your consumption if $k < k^*$ and you will be decreasing it if $k > k^*$. Hence, when $k = k^*$, $\Delta c = 0$.

Now suppose that the initial value of capital stock is $k_L < k^*$ and you must choose how much to consume. If you decide to consume $c > f(k_L)$, your consumption will reduce your capital stock and if you do the same repeatedly, you will eventually consume the entire capital stock and will be unable to consume anything. This path violates the condition $c > 0$. Suppose in turn that the initial amount of capital stock is some $k_H > k^*$ and you decide to consume $c < f(k_H)$. Then the capital stock will be growing, while your consumption is declining, until you hit again $c = 0$. Hence, neither of these paths can be optimal. In turn, suppose that at any $k_L < k^*$ you choose $c < f(k)$. Then your consumption and the capital stock will be both growing.

To determine the optimal path, we must raise one more question: Would you ever choose a path that leads to $c = f(k)$ when $k < k^*$? If you were to do this, you would not invest in the current period. Hence, you could not increase your consumption any further without reducing the capital stock. But you know that if $k < k^*$, then $\beta(1 + f_{k_{t+1}}) - 1 > 0$, so that along an optimal path you would increase your consumption. Hence, this cannot be an optimal path. An optimal path must lead to the point at which $\Delta c = 0$ and $\Delta k = 0$. This point is called the *saddle point* and the path that leads to it is called the *saddle path*.

The same is true if you think of time in continuous terms, in which case the optimal path of consumption must satisfy

$$\frac{\dot{c}}{c} = \frac{1}{\sigma}(f_k - \rho),$$

where $\rho = 1 - \beta$, and

$$\dot{k} = y - c.$$

9.4   Government and economic growth

The issue whether governments should be actively promoting economic growth is ridden with controversy. The Krueger-Westphal symposium will give you a taste: As I read it, Westphal shows that South Korea succeeded because it did precisely those things that according to Krueger governments should not do. But even an extremely cautious review of the current state of knowledge, by Grossman (1990), concludes that there are some things governments can and should do to promote growth.

The general framework of this debate is that the state has a role of play if (1) private and public inputs into production are not perfect substitutes and (2) markets do not supply the correct amount of some input, because (i) they are nonrival in consumption, (ii) they generate externalities, or (iii) they entail fixed costs. At issue here is the production function. Suppose that output is produced by two inputs, P and G, where P stands for the private input and G stands for the public input, which is either a stock or tax-financed flow of public productive services. The crucial question is whether G differs in some way from P. If it does not, then the government can do only those things that the private sector can do alone. Say that P stands for the capital stock of privately owned automobile factories and G stands for the capital stock of the publicly owned ones, Renault. As long as total capital stock, $K = P + G$, is given and the technology is the same in both sectors, it makes no difference who produces cars.

But suppose that G is somehow different from P. One way it may be different is that G generates technological spillovers (an externality) that increase the productivity of P. One classical example is that teflon, originally developed to protect the nose of space rockets, found widespread use in our kitchens. The production function is then

$$Y = F(P(G), G).$$

Differentiating with regard to G, we get

$$Y_G = F_P P_G + F_G,$$

so that increasing the public capital stock increases output in two ways – both directly and via the spillover effect, P_G, on the productivity of P – while increasing the private stock has only the direct effect. Remember (from the example of externalities we studied earlier) that if G were privately owned, it would be undersupplied, because its owners would not capture the benefits of the externality.

Another way to think of this difference is that public capital is complementary to private capital in such a way that when the two capital stocks (or the flow of public productive services) are balanced in a particular way, the output is linear in the "broad" notion of capital stock. Examples of the public productive input range from law and order to infrastructure to nonrival and nonexcludable knowledge. A government-supplied road serves private firms to deliver their products to the market. If one were to increase private capital stock given a constant level of public productive services, output would grow less than proportionately and the same is true if one increased the public productive input while holding the private capital stock constant. If there are too many factories per road, delivery slows down; if there are too many roads, they are of little use. But an increase of both inputs would increase the output proportionately as long as some mixture of them is preserved.

This is the point of departure of the Barro (1990) model. Let me first introduce his notation: k is private capital stock per worker, g is the flow of public productive services per worker, where

$$g = \tau y$$

is financed by taxes, and final demand goods are produced only by the private sector using the technology

$$y = \Phi(k, g),$$

$\Phi_{kk} < 0$, $\Phi_{gg} < 0$. We can rewrite this function as

$$y = k\Phi\left(\frac{g}{k}\right),$$

so that

$$\frac{y}{k} = \Phi\left(\frac{g}{k}\right),$$

which Barro assumes to be (Cobb-Douglas) of the form

$$\frac{y}{k} = A\left(\frac{g}{k}\right)^{\alpha},$$

$0 < \alpha < 1$. Balanced budget constraint implies that

$$g = T = \tau y = \tau k \Phi\left(\frac{g}{k}\right).$$

All households are the same (this is a *"representative household"* model). Each has a utility function

$$U(C) = \frac{C^{1-\sigma}}{1-\sigma}, \sigma \neq 1.$$

The time sequence is the following. The government chooses τ, which generates g, which is supplied to producers. Then households decide how much capital to supply, so as to maximize the present value of their consumption,

$$U = \int e^{-\rho t} U(C_t) dt.$$

The question that Barro (1990) asks concerns the optimal size of the public sector, which is $\tau = g/y$. The state is a utilitarian utility maximizer, so that it has the same objective as the households. The algebra is tricky and tedious. I reproduce it in the Appendix, to enable you to follow the model. Let me just present some results and comment on them.

The optimal size of the public sector turns out to be

$$\tau^* = \alpha,$$

which says that the government should tax and provide as public inputs a share of the gross national product equal to the elasticity of output with regard to these inputs. Note when Barro (1990) calibrates his model, he takes a surprisingly high value of $\alpha = 0.25$. Cheibub and Przeworski (1997) arrive at a similar answer econometrically. Hence, the state should provide a sizeable input into production.

The most surprising result of the model is that private investment begins to decline before the tax rate reaches its optimal level. The picture looks like this (see Figure 9.2).

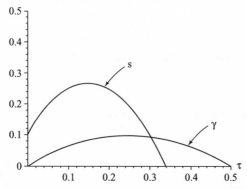

Figure 9.2. Private investment declines before the tax rate reaches optimal level.

This result has two implications. The first one is that the fact that invest-ment is falling as taxes increase does not necessarily indicate that taxes are too high. In the region of τ between the level when s reaches the maximum and when γ does, increasing taxes still increases the rate of growth, which under Barro's (1990) assumption also maximizes social welfare. Although private investment is falling, public investment is increasing, and as long as $\tau < \alpha$, the rate of growth is increasing as well. The second implication is that this political-economic equilibrium is inefficient. If the government could command private investment (or if it could use pure consumption rather than income taxes), growth would increase and so would social welfare.

9.5   Politics of economic growth

Growth is intrinsically a political process. The political aspect of economic growth arises from the fact that the relation between the current and the future consumption of each individual is mediated by decisions made by everyone else. Whereas everyone wants to consume, each wants all others to invest. Because an individual who consumes at one moment also wants to consume in the future, when the possibilities of one's future consumption depend on the stock of productive inputs accumulated by others, at each time each individual wants everyone else to invest as much as possible. This interdependence is political to the extent that some people can use political power to influence the actions of others. I want others to invest, when I can grab a part of output that is due to their investment.

Table 9.1

		Grab	
		cannot	can
	separately	I: independent	III: politically interdependent
Produce			
	jointly	II: economically interdependent	IV: politically and economically interdependent

Consider this situation in most general terms. Say there are two individuals (or types of individuals), $i \in \{1, 2\}$. At time t, a total output Y_t is produced. We need to make two distinctions.

The first one is whether this output is produced by each individual operating separately or by the two individuals working jointly. If the output is generated by the two individuals producing separately (say two self-sufficient peasants), the total output is just the sum of individual outputs, $Y_t = y_t^1(k_t^1) + y_t^2(k_t^2)$. If it is generated jointly (say by physical capital and skilled labor), $Y_t = f(k_t^1, k_t^2)$, where k^i is the input into production of individual i.

The second distinction is whether anyone can grab someone else's output. Assume that no one can take anything from anyone else, so that the output is divided between the two individuals only by the market. If individuals produce separately, each guards his income. If they work together, each gets an income that depends on the inputs each supplied to production and the contribution of these inputs to the joint output: $y_t^i = f_i k_t^i$, where f_i is the marginal product. But if it is possible for individuals to grab, then the first individual may get some amount $\beta Y_t \neq y_t^1$ while the second individual would get $(1 - \beta)Y_t \neq y_t^2$.

Because we have two dichotomous distinctions, we end up with four cases to consider (see Table 9.1).

The simplest generic formulation of the role of politics in growth that I could find is Bénabou's (1996), so let us study his story. As a benchmark, consider a simple economy in which individuals, all identical, are economically and politically independent. This a one-good economy, in which the capital stock can be used in production or consumed directly. Let k_t be the capital stock at the start of the period. This economy grows according to the linear technology:

$$k_{t+1} = r(k_t - c_t).$$

The agents have a CRRA utility function

$$u(c_t) = c_t^{1-\sigma},$$

and they maximize

$$U_t^i = \sum_{s=t}^{\infty} \rho^s c_t^{1-\sigma},$$

where $1/\sigma$ is the intertemporal elasticity of substitution (and $\rho r^{1-\sigma} < 1$).

You know everything about such economies: linear production function, CRRA utility function. Such economies will always invest at a constant rate s and will grow at a constant steady state rate. But because you have not seen one like this formally, let us go through the steps. Because $k_t - c_t = s$,

$$k_{t+1} = rsk_t,$$
$$\Delta k_t = (rs - 1)k_t,$$
$$\frac{\Delta k_t}{k_t} = rs - 1.$$

Now, to find s we must solve the maximizing problem, the same for all individuals,

$$\max_s U_t^i = \sum_{s=t}^{\infty} \rho^s c_t^{1-\sigma},$$
$$s.t. \; k_t = (rs)^t k_0,$$

or

$$c_t = (1 - s)(rs)^t k_0.$$

Substituting consumption into the maximand yields

$$\max_s \sum_{t=0}^{\infty} \rho^t \left[[(1 - s)k_0]^{1-\sigma} (rs)^{t(1-\sigma)} \right]$$
$$= \max_s k_0^{1-\sigma} (1 - s)^{1-\sigma} \sum \rho^t (rs)^{t(1-\sigma)}$$
$$= \max_s k_0^{1-\sigma} \frac{(1 - s)^{1-\sigma}}{1 - \rho(rs)^{1-\sigma}} = \max_s k_0^{1-\sigma} u(s),$$

where

$$u(s) \equiv \frac{(1 - s)^{1-\sigma}}{1 - \rho(rs)^{1-\sigma}}.$$

Table 9.2

$Group^1/Group^2$	Cooperate	Deviate
C	$\alpha_1(1-s), \alpha_2(1-s)$	$\alpha_1(1-s)-(\beta_2-\delta_2)s, \alpha_2(1-s)+\beta_2 s$
D	$\alpha_1(1-s)+\beta_1 s,$ $\alpha_2(1-s)-(\beta_1-\delta_1)s$	γ_1, γ_2

The rate of saving that solves this maximization problem is (you can check it for yourself)

$$s = (\rho r^{1-\sigma})^{1/\sigma} = \rho^{1/\sigma} r^{1/\sigma-1}.$$

This is thus just a formally slightly different economy of the kind we studied before. Remember that we have found the optimal rate of savings and the optimal rate of growth by assuming that investment decisions of particular agents are independent.

Let us thus introduce politics. Assume now that there are two groups of homogeneous agents, $i \in 1, 2$. In every period t, each group can either moderate its claims to consumption ("cooperate") or try and extract a disproportionate amount at the expense of the other group ("deviate"). Here are the shares of k that are consumed by each group, given each combination of actions (see Table 9.2).

Consider the structure of this situation. The parameters α_i capture the distribution of income in the outcome without conflict, which can be thought of as the market solution. Without a loss of generality, assume that types 1 get a lower share of k, so that $\alpha_1 \leq \alpha_2 = 1 - \alpha_1$.

The $0 < \beta_i \leq 1$ are the fractions of the resources sk_t, which are grabbed by the group i, above its independent (collectively optimal) level of consumption, which is $\alpha_i(1-s)$. Of this grab, a fraction $0 < \delta_i \leq \beta_i$ comes from raiding the capital stock and the fraction $\beta_i - \delta_i$ is at the expense of the other group's consumption. Think like this: When 2 grabs $\beta_2 s$, 1 cooperates by reducing her consumption by $(\beta_2 - \delta_2)s$. Hence, total consumption is now

$$\alpha_1(1-s) - (\beta_2 - \delta_2)s + (1-\alpha_1)(1-s) + \beta_2 s = (1-s) + \delta_2 s,$$

and investment is

$$1 - (1-s) - \delta_2 s = (1-\delta_2)s.$$

Table 9.3

Group^1/Group^2	C	D
C	0.32, 0.48, (0.20)	0.30, 0.58, (0.12)
D	0.42, 0.42, (0.16)	0.55, 0.45, (0)

Hence, δ and $\beta - \delta$ are conceptually distinct: δ stands for grabbing investment resources from the other group (*redistribution of assets*), while $\beta - \delta$ represents grabbing consumption, say via taxes and transfers.

We know what happens when both groups cooperate and when one deviates. When both deviate, that is, both try to consume above the socially optimal level, each gets some part $\gamma_i > \alpha_i(1 - s) - (\beta_{-i} - \delta_{-i})s$. The shares γ_i represent each side's strength in the political conflict, or *political power*.

With these assumptions, it is obvious that the equilibrium of the one-shot game is $\{D, D\}$. Let us stick to some specific numbers to have an intuition of what happens. Let $s = 0.2, \alpha_1 = 0.4, \alpha_2 = 0.6, \beta_1 = \beta_2 = 0.5, \delta_1 = 0.2,$ $\delta_2 = 0.4, \gamma_1 = 0.55, \gamma_2 = 0.45$. Then the game is (with total investment rates on parentheses) (see Table 9.3).

In this story, note that 2 is market rich while 1 has more political power.

The one-shot equilibrium is thus $\{D, D\}$. In equilibrium, group 1 consumes 0.55 of capital and group 2 consumes 0.45. As a result, they consume the entire capital stock. (This is just a simplification: We could make 1's share to be 0.38 and 2's share 0.43 and the point would have been made.) You can see, however, that in this equilibrium the entire capital stock is consumed, so that total utility is

$$U(D, D) = k^{1-\sigma}.$$

In turn, we know that the total utility when both cooperate is

$$U(C, C) = k^{1-\sigma}u(s).$$

To consider the range of s when the cooperative equilibrium is superior, let us study the function $u(s)$. We know that $u(0) = 1$. We also know that $u(s)$ reaches the maximum at $s^* = (\rho r^{1-a})^{1/a}$. Substituting and doing messy algebra shows that

$$u(s^*) = \frac{1}{[1 - \rho^{1/a}r^{(1-a)/a}]^a} = \frac{1}{(1 - s^*)^a} > 1.$$

Finally, when $s = 1$, $u(1) = 0$. Hence, $u(s)$ rises from 1 at $s = 0$ to some value higher than 1 at $s = s^*$ and then declines to 0 at $s = 1$. Because $u(s)$ must pass through 1 between $s = s^*$ and $s = 1$, let $\bar{s}$ be the value at which $u(\bar{s}) = 1$.

The question now is whether the cooperation outcome can be sustained in this polity. Suppose that both types adopt the following, *grim trigger*, strategy: If you cooperate, I cooperate; if you deviate, I will deviate from now on. When would type i want to pursue this strategy? We know that the value of cooperation for i is $(\alpha_i k_t)^{1-\sigma} u(s)$. In turn, if you were to deviate, you would get $\{[\alpha_i(1 - s) + \beta_i s]k_t\}^{1-\sigma}$ during the current period and

$$\rho(\gamma_i k_{t+1})^{1-\sigma} = \rho[\gamma_i rs(1 - \delta_i)k_t]^{1-\sigma}$$

during the second period, after which it will get nothing. Hence, cooperating is better than defecting when

$$(\alpha_i)^{1-\sigma} u(s) \geq [\alpha_i(1 - s) + \beta_i s]^{1-\sigma} + \rho[\gamma_i rs(1 - \delta_i)]^{1-\sigma}.$$

Note that because all the terms contain $k_t^{1-\sigma}$, it cancels, and the condition is independent of the current level of wealth. The structure of this game is independent of the level of wealth: It is the same in poor and affluent countries. This is not generally true, and in general one must consider wealth effects (Benhabib and Rustichini 1996).

We can rewrite the last expression in a form that will be more convenient to analyze the consequences, as (divide and multiply by α_i within each term in square brackets, then simplify)

$$u(s) \geq \left[1 - s + \frac{\beta_i}{\alpha_i}s\right]^{1-a} + \rho\left[rs(1 - \delta_i)\frac{\gamma_i}{\alpha_i}\right]^{1-a}.$$

If this condition is satisfied for both i, then cooperation is sustainable as an equilibrium. If it is violated for at least one player, the only equilibrium is of no growth.

Here are the consequences:

(1) There is *a maximum sustainable rate of growth*. We know that $u(s)$ increases in s and then declines. Now note that the RHS assumes the value of 1 when $s = 0$ and then increases monotonically in s. Hence, either the RHS is always higher than $u(s)$ or they must cross somewhere. Here is a picture in which they cross (see Figure 9.3).

The point at which they cross gives the maximum sustainable growth rate. Note that this rate is lower when the larger β/α and γ/α are higher

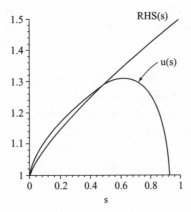

Figure 9.3. Maximum sustainable growth rates.

and δ is lower. The intuition is that when the saving rate is high, the incentive to grab increases: There is more to grab. Hence, when you invest, you must consider that your abstemiousness increases the incentives of the other people to grab your consumption.

Specifically, there are political conditions under which the first-best rate of growth is unsustainable. We know that the first-best rate occurs at $s^* = s^{FB}$. Hence, the first-best is unsustainable when

$$u(s^{FB}) = \frac{1}{(1 - s^{FB})^\sigma} < \left[1 - s^{FB} + \frac{\beta_i}{\alpha_i} s^{FB}\right]^{1-\sigma}$$
$$+ \rho \left[rs^{FB}(1 - \delta_i)\frac{\gamma_i}{\alpha_i}\right]^{1-\sigma}.$$

The second-best sustainable growth rate in an economy $\{\rho, r\}$ and a polity $\{\alpha, \beta, \gamma\}$ is thus the rate that satisfies

$$u(s^{SB}) = \left[1 - s^{SB} + \frac{\beta_i}{\alpha_i} s^{SB}\right]^{1-\sigma} + \rho \left[rs^{SB}(1 - \delta_i)\frac{\gamma_i}{\alpha_i}\right]^{1-\sigma}.$$

(2) Rates of growth that can be sustained are lower when β/α is larger: One player can grab more relative to his market share when the other player cooperates.

(3) Rates of growth that can be sustained are lower when market income inequality is greater. When one α_i is lower, the ratios β/α and γ/α are larger for this actor. Hence, given β, γ growth is maximized at $\alpha = 0.5$.

(4) Rates of growth that can be sustained are higher when political power reflects the distribution of market incomes. If the actor with higher γ has lower α, then the ratio γ/α is high for this actor. Note that this says that growth is higher when the market rich have more political power: a conclusion we encounter is several contexts. Hence, the implication here is "trickle down": The poor are better off when the rich are induced to invest.

Although we learned about the generic impact of politics on growth and we acquired some techniques for studying repeated games, all this was excessively abstract to teach us much. As political scientists, we want to know who the actors are, what they can "grab," and how they "grab." One may think that the actors are "rulers," or those who control the state, and individual economic agents: Remember the model of predatory state in Chapter 5. "Grabbing" will then consist of policies that serve the rulers, rather than the society. One may conceive of the actors as those who derive incomes from capital and from labor services, as well as governments, elected or not (Przeworski and Wallerstein 1988). Grabbing will consist of either raising wages above the competitive level or taxes and transfers. Finally, one may think that the actors are voters. Grabbing will consist of redistributions of productive assets or of taxes and transfers. But, however one thinks of the politics of growth, what we have learned is that economic growth does depend on politics.

9.6   Appendix: Some steps in the Barro (1990) model

The marginal product of private capital is $\partial y/\partial k$. The derivation is not obvious:

$$\frac{\partial y}{\partial k} = \frac{\partial}{\partial k} k \Phi\left(\frac{g}{k}\right) = \Phi\left(\frac{g}{k}\right) + k\left[\Phi'\left(\frac{g}{k}\right)\frac{1}{k^2}(-g)\right]$$

$$= \Phi\left(\frac{g}{k}\right) - \Phi'\left(\frac{g}{k}\right)\frac{g}{k} = \Phi\left(\frac{g}{k}\right) - \Phi'\left(\frac{g}{k}\right)\frac{g}{y}\frac{y}{k}$$

$$= \Phi\left(\frac{g}{k}\right) - \Phi'\left(\frac{g}{k}\right)\frac{g}{y}\Phi\left(\frac{g}{k}\right) = \Phi\left(\frac{g}{k}\right)\left[1 - \Phi'\left(\frac{g}{k}\right)\frac{g}{y}\right].$$

Now

$$\Phi'\left(\frac{g}{k}\right)\frac{g}{y} = \frac{d(Y/K)}{d(G/K)}\frac{G/K}{Y/K} = \eta,$$

where η is the elasticity, which is constant for the Cobb-Douglass production function. Hence,

$$\frac{\partial y}{\partial k} = \Phi\left(\frac{g}{k}\right)(1 - \eta),$$

at a fixed g.

Because the private rate of return to capital stock is $(1 - \tau)\frac{dy}{dk}$, we already know that the optimal consumption path of households must follow

$$\gamma = \frac{\dot{c}}{c} = \frac{\dot{k}}{k} = \frac{1}{\sigma}\left[(1 - \tau)\frac{dy}{dk} - \rho\right]$$

$$= \frac{1}{\sigma}\left[(1 - \tau)\Phi\left(\frac{g}{k}\right)(1 - \eta) - \rho\right].$$

As long as τ and thus $\frac{g}{k}$ are constant, the rate of growth of output, consumption, and capital stock will be constant. (This is just a linear model we studied before.) The initial quantity of consumption is

$$c(0) = k(0)\left[(1 - \tau)\Phi\left(\frac{g}{k}\right) - \gamma\right].$$

This is because $c = y - \tau y - \dot{k} = (1 - \tau)k\Phi(\frac{g}{k}) - \dot{k} = k[(1 - \tau)k\Phi(\frac{g}{k}) - \frac{\dot{k}}{k}]$. Hence, given the initial stock of capital, $k(0)$, the initial amount of consumption is $c(0)$, and the economy grows from then on at the rate γ.

Now go back to the growth equation. The size of government, τ or $\frac{g}{k}$, affects it in two conflicting ways. An increase in τ reduces γ via $(1 - \tau)$ but an increase in $\frac{g}{k}$ increases $\frac{\partial y}{\partial k}$, which raises γ. With Cobb-Douglass technology, the elasticity η is constant and $\eta = \alpha$. Because $\tau = \frac{g}{y}$ and $\frac{g}{k} = \frac{g}{y}\frac{y}{k} = \frac{g}{y}\Phi(\frac{g}{k})$,

$$\frac{d\gamma}{d(g/y)} = \frac{1}{\sigma}\left[-\frac{d\tau}{d(g/y)}\Phi\left(\frac{g}{k}\right)(1 - \alpha) + (1 - \tau)(1 - \alpha)\Phi'\left(\frac{g}{k}\right)\frac{d(g/k)}{d(g/y)}\right].$$

Now, $\frac{d\tau}{d(g/y)} = 1$ and

$$\frac{d(g/k)}{d(g/y)} = \frac{d}{d(g/y)}\frac{g}{y}\Phi\left(\frac{g}{k}\right) = \Phi\left(\frac{g}{k}\right) + \frac{g}{y}\Phi'\left(\frac{g}{k}\right)\frac{d(g/k)}{d(g/y)}$$

or

$$\frac{d(g/k)}{d(g/y)}\left[1 - \frac{g}{y}\Phi'\left(\frac{g}{k}\right)\right] = \Phi\left(\frac{g}{k}\right),$$

and because $\frac{g}{y}\Phi'(\frac{g}{k}) = \eta = \alpha$,

$$\frac{d(g/k)}{d(g/y)}(1-\alpha) = \Phi\left(\frac{g}{k}\right).$$

Substituting back yields

$$\frac{d\gamma}{d(g/y)} = \frac{1}{\sigma}\left[-\Phi\left(\frac{g}{k}\right)(1-\alpha) + (1-\tau)(1-\alpha)\Phi'\left(\frac{g}{k}\right)\frac{\Phi\left(\frac{g}{k}\right)}{1-\alpha}\right]$$

$$= \frac{1}{\sigma}\Phi\left(\frac{g}{k}\right)\left[-(1-\alpha) + (1-\tau)\Phi'\left(\frac{g}{k}\right)\right].$$

Setting this derivative to 0 to maximize growth yields

$$-(1-\alpha) + (1-\tau)\Phi'\left(\frac{g}{k}\right) = 0.$$

But $\Phi'(\frac{g}{k})\frac{g}{y} = \alpha$, so that

$$\frac{1-\alpha}{1-\tau} = \alpha\frac{y}{g} = \frac{\alpha}{\tau},$$

and

$$\tau^* = \alpha.$$

Hence, growth is maximized when the tax rate and the share of public productive services in output is α. You can check that when $\tau < \alpha$, the rate of growth increases in $\frac{g}{y}$ and when $\tau > \alpha$, it declines.

Now consider private savings at the tax rate that maximizes growth. The saving rate, s, is

$$s = \frac{\dot{k}}{y} = \frac{\dot{k}}{k}\frac{k}{y} = \frac{\gamma}{\Phi\left(\frac{g}{k}\right)},$$

so that

$$\frac{\partial s}{\partial(g/y)} = \frac{1}{\Phi^2\left(\frac{g}{k}\right)}\left[\frac{d\gamma}{d(g/y)}\Phi\left(\frac{g}{k}\right) - \Phi'\left(\frac{g}{k}\right)\gamma\right].$$

When the growth rate is at the maximum the first expression in the brackets equals 0. Hence,

$$\frac{\partial s}{\partial(g/y)}\bigg|_{\gamma=\max} < 0,$$

so that the rate of saving is decreasing in the tax rate at the growth maximum.

Finally, we must ask the question whether maximizing growth is the same as maximizing the utility of households. The objective U given earlier can be simplified as

$$U = \frac{[c(0)]^{1-\sigma}}{(1-\sigma)[\rho - \gamma(1-\sigma)]}.$$

Rewriting $c(0)$ is tedious but it involves only substitutions of known quantities, so I leave it to you. In the end, $c(0)$ can be written as

$$c(0) = \frac{k(0)}{1-\eta}[\rho + \gamma(\sigma + \alpha - 1)].$$

Substituting into U yields

$$U = \left(\frac{k(0)}{1-\eta}\right)^{1-\sigma} \frac{[\rho + \gamma(\eta + \sigma - 1)]^{1-\sigma}}{(1-\sigma)[\rho - \gamma(1-\sigma)]}.$$

Hence, whatever maximizes the rate of growth also maximizes utility.

CHAPTER 10

Government and redistribution

10.1   Readings

Read:

Roemer, John E. 2001. Chapters 1 through 7 of *Political Competition: Theory and Applications*. Cambridge, MA: Harvard University Press.

Besley, Timothy and Stephen Coate. 1998. "Sources of Inefficiency in a Representative Democracy: A Dynamic Analysis." *American Economic Review 88*: 139–156.

Recommended:

Fernandez, Raquel and Richard Rogerson. 1995. "On the Political Economy of Education Subsidies." *Review of Economic Studies 62*: 249–262.

Background:

Roemer, John E. 1996. "Introduction" to *Theories of Distributive Justice*. Cambridge, MA: Harvard University Press.

Dasgupta, Partha. 1982. "Utilitarianism, Information, and Rights." In Amartya Sen and Bernard Williams (eds.), *Utilitarianism and Beyond*, 199–218. Cambridge: Cambridge University Press.

Sen Amartya. 1992. *Inequality Reexamined.* Cambridge, MA: Harvard University Press.

Atkinson, Anthony B. 1970. "On the Measurement of Inequality." *Journal of Economic Theory 2*: 244–263.

10.2   Introduction

The questions whether governments should redistribute anything, what they should redistribute, and from whom to whom consume moral philosophers and have worked their way into economics. We have touched on some normative issues in the introductory chapter and will not advance much further. All I can do is to recommend Roemer's (1996) book. We also stay away from Sen's (1992) eye-opening question, which is "equality of what?" Most of this chapter concerns positive theories of redistribution, where the question is how much governments will redistribute. But we need a brief introduction to different reasons governments may redistribute, with which we begin, and we need to return to the criteria for evaluating allocations and distributions, with which we end. Hence, the chapter begins with a clarification of some normative issues, proceeds to ways of studying redistributions, and ends with a discussion of criteria to evaluate actions of governments.

10.3   Preferences for equality

We have been assuming throughout that if the collective decision maker is benevolent it maximizes utilitarian welfare. We need to look back at this maximand.

The classical utilitarian criterion, originating with Bentham,[1] was

$$W = \sum_{i \in N} U_i(.).$$

The subscript i attached to utility indicates that particular individuals may derive different utility from the same states of the world. And the empty parentheses denoting the argument of this function says that individuals may derive utility from whatever. This assumption is nowadays called *unrestricted domain*.

Thinking of social welfare in such terms may be morally appealing but it suffers from two, very different, deficiencies. The first one is that it ignores distributional aspects: By this criterion, social welfare is the same in a society in which one person is very happy and one miserable and a society in which both are moderately happy. We return to this issue later. The second aspect is practical, namely, that it is very hard, if not impossible, to assess social welfare thus defined.

---

[1] I am skirting here over some issues. Bentham's criterion was the greatest happiness of the greatest number. The latter part is ambivalent, because it may imply that the welfare of a society increases as the population increases. I read it to mean "of as many people as possible among those living."

Several comments are due. First, note that what we are summing here over all individuals is utility, not income. Even if individuals cared only about income, the utilitarian criterion would have been

$$W = \sum_{i \in N} U_i(Y),$$

allowing individuals to derive different utility from having the same amount of income. To evaluate social welfare according to this criterion, therefore, we need to make interpersonal comparisons of utility. Suppose we have to decide whether to build a dam that would lower the cost of electricity to consumers but deprive of subsistence local peasants, whose fields would be flooded. How are we to tell whether the dam enhances or reduces social welfare? Whether we can do it and under what conditions is a complicated technical issue, but the general conclusion is that such comparisons are possible only under special conditions (see Roemer 1996). We already know that we can escape interpersonal comparisons of utility if we can use the Pareto criterion. Clearly, if there exist two allocations such that one makes someone better off without anyone else being worse off, this allocation is superior. But such situations are rare and we have seen repeatedly that this criterion often fails to provide useful guidance.

What about a more general form of the utilitarian criterion? Instead of summing the utility of each individual, we could define a *social welfare function*

$$W = W(U_1, U_2, \dots, U_N),$$

increasing in all arguments and perhaps satisfying some other conditions. This will not advance us very far. For one, we can think of many such functions. In one, all the individuals can be given equal weights, as when the utilities are just summed. In another, we can restrict attention to the welfare of the individual who is the least well off, so that the criterion would become

$$W = \max \min_{i \in N} U_i.$$

Second, some such criteria would be indecisive, that is, they would fail to associate one index W to social welfare of societies characterized by some combinations of utilities.

Faced with such difficulties, we can proceed differently, reducing the degree of subjectivism in our description of individuals. Let me first pose the point starkly. Dasgupta (1993) observed that although the notion of well-being is subjective, the notion of deprivation is objective. Although individuals may differ in their subjective conceptions of their welfare when they are sufficiently affluent to be able to make choices, all individuals suffer when they do not satisfy some, the same, basic needs. Hence, although we may be unable to determine what makes individuals well-off, we can easily determine what makes them miserable. Even the most subjectivist economist needs just a few hours to conclude that what a poor village needs is clean water and a school. Hence, satisfaction of some "basic needs" or provision of "primary goods" can serve as an objective criterion of social welfare.

In practice, we often assume that the **function** that relates the states experiences by different individuals to their subjective welfare is the same for all individuals. Note that in the Laffont and Tirole (1994) book, the maximand of the benevolent utilitarian collective decision maker was the sum of incomes of all individuals in society. Even when agents cared about effort, the disutility of effort was measured in money terms. More generally, we can think that all individuals are characterized by some, the same, function $U(.)$. Assume, for example, that all individuals derive from consumption the utility

$$U(C_i) = \frac{C_i^{1-\sigma} - 1}{1 - \sigma},$$

σ given and the same for all $i \in N$ (adding -1 to the numerator just serves to make utilities positive). If we know that this is the utility function of all individuals and if we know the distribution of consumption associated with each allocation of resources, then we could evaluate allocations by the utilitarian criterion.

In a seminal article, Atkinson (1970) pointed out that we can justify the same operation in a different way. We can think that each society is characterized by some preference with regard to equality. In some societies people hold highly egalitarian values; in other societies they may be less egalitarian. The parameter σ then can be thought of as the social preference for equality. To see why, consider how societies with different preferences for equality evaluate two distributions of consumption: a very unequal one, with $C_1 = 90$, $C_2 = 10$, and a perfectly equal one, with $C_1 = C_2 = 50$. A society characterized by $\sigma = 0$ will attach the same value of $W = \sum U = 98$ to both distributions. But a society characterized by $\sigma = 1.5$ will value the unequal distribution at $1.789 + 1.367 = 3.156$ and the equal one at $1.717 +$

1.717 = 3.434. Hence, societies attaching different values to equality will have different preferences over distributions.

Finally, we must extend this discussion to a world with production. Thus far we have considered how to evaluate distributions of income, consumption, or whatever else that is associated with different allocations of resources. But governments can redistribute productive resources, not just final incomes or consumption. How then are we to think about the distribution of resources that enter into production, say land or education? Let me just sketch what is entailed in Bénabou (2000).

Suppose that the production function in some input x is concave, $y = f(x)$, $f_x > 0$, $f_{xx} < 0$. Consider two economies, in which $\sum x = X$ is the same. Then, as you already know, the output will be higher in a society in which x is distributed more equally. Now, if there were a complete set of markets, specifically a credit market, then the agents who have higher endowments of x would loan resources to agents with lower endowments, the agents with initial lower endowments would produce more, and would repay the loans. Hence, this set of markets would lead to a Pareto efficient allocation that would be Pareto superior to the initial one. But such markets are missing because poor people do not have a collateral and there is too much moral hazard. Parents may borrow to educate their talented children but they may spend the money to feed their family or the children may turn out to be lazy. Peasants may borrow money to buy land, but again they may do other things than to produce so as to repay the loans. And because the poor do not have collateral assets, loaning to them is too risky. Hence, markets will not effectuate this redistribution. It does not follow necessarily that a government that seeks to maximize total output will want to redistribute this productive resource: If redistributing has shadow costs, then governments have to weigh the deadweight loss from redistributing against the output gain from a more equal distribution. But if the government can effectuate a lump-sum redistribution – say an agrarian reform or a one-time levy to build schools – then this redistribution would unambiguously increase the total output.

Note that this argument does not hold when the production function is not concave. Suppose that $f_{xx} > 0$, so that agents with higher initial endowments produce more at the margin. Now a redistribution of productive endowments would lower total output. The only mechanisms through which poor people can be made better off is either "trickle down" through the markets or a redistribution of final consumption through taxes and transfers.

With this introduction, let us consider positive theories of redistribution.

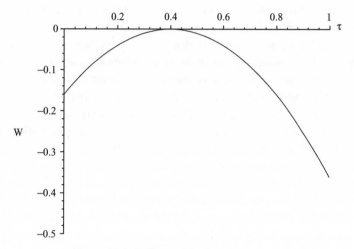

Figure 10.1. Indirect utility function.

10.4   Positive theories of redistribution

10.4.1   Models of party competition

Before we can get to redistribution, we need to learn more generally what to expect when policies are decided by voting.

Consider first a process of voting in a committee. There are N voters, N odd (or very large), each of whom seeks to maximize the utility derived from the state of the world that will result as a consequence of a particular policy. Let this state of the world be c, so that the maximand is $U(c)$, and let the policy be τ. We can now define an *indirect utility function*, that is, the utility function defined over the policies, $W(\tau)$. For example, suppose that we are to vote on a single issue: expenditures of the local school. Each voter attaches some value c to the expenditures on the school, so that each voter derives indirect utility from the tax rate, τ, financing the school.

Let the *ideal point* – the most preferred tax rate – of individual i be τ^i. Assume that the indirect utility function is

$$W^i(\tau, \tau^i) = -(\tau^i - \tau)^2,$$

plotted in Figure 10.1 for $\tau^i = 0.40$.

This utility function is *quasi-concave*, that is, utility reaches a maximum at τ^i and it declines (or at least does not increase) as τ diverges from τ^i.[2]

Each voter can propose any amount of expenditures. Suppose that there are five voters and that each proposes his or her ideal point, so that the proposals are $\tau^1 < \tau^2 < \tau^3 < \tau^4 < \tau^5$, where we have indexed voters by their ideal points. Everyone votes and a decision is reached by majority rule. Suppose that we pair τ^2 against τ^3. Then voters 3, 4, and 5 will vote for τ^3 and voters 1 and 2 will vote for τ^2. Hence τ^3 will beat τ^2 by majority vote: $\tau^3 \succ_M \tau^2$. Suppose that we now pair τ^3 against τ^4: We will get $\tau^3 \succ_M \tau^4$. Because τ^3 beats every other proposal by majority vote, τ^3 is the majority winner. Note that τ^3 is the ideal point of the voter whose peak preference is the median of all ideal points.

To generalize, assume that the distribution of ideal points is some $f(\tau^i)$, with the *cumulative distribution function* $F(\tau^i)$. The winning proposal is a proposal that obtains the votes of at least a majority of voters. Let τ^M be the proposal such that $F(\tau^M) = 1/2$. You can see immediately that there is no proposal that can beat τ^M by majority vote. Hence, τ^M is the majority winner.

This is then the median voter theorem: When preferences are quasi-concave and the decision is reached by pairwise majority rule, the winning proposal is the ideal point of the voter with the median peak preference. Initially proved by Black (1958), this theorem is the workhorse of political economy, because it permits us to identify the outcome of the collective decision-making process on the basis of just one piece of information, namely the ideal point of the median voter.

Except for some referendums, few collective decisions, however, are made in this way. Typically proposals are made by political parties. Suppose now that there are two political parties,[3] which we will call L and R. What do they have to propose so as to maximize their chances of winning the election? You can see immediately that if R were to propose τ^2 then L could propose τ^3 and win. In turn, if L were to propose τ^4 then R could

---

[2] Not all utility functions satisfy this property. A classical example is a survey conducted during the Vietnam War, in which many respondents preferred both extreme responses – "get out" and "bomb the hell out of them" – over the status quo. Hence, their utility function was convex.

[3] If there are more than two parties, the story is much more complicated, because the policy depends now on the coalitions formed after the elections. But voters can anticipate which coalitions will be formed. A classical article on this topic is Austen-Smith and Banks (1988).

propose τ^3 and it would win. In turn, if both were to propose τ^M, then each would win with some positive probability: We can assume, for example, that when parties offer the same proposal, the winner is decided by a flip of a fair coin.

In general, let the proposal of party L be τ^l and let the proposal of party R be τ^r. Then, the vote share of the left party, v, when the proposals are (τ^l, τ^r) is

$$v(\tau^l, \tau^r) = 1 - F[\tau^l - (1/2)(\tau^l - \tau^r)],$$

and the share of the right party is $1 - v$. This is because all voters for whom $\tau^i \geq \tau^l$ vote for the left party, as well as those whose ideal points are closer to τ^l than to τ^r. Note that when $\tau^l = \tau^r = \tau^M$, $v(\tau^M, \tau^M) = 1 - F(\tau^M) = 1/2$.

The probability that the left party wins is thus

$$\pi(\tau^l, \tau^r) = \begin{matrix} 0 & if & v(\tau^l, \tau^r) < 1/2 \\ 1/2 & if & v(\tau^l, \tau^r) = 1/2 \\ 1 & if & v(\tau^l, \tau^r) > 1/2 \end{matrix}$$

Hence, **if political parties care only about winning**, then they both *converge* to the position of the median voter and the winner can be decided only by some random mechanism (or a partisan Supreme Court, as the case may be). As long as the probability of winning when parties offer as their proposals the ideal point of the median voter is positive, this probability is higher than when either makes any other proposal, because otherwise the party is sure to lose. This is Downs's (1957) model of party competition.

This much is true when parties care only about winning the election and when they know for sure the ideal point of the median voter (or the distribution of voter preferences). Suppose now that **parties care only about the policy outcome**. Party L has the ideal point τ^L, party R likes most τ^R, $\tau^L > \tau^R$, so that the left party is the spender. They both know the distribution of voter preferences. What will they do? For simplicity, suppose that the distribution of voters' ideal points is *symmetric* and party R offers as its proposal some point $\tau' < \tau^M$ that is closer to τ^M than τ^L. Then if party L offers τ^L, it will get the utility $U(L) = -(\tau^L - \tau')^2$. But if L offers some point $\tau'' > \tau^M$ that is closer to τ^M than τ', it will get more, namely $U(L) = -(\tau^L - \tau'')^2$. But then the right party can get closer to the position of the median voter, win, and get utility higher than $U(R) = -(\tau^R - \tau'')^2$.

Suppose that both L and R offer τ^M. If R were to deviate from this offer to any $\tau' < \tau^M$, L could deviate to some $\tau'' > \tau^M$, which would be closer to τ^M than τ' and win. Hence, R would not want to deviate. And because the same is true for L, in equilibrium both parties offer τ^M, and the winner is decided by a flip of a coin.

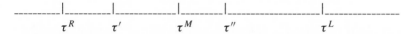

Thus far we distinguished parties that care only about winning from parties that care only about the policy outcome. Consider now the effect of uncertainty about the position of the median voter. Such uncertainty may arise because parties do not know the distribution of voter preferences or because they do not know how responsive voters are to their messages. Suppose that parties do not know the exact location of the median preference but they know the distribution of this preference.

Assume that both parties are purely opportunistic, that is, they care only about winning. The left party is now maximizing the expected probability of winning, which is $E[\pi(\tau^l, \tau^r)]$. The solution to this problem is to set $\tau^l = E(\tau^M)$. And because the problem of the right party is the same, both parties converge to the expected position of the median voter.

Finally, suppose that parties are uncertain about the location of the median voter **and** that they have policy preferences. The Nash equilibrium is a pair of strategies $\{\tau^{*l}, \tau^{*r}\}$ such that for all $0 \leq \tau \leq 1$

$$E[U^L(\tau^{*l}, \tau^{*r})] \geq E[U^L(\tau^l, \tau^{*r})],$$

$$E[U^R(\tau^{*l}, \tau^{*r})] \geq E[U^R(\tau^{*l}, \tau^r)].$$

The objective of the left party is now to maximize expected utility

$$E[U^L(\tau^l|\tau^r)] = \pi(\tau^l, \tau^r)U^L(\tau^l) + [1 - \pi(\tau^l, \tau^r)]U^L(\tau^r).$$

If the left party proposes τ^l, it wins with the probability $\pi(\tau^l, \tau^r)$, getting $U^L(\tau^l)$, and it loses with the probability $(1 - \pi)$ in which case it gets $U^L(\tau^r)$. Suppose that the position of the right party is fixed at some τ^r. First-order condition for the left party then implies

$$\frac{\partial \pi}{\partial \tau^l}[U^L(\tau^l) - U^L(\tau^r)] = -\pi \frac{dU^L(\tau^l)}{d\tau^l}.$$

This is sufficient to see that parties will not converge to the same position. If they did, then the expression in the square brackets would be zero, but the

Table 10.1

	Certain	**Uncertain**
Winning	converge	converge
Policy	converge	do not converge

right-hand side would be different from zero, so that this equality could not hold. Moreover, because (in the interval τ^M, τ^L) $\frac{dU^L(\tau^l)}{d\tau^l} > 0$ and $\frac{\partial \pi}{\partial \tau^l} < 0$, the expression in the brackets must be positive, so that $\tau^l > \tau^r$. Because the same is true of the right party, when parties care about policies and they are uncertain about the position of the median voters, then (1) they do not offer their ideal points, but (2) they do not converge to the same position.

These results can be summarized by the following table, adopted from Roemer (2001). The rows characterize the objectives of parties, the columns their knowledge, and the cell entries describe the equilibrium strategies (see Table 10.1).

This entire construction breaks down, however, when voters choose simultaneously in more than one dimension of policy space. Generically, Nash equilibria do not exist. Suppose that voters choose between two parties, each of which offers a two-dimensional proposal: how much to tax and how to allocate the tax revenue between transfers and public goods. Now voters have preferences in two dimensions and we already know that the collective choice may be intransitive. Party L will offer a proposal X, which will beat Y; Party R will offer Z, which will beat X; and Party L will counter with Y, which will beat Z, and so on. Hence, we will not know which proposal will win.

Anticipating this difficulty, Downs argued that in fact preferences are reduced to one dimension by ideology and this line of defense has been pursued by several researchers. Even if voters have preferences over multiple dimensions of the policy space – say tax rate, military spending, and religious instruction in public schools – voters are ordered in the same way in all dimensions. (Suppose, for example, that $U_i(\tau, g) = V_1(\tau) + k(y_i)V_2(g)$, with k monotonic in y and V_1, V_2 the same for all i. Such preferences are called *intermediate preferences*; see Persson and Tabelini 2000.) This argument can be given a microjustification, namely, that voters save on information costs when they are willing to be guided by ideology: They do not have to evaluate every policy proposal separately but can just classify it as being "left" or "right." Empirically, it seems that voters, both in the United States and in Europe, were aligned along a single, "left versus right" or "statist versus anti-statist" dimension. But, as we shall see, these are feeble grounds.

If the problem cannot be avoided, it must be confronted. The reason indeterminacy appears in multidimensional contexts is that political parties are free to adjust their proposals in response to each other. If this adjustment process is somehow constrained, then we can hope to get at least some definitive results. Several ways of getting around the indeterminacy have been proposed.

One is Roemer's (2001) concept of "Party Unity Nash Equilibrium," to which he refers as PUNE. His assumption is that political parties consist of three factions: (1) militants, who care only about policy, (2) opportunists, who care only about winning, and (3) reformers, who care about both. A pair of proposals is a PUNE if none of the fractions of each party wants to deviate from its proposal given the proposal by the other party. Suppose party R offers a proposal. Now party L chooses a proposal that will be accepted unanimously by the three factions, to which in turn party R responds in the same way. The effect of this refinement is to constrain the freedom of maneuver of the parties and the result is that not every pair of proposals can occur. In several applications, Roemer gets substantively interpretable results by using this approach.

Another method is the so-called citizen-candidate model (Osborne and Slivinsky 1996; Besley and Coate 1998). In this model parties are endogenous and no one adjusts. Each citizen is characterized by her preferences. Each citizen can become a candidate at some cost and announce his or her preferences. Then other citizens examine which of the candidates is closest to them and vote for the closest one. The equilibrium in such models is a set of candidates (hence proposals) such that each wants to be a candidate given all other candidates and no one else wants to become a candidate. The candidate with the most votes wins. There are again multiple equilibria but they are analytically tractable and their number is limited. We use such a model later.

Yet another is the adaptive learning model of Bendor, Mukherjee, and Ray (2002), in which the incumbents stick to the policy that made them win the election, while the opposition experiments with proposals that might beat the incumbent. Again, a limited number of equilibria emerge, even if the policy space is multidimensional.

The trick all these models share is to somehow restrict the ability of parties, or at least one party, to adjust their proposals in response to the proposal of the other party. If parties are for some reason ideologically rigid or if they cannot credibly change their stance with regard to some issues (as in probabilistic models, not discussed here), then equilibria, even if they are multiple, emerge from party competition.

10.4.2 Applications to redistribution

Positive theories of redistribution relate distributions of initial income or of productive assets to their redistribution via some political mechanism. Their general form is a society with the initial distribution $x_b \sim (\mu_b, \sigma_b^2)$ will generate a distribution $x_a \sim (\mu_a, \sigma_a^2)$ through a political mechanism P, where the subscript b stands for "before" and a for "after" the operation of P.

Consider now the following question. Suppose that individuals $i \in N$ earn a pretax income y_i. They are taxed at the rate τ. The tax revenue is then redistributed equally to everyone (or spent to finance equally valued public goods). Each individual receives a subsidy s (or benefits from public spending evaluated at g). The consumption of each individual (or "postfisc," that is tax and transfer, income), c_i, is then

$$c_i = (1 - \tau)y_i + s.$$

Assuming balanced budget, $Ns = \tau \sum y$, so that $s = \tau \frac{\sum y}{N} = \tau \bar{y}$, where $\bar{y}$ is the average income. Note that the assumptions that all tax revenue is spent on transfers (or all on public goods) and that the budget is balanced reduce the choice problem to one dimension, namely, the tax rate.

We can now rewrite consumption as

$$c_i = (1 - \tau)y_i + \tau \bar{y}.$$

The question is how incomes will be redistributed given that two parties compete to win the election (and implement their proposals if elected). Note that the redistribution to or from an individual i is

$$c_i - y_i = \tau(\bar{y} - y_i).$$

Suppose each individual wants to consume as much as possible. Then each individual will opt for a tax rate given by

$$\frac{dc_i}{d\tau} \gtrless 0.$$

Individuals for whom $\frac{dc_i}{d\tau} > 0$ will opt for a tax rate $\tau = 1$; those for whom $\frac{dc_i}{d\tau} < 0$ will opt for $\tau = 0$; those for whom $\frac{dc_i}{d\tau} = 0$ will opt for any rate $0 \leq \tau \leq 1$. Note immediately that because

$$\frac{dc_i}{d\tau} = \bar{y} - y_i,$$

people with incomes lower than average will want high tax rates, whereas people with incomes above average will want low tax rates.

To find out which voter will be decisive, we need to use a theorem by Roberts (1977), which says that the voter with the median income is the one with the median preference if the posttax income (or consumption) of individuals is monotonically ordered by their pretax incomes for all pairs $\{\tau, s\}$.

Comment. This condition, called the *single-crossing property*, concerns voters, not preferences. The single-crossing property holds in this context if the following is true. Suppose a voter with income (or some other trait) y_i has an indirect utility function $w_i(\tau, s)$ over taxes and subsidies. The voter chooses τ and receives s. Then if for some type y_i, $w_i(\tau, s) > w_i(\tau', s')$ for $s > s'$, then for all types $y' < y_i$ (or $y' > y_i$), $w'(\tau, s) \geq w'(\tau', s')$. In other words, if type y_i (weakly) prefers (τ, s) to (τ', s') and the preferred policy has a higher subsidy, then all types with lower (higher) incomes strictly prefer this policy. Hence, voters' preferences can be ordered by their incomes.

Another way to see what this property means is this. Let $U_i = U(c, g; y_i)$, where g stands for government spending and $g = g(\tau)$. The marginal rate of substitution of an individual with income y_i is then given by

$$\frac{\partial U_i}{\partial c} \frac{dc_i}{d\tau} + \frac{\partial U_i}{\partial g} \frac{dg}{d\tau} = 0.$$

But $dc_i/d\tau = -y_i$, whereas $dg/d\tau = \sum y_i = $ constant. Hence

$$\frac{\partial U_i/\partial g}{\partial U_i/\partial c} = \frac{y_i}{\sum y_i},$$

which means that the marginal rates of substitution can be uniquely ordered by individual income. (**End of comment**)

If this conditions holds, the decisive voter is the voter with median income. Hence, we know that in the societies in which the median income is lower than the average income, tax rates will be $\tau = 1$, generating complete equality of postfisc incomes.

This model can be complicated in several ways. Suppose that taxes are distortionary, so that $\frac{dy}{d\tau} < 0$. Then the optimal tax rate of the voter with median income, the decisive voter, is the rate that solves

$$\frac{dc_M}{d\tau} = \bar{y} - y_M + \tau \frac{d\bar{y}}{d\tau} = 0.$$

One way in which such distortions can occur is via the supply of labor. Suppose (Meltzer and Richard 1981) that each individual seeks to maximize the utility of consumption and leisure. The total time available to each individual is fixed and income is earned by working L hours at the exogenously given wage rate of w_i. Hence, each individual solves

$$\max_L U[(1 - \tau_M)w_i L + \tau_M \bar{y}, l],$$

with first-order condition (because $dl/dL = -1$)

$$-U_c[(1 - \tau_M)w_i] + U_l = 0$$

or

$$\frac{U_c}{U_l} = (1 - \tau_M)w_i.$$

As the tax rate goes up, the marginal rate of substitution declines, which means that each individual chooses less consumption and more leisure. Hence, taxes cause a distortion by reducing the supply of labor.

Another way in which the model can be complicated is to assume that those who vote and those who receive subsidies are not the same. For example, everyone may vote and decide to provide subsidies only to some. Suppose, following Lee (2001), that only people with incomes above some y_t vote, where t is now turnout, and a proportion r of the electorate receives the subsidies. The tax rate preferred by the individual with the median income among those voting will then be given by

$$\frac{dc_M|t}{d\tau} = (1/r)\bar{y} - y_M|t.$$

As turnout increases, poorer people vote and the median voter wants higher taxes, as in Meltzer and Richard (1981). But as the proportion of recipients increases, the median voter gains less from subsidies and prefers lower taxes.

Consider now the effect of uncertainty. A simple model of such situations is Roemer's (2001) (Section 5.2) Average-Member Nash Equilibrium, which captures a conception of a "perfectly representative democracy." I modify this model slightly to be able to derive comparative statics with regard to income inequality. The intuitive idea is the following: Take the assumptions of the median voter model introduced earlier, but now model deadweight loss of taxation explicitly. The consumption (postfisc income) of an individual $i \in N$ with prefisc income y_i is

$$c_i = (1 - \tau)y_i + \tau\overline{y}(1 - \lambda\tau),$$

where λ is the shadow cost of public funds. Each party maximizes expected average consumption of the people who vote for it. Party L proposes and implements τ_L; party R offers and implements τ_R, $\tau_L \geq \tau_R$. In equilibrium, all individuals with incomes lower than some $\hat{y}(\tau_L, \tau_R; \lambda)$ vote for party L and all those with incomes above it vote for party R.

Given any pair of tax rates, $\tau_L \geq \tau_R$, let $\hat{y}(\tau_L, \tau_R; \lambda)$ be the income level such that $c(\tau_L) = c(\tau_R)$. Then

$$\hat{y}(\tau_L, \tau_R; \lambda) = \overline{y}[1 - \lambda(\tau_L + \tau_R)].$$

The subset of individuals who prefer τ_L to τ_R is then

$$\Omega(\tau_L, \tau_R; \lambda) = \{y_i | y_i < \hat{y}(\tau_L, \tau_R; \lambda)\}.$$

If incomes are distributed according to F, then

$$F(\tau_L, \tau_R; \lambda) = F[\Omega(\tau_L, \tau_R; \lambda)] = F[\hat{y}(\tau_L, \tau_R; \lambda)]$$

is the proportion of voters preferring τ_L to τ_R, given λ.

Assume now that there are two parties, L and R. Party L represents the average voter in Ω, while party R represents the complement of this set. The income of the average member of L is then

$$y_L = \int_0^{\hat{y}} f(y_i)y_i dy_i,$$

and of the average member of R it is

$$y_R = \int_{\hat{y}}^{\infty} f(y_i)y_i dy_i.$$

Party L solves

$$\max_{\tau_L} U_L = \pi(\tau_L, \tau_R)c_L(\tau_L) + [1 - \pi(\tau_L, \tau_R)]c_L(\tau_R),$$

and party R

$$\max_{\tau_R} U_R = \pi(\tau_L, \tau_R)c_R(\tau_L) + [1 - \pi(\tau_L, \tau_R)]c_R(\tau_R),$$

where $\pi(\tau_L, \tau_R)$ is the probability that party L wins, given that the proposals are τ_L, τ_R.

The Average-Member Nash Equilibrium of this game is a triple $(\hat{y}^*, \tau_L^*, \tau_R^*)$ such that

$$(1) U_L(\tau_L^*, \tau_R^*) \geq U_L(\tau_L, \tau_R^*) \forall \tau_L \in 0, 1$$

$$U_R(\tau_L^*, \tau_R^*) \geq U_R(\tau_L^*, \tau_R) \forall \tau_R \in 0, 1,$$

$$(2) \hat{y}^* = \hat{y}(\tau_L^*, \tau_R^*; \lambda).$$

Now, if parties know everything, then $\tau_L^* = \tau_R^* = \tau_M$, $\Omega(\tau_M, \tau_M) = \{y_i | y_i < \hat{y}(\tau_M, \tau_M)\}$, $F[\Omega(\tau_M, \tau_M)] = 1/2$, and $\pi(\tau_M, \tau_M) = 1/2$, where

$$\tau_M = \frac{\overline{y} - y_M}{2\lambda\overline{y}} = \left(1 - \frac{y_M}{\overline{y}}\right)/2\lambda.$$

Note that $\hat{y}(\tau_M, \tau_M; \lambda) = \overline{y}[1 - \lambda(2\tau_M)] = \overline{y}[1 - \frac{\overline{y}-y_M}{\overline{y}}] = y_M$. Hence, party L represents the average voter among those voters whose incomes are below the median, while party R represents the average voter among those whose incomes are above the median. All voters with incomes below the median vote for L and all those with higher incomes vote for R. Parties converge to the ideal point of the median voter; they divide the electorate in halves, and the winner is decided by a flip of a fair coin.

Now introduce uncertainty. Assume that the left party believes that the shadow price of public funds is low, $\lambda = \underline{\lambda}$, while the right party believes it is high, $\lambda = \overline{\lambda}$. Neither party knows what the voters believe: All politicians know is that voters beliefs are uniformly distributed in some interval, $\lambda \sim U[\underline{\lambda}, \overline{\lambda}]$. The probability that party L wins is now

$$\pi(\tau_L, \tau_R) = \begin{matrix} 0 & \text{if } F(\underline{\lambda}) < 1/2 \\ \frac{F(\underline{\lambda})-1/2}{F(\underline{\lambda})-F(\overline{\lambda})} & \text{if } 1/2 \in F(\overline{\lambda}), F(\underline{\lambda}) \\ 1 & \text{if } F(\overline{\lambda}) > 1/2 \end{matrix}$$

Armed with this model, we can calculate party platforms and the distance between them as a function of income inequality, assuming that individual incomes y_i are distributed log-normally according to $y_i \sim LN(0, \sigma^2)$, where σ^2 is the variance of the log of incomes and $\triangle \equiv y_M/\overline{y} = \exp(-\sigma^2/2)$. The higher the $\triangle$, the more equal is the society. Here are the results (to calculate

Table 10.2

Δ	τ_M		τ_L	τ_R	$E(\tau)$	$\tau_L - \tau_R$
	$\underline{\lambda} = 0.1$	$\bar{\lambda} = 0.3$				
0.90	0.25		0.30	0.14	0.26	0.16
0.80	0.50		0.55	0.27	0.46	0.28
0.60	1.00		1.00	0.62	0.88	0.38
	$\underline{\lambda} = 0.0$	$\bar{\lambda} = 0.4$				
0.90	0.25		0.27	0.09	0.23	0.18
0.80	0.50		0.51	0.17	0.41	0.34
0.60	1.00		0.95	0.39	0.75	0.56
	$\underline{\lambda} = 0.1$	$\bar{\lambda} = 0.5$				
0.90	0.17		0.20	0.07	0.17	0.13
0.80	0.33		0.31	0.13	0.29	0.18
0.60	0.67		0.64	0.29	0.55	0.25

the separating income, in the numerical simulations, we assume that the actual realization of λ is $E(\lambda)$; see Table 10.2).

As in the case of certainty, higher inequality, as represented by Δ^{-1}, is associated with higher expected redistribution, $E(\tau)$, while higher expected deadweight losses reduce redistribution. As uncertainty increases, partisan proposals diverge. Moreover, these simulations indicate that higher inequality is associated with larger policy difference between parties.

The median model has been applied to innumerable contexts, because it is simple and gives a unique answer. But the cost of squeezing all kinds of questions into one dimension are significant. This model is a splendid example of looking for the key under the lamp post because this is where the light is. Let us go after the weaknesses of this model one by one. Note first that there are two assumptions that allow us to construct a one-dimensional model. The first one is relatively innocuous in static problems, namely, that the budget is balanced. But the second is descriptively inane and theoretically impoverishing. No government spends all of its tax revenue on income transfers (or the provision of public goods). A part of the public budget is spent on social policies, not equally valued by all individuals, on defense expenditures, on debt payment, on productive services, and on the costs of public administration. There is no reason to think that different kinds of expenditures order voters in the same way. Hence, the choice voters face is inextricably multidimensional. Moreover, net redistribution associated with a particular form of spending need not be monotonic with regard to the initial incomes. There is nothing that prevents voters from giving a net subsidy to old people even if they have higher incomes than younger people who are net contributors.

Squeezing the problem onto one dimension imposes in addition some implicit restrictions on the model. One is that the only feasible net redistributions are from the wealthier to the poorer, which flies in the face of much evidence that shows that some public expenditures are regressive. Tertiary, and in many countries even secondary, educational expenditures are the best example: They constitute a net transfer to people who are better off to begin with (Fernandez and Rogerson 1995). Another way to think about this hidden assumption is that taxes are restricted to the $0 \leq \tau \leq 1$ interval. But there is no good reason to think that taxes cannot be negative, that is, that the net transfer is not from the poorer to the richer. And there is no reason to think that they cannot be greater than 1, that is, that the poor cannot tax the assets of the rich.

Clearly, there are situations in which the median voter model provides the appropriate analytical tool. Milanovic (1999), for example, found that the degree of income redistribution among the OECD and some Eastern European countries is greater the greater the inequality of the prefisc (tax and transfer) income. But he also found that the median voter is a net loser from the redistribution that she presumably chooses, which is best understood by observing that voters receive from the government not only transfers but also all kinds of services: evidence of multidimensionality.

In the end, we are in a methodological conundrum. The median voter model is simple and analytically tractable but wildly unrealistic and limited in scope. In turn, multidimensional models suffer from multiple equilibria and are either analytically intractable (like Roemer's 2001, model) or excessively stylized (like the citizen-candidate model).

Perhaps the greatest puzzle opened by the median voter model is why the tax rates (and redistribution of incomes) are not as high as this model predicts. The model implies that if the median income is below the mean income, then the degree of redistribution is mitigated only by the distortionary effects of taxation. Now, according to the data we have, there is no country in the world in which median income is not lower than the mean. And unless marginal deadweight losses at the observed tax rates are astronomical, the actual degree of redistribution, pretty much all around the world, is much lower than the degree that the median voter model implies. The question is why the poor, equipped with political power in the form of universal suffrage, do not use their political rights to equalize incomes. This is particularly perplexing because survey after survey shows that in many countries, Latin American and Eastern European, for example, the first meaning that people attach to democracy is equality in the economic realm.

As usual, explanations abound. One is that poor people mitigate their distributional demands because they rationally believe in the prospect of upward mobility for themselves or their children (Bénabou 2001). Another is that when the policy space is two dimensional, say redistribution and religion, then the left party moderates its distributional proposals so as not to alienate the nonreligious people with high incomes who may vote for it (Roemer 2001). Still another is that poor people do not want redistribution because they are somehow ideologically dominated by the rich (Shapiro 1999). Yet another is to look beyond the voting procedures. As one casts a glance around the world, it is apparent that countries that are more equal in fact redistribute each year more income than the more unequal countries. Several categories of transfers filled with positive numbers among the OECD countries do not even appear in the Mexican National Accounts. What this observation suggests is that there may be other barriers to redistribution than those that constrain voting decisions. The most obvious is that the wealthy do not like to be taxed and that in some countries they can revert to the use of force if they are threatened with redistribution (Przeworski 2003).

10.5 Democracy and efficiency

Equipped with these analytical tools, we need to return to the problem of evaluating government policies. The basic setup is the following. Individuals differ in their productivity. There are two periods. Incomes produced during the first-period can be taxed. First-period taxes can be used either to provide transfers or to finance a public investment that increases productivity of some people during the second period. During the second period, incomes are again produced and they can be taxed, with the revenue being transferred and consumed.

Because the present decision makers cannot commit future ones, this process can lead to outcomes that are economically inefficient. To convey the intuitions, let me present some examples from Besley and Coate (1998). As often, I first introduce a simplified version of their model and then comment on its implications.

Consider first the following situation. There are two periods. In the first period, the electorate consists of two types of individuals: Exactly one-half of them have ability a_L and the other half have ability a_H, $a_H > a_L$. The high-ability types can benefit from education: If a school is built during the first period, at per capita cost γ, then the second-period ability of the high types is $a_H + \delta$; otherwise the ability of both types remains the same. Assume that $\delta/2 > \gamma$, which implies that the investment is potentially Pareto improving. Individuals maximize undiscounted utility of consumption over the two periods: $U(c) = c_1 + c_2$. Voting follows the citizen-candidate model.

Examine the second period. Regardless of the decision in the first period, during the second period a high-ability candidate will oppose a low-ability one. The high-ability candidate will propose no taxes; the low-ability candidate taxes at 100 percent. Everyone will vote for their own type and, because their numbers are equal, the election will be decided by a flip of a fair coin.

Now examine the preferences of the low type during the first period. The low type will want taxes. The question is whether he will want to undertake the investment. If the low type votes for investment, his income during the first period will be $(a_L + a_H)/2 - \gamma$ and his expected income during the second period will be $(1/2)a_L + (1/2)[(a_L + a_H + \delta)/2]$. If he votes not to invest, his income during the first period will be $(a_L + a_H)/2$ and his expected income during the second period will be $(1/2)a_L + (1/2)[(a_L + a_H)/2]$. Hence, if $\delta/4 < \gamma$, the low type votes not to invest.

In this example, the low type votes not to invest because he has to give up consumption during the first period whereas he is not certain if he will participate during the second period in the gains of productivity made possible by his sacrifice of consumption. The problem here is that investment is only potentially Pareto improving. True, the low type could be compensated for his sacrifice and the high type still would be better off. If the high-ability type could somehow assure the low type that she will share the benefits from her increased productivity, the low type would vote for investment. But such a promise would not be credible. Hence, if the high type wins the second-period election, the low type is worse off having voted for the investment during the first period.

Consider now a more startling situation, in which investment is unambiguously Pareto improving. Indeed, assume that investment is costless. Now there are three types: a_L and a_H types do not benefit from the investment but a third type, "movers," does. The first-period ability of movers is a_L but if investment is undertaken, their second-period productivity is $a_L + \delta$. To make the story work, assume that $p_L + p_M = p_H$ and that $p_M < 1/3$, where the $p's$ represent proportions of each type in the electorate.

Examine again the second period. If a low type wins, he will set taxes at 100 percent. If a high type wins, she will opt for no taxes. But the preference of the mover depends on whether investment occurred: If it did not, the mover will vote with the low types; if it did, she will vote with the high types. Hence, if investment was not undertaken, a low type will confront a high type, with the result decided by a flip of a coin. If investment was undertaken, a high type will run unopposed, because the low type is certain to lose and entry is costly.

Now go back to period one. Because investment is costless, the low type's first-period income depends only on taxes. The low type's expected second-period consumption if investment occurs is a_L. If investment does not occur, low type's second-period consumption is $(3a_L + a_H)/4$, which is greater than a_L. Hence, the low type wants taxes to be 100 percent and the revenue to be consumed. The high type wants taxes to be zero and for investment to occur. The mover wants a 100 percent tax and investment. But the mover cannot win: Because a three-candidate election would be decided by a plurality rule and because $p_M < 1/3$, no mover would enter as a candidate. Hence, movers must decide whether to vote for a low or a high type. If a mover votes for a low type, she gets $(a_L + a_H)/2$ during the first period and $(1/2)(a_L) + (1/2)[(a_L + a_H)/2]$ during the second period, for a total of $\frac{5}{4}a_L + \frac{3}{4}a_H$. If she votes for a high type, she gets a_L during the first period and $a_L + \delta$ during the second period. Hence, if $\delta < 3(a_H - a_L)/4$, the mover votes for a low-type candidate and no investment is undertaken. And note that investment is costless and Pareto superior to noninvestment: The worst that can happen to any type is that their consumption remains the same, the best that can happen is it increases as a result of the investment.

The most interesting implications of this example concern the concept of efficiency. We have started with Pareto efficiency of perfect markets. We then observed that if markets are missing, it may be for good reasons, and that we should therefore think of efficiency as constrained by the missing markets. Now we see that the political process can be a source of inefficiency. If there were a credit market for education, agents would trade to the unconstrained Pareto efficient allocation. But we already know that credit market for education will be missing, so that the market will not effectuate the investment in education. Now we learned that the state may not do it either. In a way, what is missing here is the market for political insurance. If the currently decisive voter could be somehow assured that she would get a sufficient benefit in the future, the socially optimal policy would be adopted. But she cannot be.

Besley and Coate (1998) consider the resulting inefficiency as constituting a "political failure," analogous to "market failures." In first-best terms, both are failures. But first-best is just not a reasonable criterion. All collective decisions must be made through some process. Hence, in the same way as it makes no sense to assume perfect markets to evaluate allocations in the real world of missing ones, it makes no sense to evaluate politically arrived at allocations abstracting from the political process. We must ask whether an allocation is politically constrained efficient, that is, whether someone could be better off without anyone being worse off **given the political process**. The concept of politically constrained efficiency is not normative – it is not an excuse for a particular way collective decisions are made – but analytical. It does not imply that all political decisions are politically constrained efficient. Avoidable collusion between regulators and firms or avoidable rent extraction by politicians constitute political failures. But the fact that the political process does not generate an economically efficient allocation is as irrelevant as is the fact that incomplete markets do not generate allocations that perfect markets would. The best that is possible is the best that can be reached under the constraints, and these constraints include the political process as well as missing markets.

None of the arguments above are specific to democracy. Just suppose, with Robinson (2000), that a dictator can invest in productive public goods, which promote development but also facilitate collective action against the dictator. This dictator may choose not to provide the public input, thus retarding growth. This allocation will be economically inefficient but, given dictatorship, it is not. If the dictator could somehow be assured that he will not be overthrown when the economy develops, he would reach the economically efficient allocation. But he cannot be assured: There is no market for security of dictators. Hence, the allocation is politically constrained efficient.

It is obviously a different question whether a particular allocation is politically constrained efficient and whether a different way of reaching collective decisions would generate better outcomes. We can ask, for example, whether democracy generates outcomes that tend to be economically more efficient than dictatorship (see Przeworski et al. 2000). We can also ask whether a differently organized democratic process would lead to better outcomes: We have been asking this question all along. But once a particular set of institutions is in place, all we can ask is whether a particular allocation is efficient given these institutions.

CHAPTER 11

Government and insurance

11.1   Readings

Study:

Barr, Nicholas. 1992. "Economic Theory and the Welfare State." *Journal of Economic Literature 30*: 741–804.

Read:

Moene, Karl Ove and Michael Wallerstein. 1997a. "Political Support for Targeted versus Universalistic Welfare Policies." Revised paper presented at the 1996 Annual Meeting of the American Political Science Association, San Francisco, CA.

Recommended:

Atkinson, A. B. 1999. *The Economic Consequences of Rolling Back the Welfare State.* Cambridge, MA: MIT Press.

Moene, Karl Ove and Michael Wallerstein. 1997b. "Rising Inequality and Declining Support for Welfare Spending." Notes for presentation at the seminar of the Center for Poverty Research, Harris School of Public Policy, University of Chicago.

11.2   Justifications of the welfare state

There are several reasons governments might want to ensure that no one suffers from remediable bad luck.

11.2.1   Solidarity

All throughout the book we assumed that each individual derives utility only from the states of the world he or she experiences personally. Formally, we have been assuming that $U_i = U(x_i)$, where x_i stands for the income, consumption, leisure, or what not, of the $i - th$ individual. But there is overwhelming evidence that people care about others (Bowles 1998). If they feel better when others are better off, they are altruistic.

Altruism comes in several varieties. You may care that others are happy in whatever way that makes them so. Then your utility function is $U_i = U(x_i, U_j)$: What enters into your utility function is the utility of others. But you may also care about others without letting them decide what makes them happy. You may, for example, derive utility from my reading the *Bible* but not *Lady Chatterley's Lover* (Sen 1970). You have *meddling preferences* and your altruism is *paternalistic*. Hence, your utility function is $U_i = U(x_i, x_j)$. Altruists may or may not respect preferences of the people about whom they care.

Another distinction concerns the "others," j. You may be altruistic only with regard to your children, with regard to your family, some broader community, all the way to "mankind."

Suppose all individuals are altruistic with regard to all other members of the same political community. They have a paternalistic utility function in consumption of the form $U_i = U(c_i, \alpha c_j)$, where α is a weight individual i places on the welfare of individual j. The budget constraint is $y_i + \sum_{j \neq i} y_j = Y$. Suppose that i's utility function is simply

$$U_i = U(c_i, \alpha c_j) = (1 - \tau)y_i + \tau \overline{y} + \alpha[(1 - \tau)y_j + \tau \overline{y}].$$

First-order condition then implies that the tax rate chosen by i will depend on

$$(\overline{y} - y_i) + \alpha(\overline{y} - y_j) \gtreqless 0.$$

Suppose that i is wealthy, so that she would vote against any taxes if she cared only about her welfare, $y_i > \overline{y}$. Yet if she sufficiently cares about the welfare of j, who is poor, $y_j < \overline{y}$, she will vote to tax herself and subsidize consumption of the poor.

"Solidarity," in my reading, is the following notion. I see myself as being in the same situation as many others. I observe that they have experienced bad luck and I see that it is just luck. By putative reciprocity, I think that they would have come to my rescue had I been unlucky, and I am willing to come to theirs. Solidarity implies that people who exert the same amount of effort should not receive different rewards just because of luck. Hence, it means that people voluntarily contribute to protect those like themselves against bad luck. Again, the scope of solidarity may differ: I may be solidaristic with my neighbors, with other wage earners, or with the human kind.

Solidarity can operate exclusively ex post, that is, no funds need be collected in anticipation that someone will suffer bad luck. It is sufficient that on observing bad luck of j, i comes to the rescue. If j happens to be poor through no fault of her own, i, who happens to be well-off, makes a voluntary contribution, say to an earthquake relief fund. In fact, people are willing to contribute to disaster relief even when the disaster happens to occur in distant places.

But even if people are solidaristic, why should the government get involved? It need not: Some of the early unemployment insurance schemes were operated by trade unions. Many disaster relief funds are operated by private charitable associations. As long as people contribute voluntarily, the government has no distinctive role of play.

11.2.2 Insurance

The insurance motive works in a very different way. We will study insurance in more detail soon, so this is just an introduction.

Suppose that I am currently employed and that with probability p I may be unemployed during the next period. Let my income while employed be w. The question now is how much money, π, I will contribute to an insurance scheme, which works as follows: If I am employed during the next period, someone else will get the money; if I am unemployed, I will get my contribution and his. Let the utility function be

$$U = w - \pi + \beta[(1 - p)(w - \pi) + p(2\pi)], 0 < \beta < 1.$$

First-order conditions imply that

$$\pi \gtreqless 0 \ if \ p \gtreqless \frac{1 + \beta}{2 + \beta}.$$

Hence, if my risk of losing the job is high, I contribute; otherwise I do not.

As you see, this voluntary insurance scheme is feasible only if individuals face similar, high, risks. If everyone faces low risks, no insurance is needed. If everyone faces high risks, everyone will contribute voluntarily. But if some people know that they face low risks while others face high risks, the low-risk types will not contribute voluntarily. Hence voluntary insurance schemes are not feasible when individual-specific risks differ. If such insurance schemes are nevertheless desirable, by some welfare criterion, then the state should compel everyone, regardless of the risks they face, to contribute.

11.2.3 Militarism

Solidarity and insurance motives provide two justifications for the welfare state, although in the first case it is not apparent that remedies against bad luck should be provided by the state. These are not the only motivations underlying the welfare state. Historically, one powerful argument in favor of the welfare state was **militarism**, namely, that the state must take care of poor families, so that they would raise healthy boys to fight in wars. Surprisingly, this was the argument used by the intellectual architects of the welfare state in social-democratic Sweden (Alva and Gunnar Myrdahl 1934).

11.2.4 Efficiency

Another justification is **efficiency**. Although welfare programs are often criticized as wasteful, there is abundant evidence that, when they are well designed, they are efficiency enhancing. There are about a billion people in the world who eat enough to live but not to work. A small food subsidy – it turns out about 45 cents a day – would make them productive. Indeed, Fogel (1994) estimates that 30 percent of economic growth of Great Britain since the industrial revolution was due to better nutrition. Preventative health programs save multiple of their cost in attending sick people. Education, particularly primary education, particularly for women has a very high rate of return. Hence, societies may want to assist the poor in becoming productive for efficiency reasons.

I do not know which of these motives predominates. I concentrate on the insurance motive because it raises the most interesting issues concerning the role of government.

11.3   Risk pooling and the welfare state

We now see why it is that insurance may have to be compulsory. The following is based on Barr (1992). An individual i faces the probability p_i of

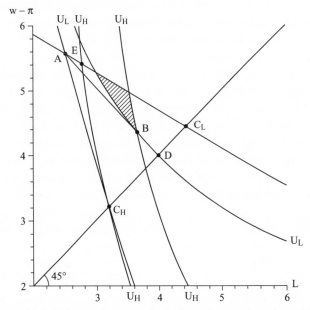

Figure 11.1. Voluntary insurance in the face of uncertainty about risks.

suffering a loss L. Competitive insurance companies must earn

$$T = \pi_i - p_i L,$$

where T is the competitive return, π_i is the premium paid by the $i - th$ individual, and $p_i L$ is the expected disbursement by the insurance company. Individuals are risk averse, so that they want to be equally well off in all states of nature.

All we need to understand what will happen is a picture that is already familiar to us in a somewhat different form. Suppose that the two possible states of nature are to be working or to be sick, but note that the argument is general: It could be working or unemployed, married or divorced, having no children and having children, and so on. Consider an individual who has some, low, probability of getting sick. When working and uninsured, this individual gets an income represented by point A in Figure 11.1 and the insurance company has zero profits. This individual is indifferent between paying low premiums (which increase as we move down along the income-when-working axis, $w - \pi$) and getting low income when sick, L, and paying high premiums and getting higher benefits. Utility of the individual increases to the North-East. The profit of the insurance company increases in premiums, π, and declines in disbursements when an individual is sick, L. Hence, profit increases to the South-West. The iso-profit line $A - C_L$ represents zero profits. The insurance company is indifferent between A and C_L, whereas the individual, who is risk averse, is better off moving along this line all the way to the sure-income locus (the 45° line). The insurance company would be better off offering a contract at some point to the South-West of the $A - C_L$ line. But then another company would offer a contract closer to this line and it would be still profitable. Hence, if the insurance market is competitive, any contract must lie at this line, and if the individual could choose, she would pick C_L.

Suppose now that there are two types of individuals: Low-risk types get sick with the probability p_L, high-risk types with the probability $p_H > p_L$. The indifference curves of the low-risk types are less steep than those of the high-risk types: If your probability of getting sick is zero, you will care only about your income when working (your indifference curves will be horizontal); if you are sure to get sick, you will care only about income when sick (indifference curves will be vertical). We already know that the line connecting the points A and C_L is the set of feasible contracts for the low-risk individuals when the insurance industry is competitive and that low-risk types will choose the contract C_L. The line connecting A and C_H is the locus of feasible contracts for the high-risk types, who will buy a contract C_H. The insurance company breaks even at any contract curve.

If the insurance company does not know who is who, it must charge a premium based on average risk:

$$\pi = [\alpha p_H + (1 - \alpha)p_L]L + T,$$

where α and $(1 - \alpha)$ are the respective proportions of the high- and low-risk individuals buying insurance. The feasible insurance contracts are now on the line $A - D$. Note that the slope of $A - D$ depends on α, the mixture of types who take the contract.

Consider now any contract B, which lies on $A - D$. Both the high-risk and the low-risk individuals would take this contract – they would *pool* – and the insurance company would break even. But if some other company could attract fewer high-risk types, it would do better. Consider a point B' anywhere in the shaded cone to the left of the indifference curve of the high-risk type and to the right of the curve of the low-risk individual, both passing through B. The high-risk type would not take B', the low-risk type would, and the firm would be better off, so that some other insurance company would bid away the low-risk types by offering a contract giving them lower incomes when sick in exchange for lower premiums. Hence, this pooling equilibrium, in which both types pay the same premium (the vertical difference between A and B) is *unstable*.

Suppose now that insurance companies offer a menu of contracts, designed to induce the two types to *separate* themselves. The contract offered to the low-risk types must lie to the left of point E on $A - C_L$: Otherwise, the high-risk types would take it. However, low-risk types would prefer the pooling contract B to any contract between A and B. So they would not take it. Thus **no separating equilibrium exists.** And even if it existed, the high-risk individuals would not be able to buy complete coverage, which is what they want to do. Hence, such an equilibrium would have been inefficient.

The general conclusion of this analysis is that when individuals face different risks, either there will be no private market for insurance at all or this market will be inefficient, leaving the high-risk types underinsured. The implication for the potential role of the state is immediate: The state can do what the market cannot, namely, to compel individuals to pool risks. The state can force individuals to insure at point D where both types pay the same premium and both have the same income whether they are working or sick.

11.4   Endogenous provision of compulsory insurance

Note that obligatory uniform insurance generates a redistribution of income. The low-risk types are willing to pay only low premiums to be fully insured. Yet under compulsory insurance, they pay the same premiums as the high-risk types. Some people are subsidizing the higher risk born by other people. Hence, we need to ask whether and what kind of a compulsory insurance scheme will be supported in a voting equilibrium.

Suppose that ex ante an individual i has the probability p_i of earning an income y_i and the probability $(1 - p_i)$ of not earning an income. The expected utility of this individual under a linear tax transfer schedule is[1]

$$EU(c_i) = p_i U[(1 - \tau)y_i] + (1 - p_i)U(\tau \tilde{y}),$$

[1] I took this setup from Karl Ove Moene (informal communication).

where $\tilde{y}$ is given by the balanced budget condition

$$\tau\tilde{y} = \frac{1}{N}\sum p_i\tau y_i = \tau\frac{1}{N}\sum p_i y_i,$$

so that $\tilde{y} = \frac{1}{N}\sum p_i y_i$.

First-order condition with regard to τ implies that

$$p_i U'[(1-\tau)y_i]y_i = (1-p_i)U'(\tau\tilde{y})\tilde{y}.$$

Assume that the utility function is CRRA, so that $U'(c) = c^{-\sigma}$. After substitution and some manipulation, which now I feel safe leaving to you, we can rewrite it as

$$\left(\frac{\tau_i}{1-\tau_i}\right)^{-\sigma} = \frac{p_i}{1-p_i}\left(\frac{y_i}{\tilde{y}}\right)^{1-\sigma}.$$

Although we can solve this equation explicitly for τ, it will be easier to analyze it in this form. Note first that the LHS decreases in τ. Hence, if the RHS increases, the optimal tax rate must decline; if the RHS declines, the optimal tax must increase. It is clear that, holding income constant, increased odds of earning an income reduce the optimal tax rate of an individual: $\partial\tau/\partial p > 0$. The comparative statics with regard to income depend on the extent of risk aversion. To derive them, however, we need to consider first the relation between income and risk. It is plausible to think that the probability of earning an income is some function of the potential income, so that $p_i = p(y_i)$. For example, skilled workers may have higher potential income **and** higher job security than unskilled ones: The correlation between income and security is positive. But it may be that spouses of people with higher potential income are more likely to divorce: I know the example is far-fetched, but it is not easy to think of situations where this correlation would be negative.

If income security is a function of the potential income, the derivative of the RHS with regard to income is

$$\frac{d}{dy}\frac{p(y_i)}{1-p(y_i)}\left(\frac{y_i}{\tilde{y}}\right)^{1-\sigma} = K\left[(1-\sigma)p + \frac{y_i}{1-p(y_i)}\frac{dp}{dy}\right],$$

where K is some positive quantity. This derivative is positive if

$$\sigma < 1 + \frac{\eta}{1-p},$$

where $\eta \equiv \frac{dp}{dy}\frac{y}{p}$ is the elasticity of p with regard to y, assumed to be constant. When this condition holds, people with higher incomes prefer lower taxes, so that $d\tau/dy < 0$. Note that if income and security are positively related, then people with higher potential income unambiguously prefer lower taxes unless they are extremely risk averse. If, however, for some reason people with higher potential income face a higher risk, then voters are pulled in opposite directions: High potential income inclines them to opt for low taxes but high risk makes them want high taxes. Under such conditions, a voting equilibrium may fail to exist.

Assume, quite plausibly, that higher potential incomes are not associated with higher risks or at least that the condition on σ holds. We need to ask one more, the last, question. What is the impact of risk dispersion on the tax rate preferred by the decisive voter? Moene and Wallerstein (2001) have shown that the tax rate will be higher when income dispersion is lower. But what about risk dispersion? Say that as a result of globalization, the probability of holding the job increases for the skilled workers and declines for the unskilled ones. What will be the impact on the tax rates that finance unemployment insurance? This is a difficult problem and I do not know how to solve it; moreover, I could not find anyone who did. But we can think intuitively. Suppose first that risks are the same for everyone, independent of income. Then each voter opts for

$$
\tau_i = \left\{ 1 + \left[\frac{p}{1-p} \left(\frac{y_i}{\tilde{y}} \right)^{1-\sigma} \right]^{\frac{1}{\sigma}} \right\}^{-1}
$$

and the median voter theorem holds, so that we can get the solution by substituting M in place of i. Suppose now that risks become differentiated in such a way that everyone with incomes above the median is more secure and everyone with incomes lower than that is less secure, whereas the risk faced by the voter with the median income remains the same. Because risks would then rank all individuals the same way as income, the preference of the voter with the median income, who would still be the decisive voter, would not change. Suppose, however, that everyone else's risks changed as before but the voter with median income faces a higher (lower) risk. Note that any two individuals, i and j, opt for the same tax rate if $\Delta_i(y_i)^{1-\sigma} = \Delta_j(y_j)^{1-\sigma}$, where $\Delta = \frac{p}{1-p}$ are the odds that an individual earns her potential income. Hence, the voter with the median income opts for the same tax rate as the person whose income is

$$
y_i = \left(\frac{\Delta_M}{\Delta_i} \right)^{\frac{1}{1-\sigma}} y_M.
$$

Hence, if the security of the median voter increases (declines), she opts for the same tax rate as a person with a higher (lower) income, and tax rate chosen by the decisive voter declines (increases).

This analysis provides only an intuition of what happens when the conditional distribution of risk changes. One can guess that if the people in the middle of income distribution discover that they face higher risks, demand for insurance will increase. It is not generally true, therefore, as Rosenvallon (1995) melodramatically conjures, that as we learn more about individually specific risks, the political support for the welfare state must decline. If, however, insecurity is concentrated at the bottom of income distribution, then the demand for insurance falls even if the average level of risk had increased. Note that around the turn of the twentieth century, a large part of the labor force was employed in manual industrial tasks. Their incomes were very similar and so were their risks of industrial accidents or unemployment. Under such conditions, there is political support for a high level of compulsory risk pooling. But if risks become concentrated at the bottom of income distribution (or if people learn they are), low-risk individuals, who will be a majority, will want to pool their risks separately from the high-risk individuals. They will vote against high levels of compulsory insurance, insure privately, and leave the high-risk individuals underinsured. Hence, political support for the compulsory insurance schemes depends on the distribution of individually specific risks.

CHAPTER 12

Epilog

Read:

Dixit, Avinash. 1996. Chapters 1 and 2 of *The Making of Economic Policy: A Transaction-Cost Politics Perspective*. Cambridge, MA: MIT Press.

This has been a long journey and I will not retrace it, just draw the central lessons. But before summarizing what we have learned, the time has come to look with some distance at the entire approach.

Modern political economy differs from classical political economy in its treatment of politics. Classical political economy treated politics as exogenous, assuming that the institutions that are required for markets to exist are neutral with regard to market allocations. Whatever these institutions may be, they are innocuous. To think somewhat differently, these institutions are not "populated": They are there but they do not act. This was true even of Marx. Whereas Marx treated the state as an instrument of a class, politics plays no role in affecting economic allocations in *The Capital*. Class struggle can only accelerate or slow down the development of capitalism, but this development is inevitable and cannot be affected by politics. What brings capitalism down in Marx's theory is market competition among capitalists not a political struggle between workers and capitalists. Workers will make a revolution, but only when the economics of capitalism works itself out.

With the discovery of traditional market failures, the state acquired a role to play in the economy. But it was simply assumed that the state would act correctly, that it will do what it should and not do what it should not. The theory of the state associated with the theory of market failures was functionalist: The assumption was that whenever the market develops gaps,

213

societal institutions will rise to fill it. One could deduce what the state will do from what it should do.

It was only in the mid-1970s that the question about the state was raised. The initial impetus had strong ideological overtones: It was a single-minded attack on the state. Stigler (1975) argued that the state is populated by the same actors as the market, that these agents are self-interested, and that their actions are economically injurious. In my reading, modern political economy was born as a response to this claim. We were forced to ask not just what the state needs to do but what rulers will want and be able to do.

Modern political economy treats the state and its relation to the economy as endogenous. It accepts the economic principle that the institutions that constitute the state, including the institution of citizenship, are populated by actors who have interests and pursue them. The issue whether their objectives are the same as those of the same people acting as economic agents or more noble seems to be more a matter of risk aversion on our part than of empirical judgments. I suspect that few people would agree with Stigler that public officials are in fact inevitably guided by their own interests. The motivation to treat public institutions as if they were populated by such people goes back to Madison: Perhaps some people are angels but when we think of institutional design we should admit the possibility that they may not be. The normative quest of modern political economy, I believe, is to think of institutions that would function well even if they were populated by people who are either corrupt or corruptible. In this sense, modern political economy is Madisonian.

Interestingly, the temptation to look for some angels somewhere permeates even the modern political economy: even Laffont (2000, p. 4) succumbs to it. That regulators or bureaucrats may have interests of their own, different from and costly to politicians and the public, has long been accepted. So it has been that even elected politicians may want to do things other than those that maximize the welfare of the society or even of the majority that elected them. But, on the one side, judges, central bankers, officials of independent oversight agencies and, on the other side, citizens associated in nongovernmental organizations are often exempted from this suspicion. A part of the reason may be theoretical: It is hard to think what judges may want other than to apply the law or central bankers other than to control inflation. But as we accumulate and reflect upon experience, it becomes apparent that people who populate such institutions are not different from anyone else. Some have an ideological ax to grind, some favor the interests of the rich, some seek publicity, some rents.

To understand how the state works in a market economy, therefore, we need a full political-economic equilibrium, that is, an understanding of what each actor will do, given what it wants and can do and what others are doing, under changing circumstances. This is, however, not a feasible research strategy: As someone remarked, all science is science of partial equilibria. Hence, we can get only partial answers. But we cannot treat as exogenous the action of actors who are affected by a particular set of outcomes. If regulators affect the welfare of the regulated, we must ask what the potentially regulated will do to affect the regulation and with what consequences. If politicians affect the welfare of citizens, we must inquire how citizens will attempt to control politicians and with what consequences.

Even if we cannot think in terms of a general equilibrium that includes politics, we can learn a lot piecemeal. The analyses in which we have engaged offer several generic conclusions about the role of the state in a market economy, about the organization of the state, about the relation between the people and the government. I do not try to extract substantive conclusions, because my intent was mainly methodological: just to offer tools. But a substantive hypothesis did organize the course.

We have seen throughout examples that the quality of state regulation of the economy should depend on the institutional design of state institutions. If citizens can control the elected representatives, if the elected representatives have proper incentives to want to and proper instruments to be able to control appointed officials, if the regulators have incentives and instruments to regulate in the public interest, then the state will do all it should and will not do what it should not. This is the Holy Grail of modern political economy. It is not to assume that the people who populate public institutions are angels, nor that they know enough to do whatever they want to do, but to design institutions that function as well as it is possible under all the constraints. To put it as a slogan, "Better democracy, better economy."

CHAPTER 13

Additional references

Ackerlof, George. 1970. "The market for 'Lemons': Qualitative Uncertainty and the Market Mechanism." *Quarterly Journal of Economics 86*: 488–500.

Arnold, Douglas. 1993. "Can Inattentive Citizens Control Their Elected Representatives?" In L. C. Dodd and B. I. Oppendheimer, eds., *Congress Reconsidered*, 5th ed. Washington, DC: CQ Press.

Arrow, Kenneth A. 1954. *Social Choice and Individual Values*. New York: Wiley.

Austen-Smith, David. 1990. "Credible Debate Equilibria." *Social Choice and Welfare 7*: 75–93.

Austen-Smith, David and Jeffrey Banks. 1988. "Elections, Coalitions, and Legislative Outcomes." *American Political Science Review 82*: 405–422.

Becker, Gary S. 1983. "A Theory of Competition among Interest Groups for Political Influence." *Quarterly Journal of Economics 98*: 371–400.

Bénabou, Roland. 2000. "Unequal Societies: Income Distribution and the Social Contract." *American Economic Review 90*: 96–129.

Bénabou, Roland, and Efe Ok. 2001. "Social Mobility and the Demand for Redistribution: the PUOM Hypothesis." *Quarterly Journal of Economics 116*: 447–487.

Bendor, Jonathan, Dilip Mukherjee, and Debraj Ray. 2001. "Adaptive Political Parties in Downsian Competition." Paper presented at the Annual Meeting of the American Political Science Association, San Francisco, CA, August 30-September 2.

Benhabib, Jess and Aldo Rustichini. 1996. "Social Conflict and Growth." *Journal of Economic Growth 1*: 125–142.

Bhagwati, Jagdish and T. Srinivasan. 1980. "Revenue Seeking: A Generalization of the Theory of Tariffs." *Journal of Political Economy 88*: 1069–1087.

Black, Duncan. 1958. *The Theory of Committees and Elections*. Cambridge: Cambridge University Press.

Bobbio, Norberto. 1984. *The Future of Democracy*. Minneapolis: University of Minnesota Press.

Bowles, Samuel. "Endogenous Preferences: The Cultural Consequences of Markets and Other Economic Institutions." *Journal of Economic Literature 36*: 75–111.

Buchanan, James and Gordon Tullock. 1962. *The Calculus of Consent: Logical Foundations of Constitutional Democracy.* Ann Arbor: University of Michigan Press.

Cheibub, José Antonio, Adam Przeworski, and Sebastian Saiegh. 2002. "Government Coalitions and Legislative Effectiveness under Parliamentarism and Presidentialism." *Ms.* Department of Politics. New York University.

Coase, R. H. 1960. "The Problem of Social Cost." *The Journal of Law and Economics 3*: 1–44.

Cunill Grau, Nuria. 1997. *Repensando lo público a través de la sociedad.* Caracas: Nueva Sociedad.

Dahl, Robert. 1971. *Polyarchy: Participation and Opposition.* New Haven, CT: Yale University Press.

D'Arcy Finn, T. 1993. "Independent Review Agencies and Accountability: Snapping at the Heels of Government?" *Optimum: The Journal of Public Sector Management 24*: 9–22.

Dasgupta, Partha. 1993. *An Inquiry into Well-Being and Destitution.* Oxford: Clarendon Press.

Dixit, Avinash. 1996. *The Making of Economic Policy: A Transaction-Cost Politics Perspective.* Cambridge, MA: MIT Press.

Downs, Anthony. 1957. An Economic Theory of Democracy. New York: Harper and Row.

Drazen, Allan. 2000. *Political Economy in Macroeconomics.* Princeton, NJ: Princeton University Press.

Dunn, John. 1999. "Situating Democratic Accountability." In Adam Przeworski, Susan C. Stokes, and Bernard Manin, eds., *Democracy, Accountability, and Representation*, 329–344. New York: Cambridge University Press.

Dworkin, Ronald. 1981a. "What is Equality? Part 1: Equality of Welfare." *Philosophy and Public Affairs 10*: 185–246.

Dworkin, Ronald. 1981b. "What is Equality? Part 2: Equality of Resources." *Philosophy and Public Affairs 10*: 283–345.

Dworkin, Ronald. 1986. *Law's Empire.* Cambridge, MA: Belknap Press.

Elster, Jon. 1992. *Local Justice: How Institutions Allocate Scarce Goods and Necessary Burdens.* New York: Russell Sage Foundation.

Ferejohn, John and Pascuale Pasquino. 2003. "Rule of Democracy and Rule of Law." In José Marìa Maravall and Adam Przeworski, eds., *Democracy and the Rule of Law*, 242–260. New York: Cambridge University Press.

Fogel, Robert W. 1994. "Economic Growth, Population Theory, and Physiology: The Bearing of Long-term Processes on the Making of Economic Policy." *American Economic Review 84*: 369–95.

Giddens, Anthony. 1998. *The Third Way. The Renewal of Social Democracy.* Cambridge: Polity Press.

Grofman, Bernard and Scott Feld. 1989. "Rousseau's General Will: A Condorcetian Perspective." *American Political Science Review 82*: 567–576.

Grossman, Gene M. and Elnhanan Helpman. 2001. *Special Interest Politics*. Cambridge, MA: MIT Press.

Guarnieri, Carlo. 2003. "Courts as Instruments of Horizontal Accountability." In José Marìa Maravall and Adam Przeworski, eds., *Democracy and the Rule of Law*, 223–241. New York: Cambridge University Press.

Habermas, Jurgen. 1975. *Legitimation Crises*. Boston: Beacon.

Hahn, Frank. 1990. "Information Dynamics and Equilibrium." In Frank Hahn (ed.), *The Economics of Missing Markets, Information. and Games*. Oxford: Clarendon Press.

Hardin, Russell. 1989. "Why a Constitution?" In Bernard Grofman and Donald Witman, eds., *The Federalist Papers and the New Institutionalism*, 100–120. New York: Agathon Press.

Holmes, Stephen. 1995. *Passions and Constraint: On the Theory of Liberal Democracy*. Chicago: University of Chicago Press.

Kelsen, Hans. 1929. *Vom Wesen und Wert der Demokratie*. Aalen: Scientia Verlag.

Krueger, Ann. 1974. "The Political Economy of Rent Seeking." *American Economic Review 64*: 291–303.

Kydland, Finn E. and Edward C. Prescott. 1977. "Rules Rather than Discretion: The Inconsistency of Optimal Plans." *Journal of Political Economy 85*: 473–491.

Laffont, Jean-Jacques. 2000. *Incentives and Political Economy*. Oxford: Oxford University Press.

Laffont, Jean-Jacques, and Jean Tirole. 1994. *A Theory of Incentives in Procurement and Regulation*. Cambridge, MA.: MIT Press.

Laver, Michael and Kenneth A. Shepsle. 1996. *Making and Breaking Governments: Cabinets and Legislatures in Parliamentary Democracies*. New York: Cambridge University Press.

Lee, Wojin. 2001. "Is democracy harmful to growth? De Tocqueville revisited." Ms. Department of Economics, Northern Illinois University, DeKalb, IL.

Lowi, Theodore J. 1979. *The End of Liberalism: The Second Republic of the United States*. New York: W.W. Norton.

Manin, Bernard. 1994. "Checks, Balances, and Boundaries: The Separation of Powers in the Constitutional Debate of 1787." In Biancamaria Fontana, ed., *The Invention of the Moden Republic*, 27–62. Cambridge: Cambridge University Press.

Manin, Bernard. 1997. *Principles of Representative Government*. Cambridge: Cambridge University Press.

Maravall, José Marìa. 2002. "The Rule of Law as a Political Weapon." In José Marìa Maravall and Adam Przeworski, eds., *Democracy and the Rule of Law*, 261–301. New York: Cambridge University Press.

Marx, Karl. 1952. *The Class Struggles in France, 1848–1850*. Moscow: Progress Publishers.

Marx, Karl. 1952 [1867]. *Wage Labour and Capital*. Moscow: Progress Publishers.

McKelvey, Richard D. 1976. "Intransitivities in Multidimensional Voting Models and Some Implications for Agenda Control." *Journal of Economic Theory 12*: 472–482.

Meltzer, Allan H. and Scott F. Richard. 1981. "A Rational Theory of the Size of Government." *Journal of Political Economy 89*: 914–927.

Milanovic, Branko. 1999. "Do More Unequal Countries Redistribute More? Does the Median Voter Hypothesis Hold?" *Ms.* Washington, DC: The World Bank.

Miller, Nicolas R. 1986. "Information, Electorates, and Democracy: Some Extensions and Interpretations of the Condorcet Jury Theorem." In Bernard Grofman and Guillermo Owen, eds., *Information Pooling and Group Decision Making*, 173–192. Greenwich, CT: JAI Press.

Minford, Patrick. 1995. "Time-Inconsistency, Democracy, and Optimal Contingent Rules." *Oxford Economic Papers 47*: 195–210.

Moene, Karl Ove, and Michael Wallerstein. 2001. "Inequality, Social Insurance, and Redistribution." *American Political Science Review 95*: 859–874.

Mueller, Dennis C. 1989. *Public Choice II*. Cambridge: Cambridge University Press.

Myrdahl, Alva and Gunnar. 1934. Kris i Befolkninsfrågan. Stockholm: Tiden.

Niskanen, William. 1971. *Bureaucracy and Representative Government*. Chicago: Aldine-Atherton.

North, Douglas. 1990. "A Transaction Cost Theory of Politics." *Journal of Theoretical Politics 2*: 555–567.

Okun, Arthur M. 1975. *Equality and Efficiency: The Big Tradeoff*. Washington, DC: The Brookings Institution.

Olson, Mancur. 1991. "Autocracy, Democracy and Prosperity." In R. Zeckhauser, ed., *Strategy and Choice*, 131–157. Cambridge, MA: MIT Press.

Osborne M. J. and Slivinsky A. 1996. "A Model of Political Competition with Citizen-Candidates." *Quarterly Journal of Economics 111*: 65–96.

Persson, Torsten and Guido Tabelini. 2000. In *Political Economics: Explaining Economic Policy*. Cambridge, MA: MIT Press.

Pigou, A. C. 1932. *The Economics of Welfare*. 4th ed. London: Macmillan.

Pitkin, Hanna F. 1967. *The Concept of Representation*. Berkeley: University of California Press.

Polanyi, Karl. 1957. *The Great Transformation*. Boston: Beacon Press.

Posner, Richard A. 1987. "The Constitution as an Economic Document." *The George Washington Law Review 56*: 4–38.

Przeworski, Adam. 2003. "Democracy as an Equilibrium." Ms. Department of Politics. New York University.

Przeworski, Adam, Michael E. Alvarez, José Antonio Cheibub, and Fernando Limongi. 2000. *Democracy and Development*. New York: Cambridge University Press.

Przeworski, Adam and Michael Wallerstein. 1988. "Structural Dependence of the State on Capital." *American Political Science Review 82*: 11–29.

Przeworski, Adam, Susan C. Stokes, and Bernard Manin (eds). 1999. *Democracy, Accountability, and Representation*. New York: Cambridge University Press.

Rawls, John. 1971. *A Theory of Justice*. Cambridge, MA: Harvard University Press.

Raz, Joseph. 1994. *Ethics in the Public Domain*. Oxford: Clarendon Press.

Riker, William. 1965. *Democracy in America*. 2d ed. New York: Macmillan.

Roberts, K. W. S. "Voting over Income Tax Schedules." *Journal of Public Economics* 8: 329–40.

Robinson, James. 1998. "Theories of Bad Policy." *Policy Reform 1*: 1–14.

Robinson, James A. 2000. "When is a State Predatory? Ms. Department of Political Science. University of California, Berkeley, CA.

Roemer, John E. 1996. *Theories of Distributive Justice*. Cambridge, MA: Harvard University Press.

Rosenvallon, Pierre. 1995. *La Nouvelle Question Sociale*. Paris: Seuil.

Sah, Raaj K. and Joseph Stiglitz. 1988. "Committees, Hierarchies and Polyarchies." *The Economic Journal 98*: 451–470.

Samuelson, Paul. 1954. "The Pure Theory of Public Expenditure." *Review of Economics and Statistics 36*: 387–389.

Schumpeter, Joseph. 1986 [1946]. *The Dynamics of Market Economies*. New York: McGraw-Hill.

Sen, Amartya. 1970. "The Impossibility of a Paretian Liberal." *Journal of Political Economy 78*: 152–157.

Sen, Amartya. 1992. *Inequality Reexamined*. New York: Russell Sage Foundation.

Skidelsky, R. (Ed.). 1977. *The End of the Keynesian Era: Essays on the Distintegration of the Keynesian Political Economy*. New York: Holmes and Meier.

Stigler, George. 1975. *The Citizen and the State. Essays on Regulation*. Chicago: University of Chicago Press.

Stiglitz, Joseph E. 1994. *Whither Socialism*? Cambridge, MA: MIT Press.

Sutherland, S. L. 1993. "Independent Review and Political Accountability: Should Democracy Be on Autopilot?" *Optimum: The Journal of Public Sector Management 24*: 23–41.

Tirole, Jean. 1994. "The Internal Organization of Government." *Oxford Economic Papers 46*: 1–29.

Tsebelis, George. 1995. "Decision-Making in Political Systems: Veto Players in Presidentialism, Multicameralism, and Pluripartism." *British Journal of Political Science 25*: 289–325.

Weber, Max. 1964. *Political Writings*. Edited by Peter Lassman and Ronald Speirs. Cambridge: Cambridge University Press.

Weber, Max. 1968. *Economy and Society*. New York: Bedminster Press.

Weber, Max. 1994. *Weber: Political Writings*. Edited by Peter Lanssman, translated by Ronald Speirs. New York: Cambridge University Press.

Weingast, Barry R. 1997. "Political Foundations of Democracy and the Rule of Law." *American Political Science Review 91*: 245–263.

Williamson, Oliver. 1989. "Transaction Cost Economics." In R. Schmalensee and R. Willig, eds., *Handbook of Industrial Organization*, Vol. I, Amsterdam: North Holland.

Index